HEEDING
THE
VOICES
OF OUR
ANCESTORS

HEEDING

THE

VOICES

OF OUR

ANCESTORS

Kahnawake Mohawk Politics and the Rise of Native Nationalism

GERALD R. ALFRED

TORONTO NEW YORK OXFORD
OXFORD UNIVERSITY PRESS
1995

Oxford University Press
70 Wynford Drive, Don Mills, Ontario M3C 1J9

Oxford New York
Athens Auckland Bangkok Bombay
Calcutta Cape Town Dar es Salaam Delhi
Florence Hong Kong Istanbul Karachi
Kuala Lumpur Madras Madrid Melbourne
Mexico City Nairobi Paris Singapore
Taipei Tokyo Toronto

and associated companies in
Berlin Ibadan

Oxford is a trade mark of Oxford University Press

Canadian Cataloguing in Publication Data
Alfred, Gerald R.
   Heeding the voices of our ancestors : Kahnawake Mohawk
politics and the rise of native nationalism

Includes bibliographical references and index.
ISBN 0–19–541138–2

1. Kahnawake Indian Reserve (Quebec) – History.
2. Mohawk Indians – Politics and government.
3. Mohawk Indians – Government relations.
4. Indians of North America – Quebec (Province) – Montreal Region
– Politics and government.   I. Title.

E99.M8A54 1995   971.4'34   C95–930862–8

Design: Brett Miller

1 2 3 4 — 98 97 96 95

This book is printed on permanent (acid-free) paper ∞

Printed in Canada

TABLE OF CONTENTS

ACKNOWLEDGEMENTS

I would like to acknowledge and thank with a few simple words those people who were important to me during my graduate studies at Cornell, and in the much more difficult introspective process of coming to an understanding of my own community. I must first say that this book is a reflection of my parents' commitment to my education and unwavering faith in my abilities.

The people of the Mohawk nation have, through their actions and words, instilled in me a sense of pride and confidence which has compelled me to confront an infuriating history and sometimes painful present, and speak a difficult truth.

My Special Committee at Cornell, Norman Uphoff, Milton Esman and Daniel Usner, gave me much more than sage advice on negotiating the demands of academe. As mentors, they imparted in me a sense of academic integrity and taught me the skills I needed to succeed, all the while encouraging me to remain rooted in the experience and wisdom of my people.

My friend Kenneth Bush has contributed greatly by setting a standard in terms of energy and ability which I respect and work hard to meet. I would also like to thank all my other friends and colleagues who have helped me along the way, especially Ron Lafrance, Sandra Rourke, Mike Wilson, Nat Hemlock, Audra Simpson, Arnold Goodleaf, Davis Rice, Gail Valaskakis, and Toby Morantz.

And to Rose E., whose love inspires me, *niawen'kowa*.

DEDICATION

I saw the scene of the fight...I passed quickly; I would not look upon the blood of my people...I turned my eyes away so I would not be angry.

I heard the voices of my ancestors crying to me in a voice of love, "My grandson, my grandson, restrain your anger; think of the living; rescue them from the fire and the knife." When I heard their voices I journeyed hither.

Kiosaton, Mohawk

PREFACE

It has been said that being born Indian is being born into politics. I believe this to be true; because being born a Mohawk of Kahnawake, I do not remember a time free from the impact of political conflict. Kahnawake shares with other communities many of the features, both positive and negative, of a modern Indian existence. But early on I realized that, as a community, the Mohawks of Kahnawake were unique in the militancy and aggressiveness embedded in the character of our political culture, and to a certain degree in other aspects of our society. It is a difficult existence that at times brings frustration, but which has also brought huge rewards. This is the context that provides the energy for my work, and this book represents my best attempt to understand and explain the turmoil which has been a constant feature of life in Kahnawake ever since I can remember.

Academics intellectualize what to others may seem obvious. The framework of understanding I put forward here contains elements which are surely the innate knowledge of anyone who lives on or near Kahnawake, and has experienced the conflictual processes I describe. In this sense, I do not pretend to any higher wisdom on Mohawk culture or tradition. My intended contribution, and my aspiration, is to present a view firmly rooted in a Native world and solidly grounded in the scholarly world. As one who is fortunate enough to walk in both, I take it as my responsibility to create bridges between the two worlds that others may use to heal the rifts that have developed between us. So this book should be read as an authentic and uncompromised description of the passion that infuses Mohawk nationalism, but also as a disciplined analysis informed by the need to create a framework in which the concepts, values and ideals of Mohawk nationalism can be appreciated by others.

The book began as my PhD dissertation, and under the tutelage of Norman Uphoff underwent a number of transformations before it emerged as a study framed within the context of nationalism. The 1990 Crisis, during which the Mohawk communities of Kahnawake, Kanehsatake, and Akwesasne were involved in an intense internal conflict leading to a military confrontation with Canada (Alfred 1991), and its aftermath, formed the actual backdrop to my research and writing. The 1990 Crisis forced me to search for deeper meaning to what seemed, from the inside, an incoherent or contradictory set of events. I began to understand Mohawk politics in terms of the creation of a political ideology based on tradition, or more accurately, the revitalization of key aspects of tradition. It then became apparent that the best way to understand Mohawk politics was through a framework which assimilated an understanding of the dynamics involved in the re-creation of community and the assertion of powers and rights based on the re-orientation of social, cultural, and political boundaries.

In the context of Mohawk nationalism, the 1990 Crisis and other confrontations with the state are not so important in and of themselves, but are significant as benchmarks in the progress of the Mohawk people toward actualizing their goals. Each crisis heightens the expectation of an eventual resolution of the community's long-standing grievances against the state, and brings out internal contradictions which are yet to be resolved within the community itself. Crises and conflict in effect provide the impetus for the re-evaluations of history and culture essential to maintaining a salient set of political values.

I came to understand political conflict as the necessary by-product of rejecting the legacy of an unjust history and the struggle to re-integrate traditional values in the community. Different views on the nature and meaning of tradition lead to internal factionalism and conflict; challenging the laws and structures of a colonial regime leads to reaction by, and confrontations with, the state. This is the price to be paid for engaging in a nationalist assertion—for being true to the wisdom and integrity of our tradition, for heeding the voices of our ancestors.

COMMUNITY PROFILE

Kahnawake is located on the south shore of the St Lawrence River, 15 km south of downtown Montreal. Kahnawake's land base of 12,000 acres includes what is known as the Kahnawake Indian Reserve, supplemented by the Doncaster Indian Reserve, a territory near Ste-Agathe-des-Monts, Quebec, shared with the Mohawks of Kanehsatake. Additionally, the Mohawks of Kahnawake claim ownership of the Seigneurie de Sault St-Louis, a 1680 seigniorial grant which includes the current Reserve as well as approximately 24,000 acres of additional land on the Reserve's eastern border, presently alienated from the Mohawks and occupied by a number of non-Indian municipalities.

At $30,000, the Mohawks of Kahnawake have one of the highest per family annual incomes of any Native community in Canada. The Mohawks have traditionally engaged in mobile employment, most notably high steel construction occupations. They have recently refocused their efforts on developing the local economy, and most Mohawks now derive their incomes directly or indirectly from either government sources or local business. The most recent statistics compiled on Kahnawake's overall cash flow indicate that 66% of income is derived from government transfer payments, 20% is derived from off-Reserve salaries, 13% from local business, and 1% from investment income. These figures do not include substantial incomes which were until recently derived from Mohawk employment and entrepreneurship in the underground economy rising from the trade and distribution of tax-free tobacco products.

The Territory of Kahnawake is governed by a Band Council called the Mohawk Council of Kahnawake (MCK). The Council is composed of a Grand Chief and eleven Council members elected by a plurality of votes in a biennial general election. An Executive Committee made up of two Council members, three senior staff, a manager, and the Grand Chief has been delegated operational authority.

There are three parallel institutions modelled on the traditional Iroquois model called Longhouses which represent, on a political level, those Mohawks who deny the legitimacy of the Indian Act-chartered MCK. The traditional Iroquois-style governments represent the focal point of social, cultural, and political activity for a significant minority of Kahnawake Mohawks. While there are conflicting opinions on the institution most appropriate to represent and govern the community on the political level, administrative and financial responsibility is exclusively vested in the MCK.

Kahnawake has reassumed authority over programs and services in a number of jurisdictional areas. This includes control in whole or in part in the following sectors: justice (Court of Kahnawake and the Kahnawake Peacekeepers), education, social services, health, and economic development. Institutions in all of these sectors have been created by MCK directive or by grass-roots initiative. Most are governed by a Board or Committee of community members representing a cross-section of the population.

Kahnawake has also developed a dense infrastructure of non-governmental activities. There are a number of youth programs and initiatives, social clubs, language retention and cultural development programs, and an active sports program especially strong in wrestling, hockey, softball, and lacrosse. Kahnawake has a local radio station, a newspaper, and a bookstore.

OUTLINE OF CHAPTERS

The purpose of this study is to examine the process of goal formation in the context of Native North American community politics. Its particular focus is to explain the resurgence of a set of goals and strategies embedded within the traditional political culture of a Native community leading to the assertion of a radical form of Native sovereignty, as opposed to a process of political change leading to further integration with Canada or the United States.

The Mohawks of Kahnawake were selected as a case study because of their prominence in the assertion of what has been termed Native sovereignty. Investigation of the ideological basis for the Mohawk rejection of imposed institutions leads to the adoption of a theoretical framework based upon theories of nationalism.

Chapter Two details the emergence of Kahnawake as a distinct political entity, as the people who left their ancestral villages in the Mohawk River Valley for Kahnawake sought to create a unique community, consciously drawing on elements from the Iroquois culture while adapting themselves to the political reality formed by the consolidation of European colonial empires within their territory.

The unique role the Kahnawake Mohawks played during the colonial era created a political culture oriented primarily toward the preservation of local autonomy, and the maintenance of cultural and political boundaries between Kahnawake and other political communities—Native and newcomer alike.

Chapter Three outlines the modern history of Kahnawake, illustrating how the community's initially uneven accommodation of the industrial age led to a rupture in the traditional political culture developed within an Iroquoian paradigm. A transition phase was characterized by disjuncture between the dominant elements of the traditional paradigm, formed in an age of power and influence, and the institutional framework reflective of the community's reduced political power and stature. Within the community there was disagreement as to the best strategy for guaranteeing Kahnawake's long-term viability—a return to traditions or further integration into the economy and institutional framework of the Euro-American states. Eventually two opposing political blocs formed, each reflecting the inability of Mohawks during the transitional phase to unify elements of their traditional culture with 20th-century political exigencies.

During the 1970s and 1980s, the values and principles representative of the traditionalist philosophy became the dominant ideology in Kahnawake. Traditional institutions—represented by the increased saliency of the *Kaienerekowa* within the community, the adoption of key concepts from the historical tradition of the Mohawk nation's external relations, and revitalized links to the Iroquois Confederacy's political structure—in the perception of Mohawks supplanted the system of government imposed by Canadian authorities as the appropriate framework for politics in Kahnawake.

Chapters Four and Five incorporate a perspective of nationalism outlined in the introductory discussion, and describe the evolution of traditionalism and the consolidation of a nationalist ideology based on the tenets of a modified Iroquois system of political thought and traditional Iroquois institutions.

Chapter Six describes how traditionalism has permeated the entire political culture in Kahnawake. It will show how the band council, originally chartered under the auspices of the Indian Act, has been transformed into an instrument of Mohawk self-government. Indeed, the community has taken the impetus provided by the original traditionalist activists and transformed traditionalism from a marginal religious and cultural movement into a mainstream vehicle for the assertion of Mohawk power.

Chapter Seven examines the effect of two key events in the community's history and presents a framework for understanding the increased urgency and stronger assertion of Mohawk nationalism since the 1970s. In a 'self-conscious traditionalism' various elements within a culture are highlighted or downplayed in an effort to create a framework for the assertion of power which accommodates essentially stable core cultural values, yet is appropriate to the shifting demands of the evolving political environment. Interaction between Kahnawake and Canada in effect creates an environment conducive to the development of alternative identities and the positing of alternative institutional frameworks better suited to the achievement of goals flowing from the imperatives of the revived traditional Iroquoian culture.

CHAPTER ONE

RECONCEPTUALIZING NATIONALISM

We are born Freemen, and have no dependence either upon Onontio or Colar. We have a power to go where we please, to conduct who we will to the places we resort to, and to buy and sell where we think fit. If your allies are your slaves or your children, you may even treat them as such, and rob them of their liberty of entertaining any other Nation but your own.[1]

Iroquois Chief, 17th Century

During the five centuries of European occupation of their lands, Native peoples have been diseased, defeated, and dispossessed almost to the point of extinction.

Entire nations were destroyed by invading armies; Native spiritual beliefs and religious systems were disrupted and devalued by religious zealots; languages were taught out of existence by cultural imperialists; vast territories were stolen and indigenous social and political institutions were undermined and outlawed in the interest of White people. This is North American history from the Native perspective. It is a tragedy with a continuing legacy of social pathology shadowing the existence of every Native person.

Indians and Inuit are still dealing with the shock these devastating losses have wrought upon their societies. But there is a growing conviction among Native peoples that the Dark Ages are over. Some are even venturing to celebrate. With a growing realization of their own inherent ability to survive as people and persist as nations, Native societies are developing the confidence to assert themselves both culturally and politically. In the area of culture, this confidence is manifested in a willingness to revive cultural traditions and use them as a basis for developing new means of expression and celebration. From pow-wows, sun dances, and sweet grass ceremonies to short stories, rock music, and dance, all are charged with pride. Always firmly rooted in the past, Native art forms, ceremonies, and writing take the values embedded in traditional forms and express them in a new way for today's generation, in effect creating novel devices for the transmission of ancient values and a revitalized Native culture.

Native politics is infused with much the same dynamic energy. In the political sphere, Native societies are abandoning institutions and values which were imposed on them by force or through the insidious operation of assimilation programs. They are re-examining the roots of their own Native political institutions and the canon of Native thought in a conscious effort to re-discover a set of values and political principles. And in this process of political revitalization, Native political thinkers have been as innovative as the most creative artist in re-orienting traditional forms to suit a new political reality.

Observers of the political process from within and from outside Native societies have tended thus far to characterize the revitalization as a movement towards enhanced 'self-government' powers or an expanded concept of 'aboriginal rights'. But these are narrow views which assume that Native politics functions in an environment created exclusively by non-Natives. Those who see the defining feature of modern Native politics as an attempt to synchronize Native values and institutions with those of the dominant society are trapped within a paradigm expressly created to subdue Native peoples.

In considering the development of their nations, Native peoples do not take the present internal-colonial system as their reference point. Lost on many observers is the fact that most Native peoples view non-Native institutions as transitory and superfluous features of their political existence. The structures which have been created to colonize Native nations do not represent an acceptable framework for co-existence between the indigenous and newcomer societies.

In the relationship between Native peoples and the dominant society, there was for centuries a one-way transfer of knowledge and erosion of Native culture resulting from efforts to assimilate Native people into new social and cultural institutions. The same mindset which drove scholars and policy-makers to call for the destruction of Native languages, religions, and ceremonies on the basis of their supposed obsolescence is now influencing scholars and policy-makers who insist that Native societies accommodate reality by shifting their values, goals, and objectives to correspond to the values, goals, and objectives of the dominant society.

The radical challenge to the existing order which Native political goals represent is misread by those scholars who focus on a small and insignificant part of the movement, which is in essence the rationalization of the colonial administration. 'Self-government' has been analysed as self-management and as constitutional reform, but with the same one-way compromise of principle and fundamental change which characterized efforts at assimilation in decades past (Barsh and Henderson 1980; Englestad 1992; Fleras and Elliot 1992).

A fundamental flaw in such analysis is the lack of appreciation for the basic premise of the movement from the Native perspective: 'national' sovereignty is not seen as opposed to self-management or a limited conception of 'aboriginal rights' within the confines of a Euro-American political framework. In many active Native communities, the sovereignty movement is now characterized by efforts to re-construct the elements of nationhood rather than to develop the means for further integrating Natives into the institutions of the dominant society. Relying on indigenous values and principles and on unique conceptions of key terms in the debate, many Native communities have embarked on a radically different path than the integrative processes represented by claims for self-government or aboriginal rights.

A number of scholars have recognized the indigenous nature of the path of political development now under way in many Native communities, focusing on the largely internal engine driving the political process among Native peoples (Boldt 1993; Cornell 1988; Long 1990). This book will build on the groundwork laid by those who have analysed the process as a consistent struggle to revitalize various indigenous cultural and political institutions in the hope of restoring the integrity of national communities. It investigates the process by which a prominent Native community has developed an ideology of national political revitalization, and moves beyond its construction of a framework of understanding for Mohawk politics to an analysis of factors of broader significance in comparing other cases of political change rooted in ethno-nationalist movements.

While the theoretical literature surrounding the issue of nationalism ignores the particular form of nation-centred political activity evident in Native communities, there has been a broadening of the concept from an initially state-centred model to one that encompasses various ethnic and sub-state political communities.[2] This has made room for a deeper understanding of nationalism and encouraged the creation of an analytic tool appropriate to the Native context.

Most earlier formulations of nationalism were based on the imposition of a common culture and the gradual homogenization of values within a society. In equating shared cultural attributes with nationhood, there was an evident bias toward the particular experience of European societies and against non-Western values. There was as well an inherent rejection of the idea of cultural diversity within a society. On the whole, nationalism was narrowly seen as the development of institutions specific to the Western context or their imposition through European colonization in various parts of the world. In this view, nationalism is:

the general imposition of a high culture on society, where previously low cultures had taken up the lives of the majority, and in some cases the totality, of the population. It means the generalized diffusion of a school-mediated, academy-supervised idiom, codified for the requirements of reasonably precise bureaucratic and technological communication. (Gellner 1983: 57)

The inherent bias toward the particularly Western form of the nation-building process is reflected again in the linkage of nationhood to exclusively Western forms of social relations, that is:

the establishment of an anonymous, impersonal society with mutually substitutable atomized individuals held together above all by a shared culture . . . in place of a previous complex structure of local groups, sustained by folk cultures reproduced locally and idiosyncratically by the micro-groups themselves. (Gellner 1983: 57)

More recent formulations of nationalism have developed a sophisticated understanding of the complexities involved in the consolidation of national entities. Brass's excellent essay (1991) highlights the role of élite competition and leadership actions in the process. From this perspective, nationalism is more than the imposition of a higher culture on a previously diverse society. It involves explicit consideration of the nature and use of political power in the process of creating and maintaining governmental authority (Brass 1991: 26).

Brass explicates the interaction of factors such as the distribution of material and organizational resources and emphasizes context in the consideration of governmental responses and the general political context (1991: 41). This formulation provides the basis of an adequate theoretical framework, yet by itself it remains insufficient due to its singular focus on the transition of ethnic group movements into states. As with previous theorists, Brass sees nationalism within a perspective solely oriented toward territorial statehood, to the neglect of what may be termed 'non-statist' nationalist ideologies.

The dominant formulation of nationalism lacks the necessary depth to incorporate the experience of political communities reacting to Western political and cultural hegemony. To a certain extent it represents a theoretical construct and understanding of history which has come to signify Western civilization, yet it truly incorporates a selective memory of the European experience in nation-building. Theorists have created a model of nationalism based upon a narrow view of one aspect of European history and applied it as the global standard.

These models were designed within a paradigm which values, or at least accepts, the set of assumptions that undergirded colonialism. By defining nationalism in terms of the creation of a synthesizing 'high' culture, or even of the achievement of bureaucratic structures and other state institutions in the development of ethnic movements, these theories rationalize the fact of Western colonial domination of various and diverse political communities, and one particular set of values within the West itself.

In the post-war era conflict has arisen as deep contradictions have emerged in the system of nation-states. There are many sub-national efforts to reset the terms of political relationships or to reevaluate the existing distribution of power and representation. Moreover, a number of communities are struggling to re-establish their political independence and preserve the separate national identities eroded through the operation of Western colonialism. It is within this context that political activity among North American Indian and Inuit peoples must be analysed. And theorists who have dealt with the post-colonial experience in other parts of the world provide useful insights into the development of an appropriate framework for Native politics. Ra'anan's work (1990) is particularly useful for its introducing non-Western perspectives and values into the development of a theory of nationalism which transcends outmoded conceptions equating nationalism with statehood and territoriality.

As Ra'anan points out, 90 per cent of countries are experiencing some form of discontinuity between national and state boundaries (1990: 8). He has offered a revised definition of nationalism focusing on the sub-national struggle. With the consolidation of nation-state hegemony, the level of analysis should be shifted to 'sub-national' or substate political communities. Nationalism from this perspective is most appropriately defined as:

> The self-assertion of ethnic groups, ranging from primary cultural, religious and educational endeavors, via political organization, to the ultimate step of struggling for territorial or state power. (Ra'anan 1990: 8)

Such a concept of nationalism can serve as a useful tool in understanding Native politics in North America. From this point of view, movements lumped together and labelled 'self-government' or 'aboriginal rights' are in fact assertions of nationhood which are manifested in many different forms all along Ra'anan's spectrum, from limited endeavours to broad assertions of state identity and power. Coupled with Ra'anan's concept of the 'nation-state fallacy'—the mistaken notion that the present system of nation-states can adequately deal with latent or demonstrated nationalism among various non-state political communities—there is a sound basis for analysing Native politics from a theoretical perspective rooted in nationalism.

The basic premise of Ra'anan's critique is that there are fundamental differences between Western and non-Western forms of nation-building. The Western form is not necessarily or always an archetype, nor is it an ideal type generalizable to other cultural contexts. The territorial and legal bases for Western nationhood are the specific products of the European experience of territorial consolidation and rationalism. Non-Western forms have various other bases for nationhood, such as religion, kinship, or culture, which contradict the Western framework based on territorial boundaries and the normalization of key Western values.

In many societies, conquest or colonization of non-Western peoples by Europeans has led to the creation of superstructures based upon the Western conception of nationhood. Canada and the United States are two examples of societies which are coming to terms with a questionable nation-state construct. Contemporary Native politics in North America represents the interaction of a non-Western (ethnic) nationalism at the political and economic centre of Western society. There is a clear contrast between the Native societies, which are mainly traditional in terms of their dominant values and political culture, and non-Native populations.

The contrast is most evident in the different sources of ethnicity for Natives and non-Natives. In Native societies, the various cultural, spiritual and political affiliations which comprise ethnicity are at root primordial and fixed, whereas in the general population there is a transience of ethnic identity. A recent study of ethnicity in the United States illustrated how factors as diverse as surname and appearance determine people's choice of ancestry and ethnicity (Waters 1990: 57).

Connor has spoken to the issue of nationalism among non-state political communities in other parts of the world (1978). With particular relevance to those communities usually relegated to the category of tribes, he has concluded that an intellectual framework which discounts the inherent nationalist core in their political goals is inappropriate:

> Calling this tribalism, while reserving nationalism to describe attachment to the new states, both reflects and strengthens a presumption that the loyalty of the individual will assuredly over time be transferred from the part (which is actually the nation but called the tribe) to the whole (actually the state but called the nation). (Connor 1978: 392)

Since the consolidation of the Euro-American nation-states during the last century, Native societies have been forced to compromise their concept of nationhood to accommodate one emanating from a Western perspective. The unstated premise is that both Canada and the United States were constructed through the suppression rather than the integration of Native nations. Thus the challenge facing a political community like the Mohawk nation at this point is to re-assert its nationhood in spite of the continuing domination of institutions explicitly designed to destroy the distinct culture, identity, and indigenous institutions which comprise the core of Mohawk nationality.

NATIVE POLITICS AS NATIONALISM

Each Native community in North America possesses a distinctive culture and set of historical experiences. This multiplicity of cultures, values, and forms of social and political organization has led to the development of many different identities among what is usually assumed to be a monolithic group. There are major commonalities among the thousands of North American Indian and Inuit communities, yet the differences are so substantial as to make the concept of a single affiliation impossible. There is no doubt that at the community level, each tribe, band, or nation constitutes a political community which is best thought of in terms of a distinct group. There is within each community a clear set of axes around which identities and institutions are formed. These differ radically from those of non-Native society and substantially from those of other Native communities.

The efficacy of analysing Native politics in terms of community-level assertions of nationalism is evident, for example, in the failure of Indian people to develop any form of effective pan-Indian political organization. Heisler (1990: 43) has identified certain inherent problems of organizing politics around ethnicity in the West. Numerous attempts at pan-Indian organization have failed due to precisely the sort of weaknesses that Heisler's model predicts would forestall organizations attempting to base themselves on apparent but illusory ethnic affiliations. The problems may be summarized as: 1) a lack of structural integrity and continuous saliency; 2) the difficulty of achieving groupings operating at different social and economic levels; 3) the difficulty of organizing people on the basis of ascriptive labels; and 4) the difficulty of representing ethnic groups politically.

Native communities, on the other hand, have been quite successful in organizing political activity around their specific national identities. Each of the major problems identified by Heisler and responsible for the failure of pan-Indianism has been confronted successfully by those Native communities that have become involved in reasserting their nationhood: Structural integrity and continuous saliency are provided through the preservation of ancient cultural values and the persistence of traditional forms of social organization within the communities. Social and economic disparities are almost non-existent due to generally depressed economies, or to the levelling effect of social welfare programs. The labels attached to Native peoples are not ascriptive as are other ethnic labels in the West. Political representation is an established fact among Native peoples, either through the re-implementation of traditional forms or through adopted Western-style institutions.

Emerging from a dark age of active oppression, Native communities in the latter half of this century have found themselves surprisingly sound with respect to the type of organization necessary to engage in political battle. Forming various self-contained ethnic groups, Indians and Inuit have begun to attack the state institutions which have been the source of their discontent. And the attack has been taken to the enemy using many different strategies and tactics. Each community has taken a particular approach toward the assertion of its goals. Conceptualizing each community's struggle in terms of a distinctive nationalist movement is the most effective way of understanding what at times may seem like a confusing array of tactics, strategies, and goals. But they remain confusing only as long as the observer fails to recognize the localized basis for Native organization and the nationalistic (not just tribal) nature of Native objectives.

Understood properly, Native politics is the self-assertion of nationhood on different axes and to differing degrees by various distinct political communities. By utilizing this nationalist perspective and integrating the concept of a spectrum of assertion ranging from very limited local endeavours to comprehensive demands for territorial sovereignty and state power, this book proposes a broader perspective on Native politics. But it is not enough to re-categorize. The study goes further and develops an analytical framework to deal with these issues on a comparative basis. The nationalist perspective is embedded in the study's efforts to explain key elements in the process of politics within Indian and Inuit communities and the evolution of nationalist ideologies in other contexts.

Anthropologist Katherine Verdery's recent analysis of the state of scholarship on these issues, and the notion that nationalism is fading, recognized the saliency of such a reorganization:

> The size requirements of viable nationhood are decreasing. In addition, people are being compelled into single identities—alternatives are being stripped away from those who would have multiple allegiances . . . while xenophobia and multiculturalism normalize these identities as the basic elements in socioeconomic competition and conflict. This suggests that although the nation with which we have been familiar may indeed be past its peak, being born into something as a natural condition will remain fundamental to human experience and scholarship. (Verdery 1993: 44)

With this understanding of the nature of nationalism in the contemporary era, the framework recognizes and integrates three methodological foundations in the study of nationalism. To be properly understood, a formulation of nationalism must be considered in context, using tools and terminology appropriate within the specific culture and times. The symbolic aspect of nationalism must be recognized, and the multiple meanings of various symbols and words must be integrated into the analysis. Finally, the ideological nature of nationalism must be realized, and scholars should be critical in their analysis of definitions and ideas contained within the rhetoric of nationalist movements (Verdery 1993: 39).

Nationalism is best viewed as having both a relatively stable core which endures and peripheral elements that are easily adapted or manipulated to accommodate the demands of a particular political environment. Just as mythographers have identified the co-existence of persistent core messages and changeable tellers and audiences as key to the process of transferring cultural knowledge over time in oral traditions (Vecsey 1991: 21), some social scientists have recognized the essentialist nature of nationalism co-existing with self-conscious ascriptions of distinctiveness appropriate to shifting temporal and political environments:

> It is this group notion of kinship and uniqueness that is the essence of the nation, and the tangible characteristics such as religion and language are significant to the nation only to the degree to which they can contribute to this notion or sense of the group's self-identity and uniqueness. And it is worth noting that a nation can lose or alter any or all of its outward characteristics without losing its sense of vital uniqueness which makes it a nation. (Connor 1978: 389)

Some distinction must be made at this point between the different forms of nationalist ideology and the significance of this study's focus. Early formulations of nationalism, identified above as being inappropriate to this study's level of analysis, concentrate on what may be referred to as *State Nationalism*, a form oriented toward incorporating groups into a larger community and creating a common identity which supports the development of hegemonic state institutions. Conventional approaches to the study of non-state nationalism (Meadwell 1989) focus on what may be termed *Ethno-Nationalism (Statehood)*, a form clearly oriented to the achievement of political independence and the promotion of cultural distinctiveness among a group within an existing state. This study extends the analysis to what may be termed *Ethno-Nationalism (Autonomy)*, a form which seeks to achieve self-determination not through the creation of a new state, but through the achievement of a cultural sovereignty and a political relationship based on group autonomy reflected in formal self-government arrangements in cooperation with existing state institutions.[3]

'Community sovereignty' and 'state-based' nationalist movements have essentially different natures. Whereas the state-based form undermines the structural integrity of the state within a specified territory in the attempt to replicate state institutions for a more limited constituency, the community sovereignty form seeks only to limit the extent of the state's jurisdictional authority in the attempt to promote the distinctiveness of a limited constituency. Where the state-based nationalist project is geared toward displacing the existing state in the creation of a new one, community sovereignty nationalism accepts the state's present existence and attempts an accommodation that preserves the integrity of both the challenging ethnic group and the state itself.

The social science literature contains some material relevant to an explanation of Native political activity as a variant of ethno-nationalism. Cornell has analysed the social and cultural roots of a bifurcation of Indian identity and offered an explanation based on two distinct aspects of the process by which the society is transformed (1988: 45). In his view, the simultaneous development of localized and supra-tribal identities among different groups is based on the transformation of institutions and the gradual emergence of new goals and strategies for self-government. While Cornell provides a sound philosophical basis for understanding the movement as a social-cultural phenomenon, he does not offer any suggestions or analytical tools to apply his theoretical insights in the political sphere.

Boldt's recent work (1993) is a starting point for the ethno-nationalist analysis; in it he presents a re-evaluation of the goals being pursued by Indian communities in Canada. In doing so he makes a clear distinction between what he sees as the basic tools for survival and extraneous demands. He argues that cultural survival and practical progress should form the primary objectives of Native communities, in clear contrast to goals derived from an explicitly political process of competition for resources or power within or against the Canadian state. Boldt recommends abandoning essentially political goals such as legal sovereignty and territorial consolidation in favour of objectives that will ensure the continuity of cultural distinctiveness and an improvement in the material well-being of Indian people. The cultural and practical goals form what he considers the basis of a 'traditional cultural nationhood' (Boldt 1993: 136).

The problem with Boldt's recommendation is its inherently restrictive framework. Will Indians and Inuit be content merely to 'survive'? Boldt does not rise above the limitations of his own Canadian perspective. He is quite willing to allow Indians to survive as distinct cultural communities and to improve their standard of living within the Canadian federation. His analysis is decontextualized in the sense that it does not question the philosophical bases of the political framework, nor does it challenge the assumption of the supremacy of Canadian law within Native communities. In fact he tries to dissuade Indians from orienting their politics toward a stronger assertion of explicitly political objectives.

The fact is that there are Indian and Inuit communities already struggling to preserve their culture and prevent the complete destruction of their lands and traditional institutions by Canadian authorities. In this context Boldt's proscriptions may be heartening and even useful. But there are many more Indian and Inuit communities for whom the framework is irrelevant. The majority of communities in North America are no longer threatened with imminent extinction. Cultural survival or revival and the achievement of a basic level of material well-being have become only the prerequisites for a movement seeking a more consciously political set of objectives. The Mohawks of Kahnawake are one of those communities who have advanced beyond the survival mode to an explicit assertion of nationalist goals.

Boldt has identified economic self-sufficiency and a negotiated set of jurisdictional power-sharing arrangements as prerequisites for 'survival' (1993: 138, 259). The Mohawks of Kahnawake have made substantial progress in regaining jurisdictional authority over key areas within the community, particularly in the areas of education, health and social services, policing, and infrastructure. They have also developed the means to reduce their economic dependence upon the Canadian government. The Canadian government still injects over 30 million dollars per year into the community, but as a result of the extensive Mohawk participation in the wage economy, quasi-legal enterprises, and the development of a more conventional economic base on their territory, the community is no longer totally dependent upon federal transfer payments for the material well-being of its population.

The community's success in divesting itself on a governmental level from the practical application of the federal Indian Act, combined with achieving an independent economic base, has led to Kahnawake's assuming a leading role in challenging the legal and political relationship between Native communities and the Government of Canada. At this point in their history the Mohawks of Kahnawake are capable of pressing for a more ambitious set of political goals than those identified by Boldt as being necessary for survival. Moving from a survival ethic embedded within the larger framework of Canadian federalism, the Mohawks of Kahnawake have enunciated an ideology which is predicated on the assertion of nationhood at all levels of interaction with Canadian authorities.

MOHAWK AND QUEBEC NATIONALISM

This book does not place a great emphasis on the relationship between the Mohawks of Kahnawake and the Province of Quebec. This may not make sense to those familiar with the structure of Canadian federalism and the apparent influence of Quebec institutions upon politics in the Mohawk community. But despite the enhanced powers of Quebec within Canada with regard to many jurisdictional areas, including claims of legal authority in Indian reserves, structural links between the Province and the Kahnawake Mohawks are almost non-existent—the exception being in the areas of health care and funding of social service programs. Considering the salient variables in shaping the process of identity and goal formation, the Mohawks relate on an institutional level exclusively with federal authorities.

The real impact of Quebec on Kahnawake has been as an instigator of conflictual processes which have increased the intensity of the Mohawks' nationalist assertions. Quebec poses a clear and present threat to the Mohawks' efforts to develop autonomous institutions in such areas as policing and education. Kahnawake Mohawks have rejected the legitimacy of Quebec institutions within their community and responded to the perceived danger of an imposed Quebec sovereignty in their community by developing 'alterNative' institutions.

Language differences are at the root of many of the problems between the Mohawks and the Province. Quebeckers have failed to develop means of accommodating Mohawk nationalism within the dominant perspective, which sees Quebec on a path toward eventual separation from the Canadian federation and statehood. Quebec nationalism is predicated on a political community constructed around the French language and the desire for preserving what is viewed as a distinctive French-Canadian culture—it is in essence a linguistic nationalism. Mohawks on the whole do not speak French and partake of a radically different culture. Indeed, Mohawks are viewed as 'Anglos' by the majority of francophone Quebeckers who see the Mohawk intransigence on the sovereignty issue as tantamount to a tacit alliance with the English-speaking minority within the Province against the French-speaking majority's political goals. This Anglo-Mohawk conspiracy theory is widespread in Quebec (Philpot 1991) and forms a real barrier to the development of a dialogue between Mohawks and Provincial authorities.

The most sober and informed Quebec intellectuals have a pessimistic view of the prospects for reconciling Mohawk and Quebec nationalism. The consensus is that the institutional structure of Canadian federalism precludes the satisfaction of both Native and Quebec nationalistic goals (Salée 1993). There is an appreciation of the nature of Native goals with respect to the achievement of autonomous control over Native communities, as Salée's analysis illustrates:

> The manifestation of the Aboriginal identity includes demands which go far beyond the claims expressed by most cultural communities *vis-à-vis* Quebec. It places itself squarely outside any sense of fealty to Quebec society and engages in a face-off of parallel identities in which the threat to survival permits neither the one nor the other to suffer any compromise. (Salée 1993: 24)

Yet even in such an informed analysis, the language barrier and failure to develop a sustained dialogue or structural linkage results in a misapprehension of the non-statist nature of Native nationalism. On the basis of an interpretation of Native political rhetoric, Salée concludes that 'It is autonomous, parallel power that First Nations are claiming . . . a power which will make them into sovereign political communities, independent from the Canadian political community' (Salée 1993: 25).

It is, rather, Quebec's demand for autonomy and an outstanding level of power within the Canadian federation and relative to Native nations within its administrative boundaries that has led to the conflicts involving Natives across the Province. As Quebec's determination to undermine Canada's federal structure advances, Mohawks (and other Native groups) have become a convenient pawn in the tussle between federal and provincial authorities—representing as they do an established federal jurisdiction in a province demanding an increasingly higher degree of control within its perceived territorial boundaries. The intransigent Mohawk position denying Quebec's legitimacy as an authority on Mohawk lands makes the community an obvious target. This dynamic defines the volatile atmosphere which has existed for at least a generation, and which continues to form a crucial element of the federal-provincial-Mohawk relationship in Quebec today.

NESTED MOHAWK IDENTITY

This book will present a challenge to those who see identities as clearly delineated, and whose view of community does not recognize the cross-cutting allegiances which arise over the course of a people's history. The thesis presented here integrates a conception of 'identity' which does not place strict boundaries between (a) localized Kahnawake, (b) national Mohawk, (c) broader Iroquois, and (d) pan-Native identities which are present to varying degrees within the Kahnawake community. It recognizes that these identities are 'nested'. The Iroquois world, of which Kahnawake Mohawks are a key element, is a complex set of linked Native American communities in the area between New York State and Quebec which also includes other villages of the Seneca, Onondaga, Oneida, Cayuga, and Tuscarora nations. The Mohawk nation, as it is referred to in this study, is a collection of persons descended from speakers of the Mohawk language who before Europeans came to North America lived in what is now central New York State along the Mohawk River. Today, Kahnawake is one of seven Mohawk communities. Thus people of Mohawk descent who live in Kahnawake have a multi-layered identity which incorporates each one of the 'communities' he or she has inherited, and which also includes a broader Native—or the more common 'Indian'—identity flowing from their racial affiliation and identification as the indigenous peoples of North America.

The Mohawk language terms used for each of these layers express the subtleties very well: Natives are *Onkwehonwe*, or 'original beings'; Iroquois are *Rotinohshonni*, or 'people of the Longhouse'; Mohawks are, in addition to being Iroquois, *Kanienkehaka*, or 'people of the flint', while Kahnawake Mohawks are *Kahnawakero:non*, or 'people who live by the rapids'. In telling the story of the Mohawks of Kahnawake some ambiguity with respect to labels is unavoidable.[4]

THEORETICAL FRAMEWORK

The contemporary manifestations of Kahnawake's nationalism are best analysed from the perspective of comparative analysis. A recent series of essays entitled *Structuring Politics* presents an approach to explaining the political process within specific national cases (Steinmo et al. 1992). This approach, termed 'historical institutionalism', is concerned principally with strategies and goals shaped by the institutional context. It is an appropriate framework because, as Kahnawake has moved from consolidating the forces necessary for survival to an active advancement of its political interests *vis-à-vis* the Canadian state, the process has largely been one of regaining control of and reforming institutions.

Focusing upon the relationship between identity and institutional variables relevant to the Kahnawake case—traditional structures, imposed institutions, the legal framework of this relationship, and formalized political values—our study places institutions at the centre of its explanatory model. The analysis will also integrate Ra'anan's idea about degrees of assertion for measuring political goals as the dependent variable. Classifying the character of the community's nationalism along a spectrum is done according to three independent variables adapted from those identified in Steinmo's model as formal rules, structures, and practices: 1) identity manifested in political symbols and traditions; 2) institutions manifested in the structures of self-government and the legal structure of the relationship with the federal government; and 3) forms of interaction manifested in key historical events.

Interactions, or key events in the community's history incorporating the implicit influence of a multiplicity of variables, force the institutions to respond by constraining and refracting their energy. Institutional responses channel the energy inherent in interactions and result in the emergence of goals or policies characteristic of a specific form of nationalism. These goals can be analysed in a comparative context by placing them along a spectrum designed to gauge the degree to which the particular community is asserting its nationhood.

The model acknowledges the mutual influence between the processes of institutional response and goal formation. Goals are essentially a function of the institutional mediation of inputs derived from crisis energy, but as soon as the goals are formalized there is a reciprocal pattern of influence in which the goals begin to influence the institutions. In considering the shift in goals from one end of the spectrum to the other, the environmental factors termed interactions intervene in what would otherwise be a self-contained process of ongoing reciprocal relationships between institutional response and the crystallizatibn of political goals.

Here another concept derived from historical institutionalism becomes relevant. The principle of 'institutional dynamism' (Steinmo et al. 1992: 16) is pivotal to understanding the non-static nature of all the institutions in the model: the symbols of nationhood and structures. In order to remain salient, institutions must exhibit a certain dynamism and evolve to remain appropriate within the revised context created through the formation of new goals. Transpose the explanatory model into the present era: The three independent variables which form the institutional context in Kahnawake are the *Kaienerekowa*—an ancient mythic narrative which contains a description of Iroquois political and social structures and constitutes the core of the community's political tradition; the band council which arises from the cluster of structures determining the community's institutional capacity for self-government; and the federal Indian Act and other legislation which form the structure of the community's legal relationship with Canada. Energy flowing from the crises which arise during the course of Kahnawake's interactions with other political communities is mediated and refracted through these three institutions, leading to the formation of a particular set of goals in Kahnawake.

The *Kaienerekowa* moved from latency to saliency in response to broad changes in the political context as a result of both the Seaway and Membership crises, discussed in Chapter Seven. It has emerged as the legitimate expression of political principles and as the central reference point for the derivation and validation of traditional values. The Indian Act, on the other hand, has failed to exhibit the dynamism necessary to remain an appropriate institutional framework within Kahnawake. During the Seaway crisis, the band council failed to counter the manifest threat to the Mohawk land base through the powers afforded it under the Indian Act; it appeared that the Indian Act was instead a tool for the further erosion of Kahnawake's territorial base by Canadian authorities. During the Membership crisis, the band council could not develop an appropriate response to the imposition of foreign rules and the ensuing disruption in the community, within the parameters of Canadian law. The Indian Act was again demonstrated to be a legislative tool for the control of Mohawk people.

The principle of institutional dynamism can be used to explain the response of each of these Kahnawake institutions in two interactions or crises: the expropriation of large amounts of Mohawk territory during the 1950s for the construction of the St Lawrence Seaway, and the impact of amendments to the federal Indian Act in the 1980s which imposed new and controversial criteria for membership. The principle helps explain how the institutional dynamism of one set of institutions (traditional) and the failure of the other (colonial) to adapt to changes in context has led to the reformulation of political goals and identity in Kahnawake—manifested most clearly in the re-formation of the band council itself.

The refraction of the energy contained in these crises through the responses of the band council and the community has led to the formation of a set of goals which reflects the increased saliency of the *Kaienerekowa* and the decreased legitimacy of Canadian institutions. Over the course of the community's recent history, institutions based on traditional Iroquois structures and values have emerged as the most appropriate framework for Kahnawake's assertion of nationhood. Kahnawake's political identity now reflects more the values and principles contained in Iroquois tradition, as opposed to Western or any other values and principles. This has led to a shift from a localized assertion of nationhood implicit in the band council system and acceptable within the Indian Act framework, and a re-orientation of goals to reflect the political autonomy and assertion of broad state-like powers inherent in the Iroquois tradition.

Key Themes

Reviewing the experience of the Mohawks of Kahnawake will elucidate a number of key themes which run through the analysis of politics in the community and which provide general insights into the operation of nationalism in other contexts:

I. *The Adaptiveness of Tradition*: the study disagrees with approaches to understanding collective identity and tradition which assume strict primordialist or instrumentalist perspectives. A proper understanding of the process in which collective identities are formed must strike a balance between the two.

II. *Identity is not Sufficient as an Explanatory Factor*: in consideration of the process in which goals are formed within political communities, the historical and cultural context is important but not sufficient as an explanation unless it is paired with an appreciation of the institutional context of politics and the impact of exogenous influences upon the endogenous process itself.

III. *The Intermittent Influence of Exogenous Factors*: external factors play a key role in the transformation of identity and the process of goal formation, but they operate only intermittently as shocks or stimuli to a largely endogenous process in which history and reality are constantly re-interpreted by internal actors. At different times in the process, the relative importance of exogenous and endogenous factors fluctuates, but the overall character of the process remains mostly internally driven.

This book is an interpretive endeavour. It has drawn on relevant approaches in the social sciences and integrated them into an appropriate set of lenses through which to view the institutional framework and the re-orientation of Mohawk nationalism. This interpretive approach centres on the identification, extraction, and elaboration of theoretical import and meaning from historical and contextual variables.

Almond (1990) has discussed the relationship between ideology and methodology. There is an inherent value in staking out an ideological and methodological position. Everyone needs to make clear the point of reference from which he or she tries to develop a useful perspective on events. While meaning and context are important factors to consider, they do not explain anything by themselves. Almond assumes that the task of political science is to discover regularities amidst the confusion and complexity of the real world. He asserts that political science should offer solutions to persistent problems and evaluate courses of action. In this task, a sustained focus on the various elements of the process such as institutions, history, and ideology is more revealing than 'harder' reductionist analyses relying on other means.

As discussed above, the tools of 'historical institutionalism' will form the basis of this study's methodology. Comparing political communities organized on the state level (Steinmo et al. 1992) is primarily a case study approach which seeks to derive conclusions about the role of institutions through the investigation of specific contexts and processes. It focuses on intermediate level institutions rather than on any specific methodological tactics. Employing the approach to analyse Kahnawake necessitates the use of a variety of research methods. This study utilizes a number of research tactics, all within the category of what may be termed qualitative research methods.

While there is no standard strategy in qualitative research, there are ways of ensuring that the research achieves a standard of verifiability and that the research design conforms to accepted principles of social scientific value and logic. Marshall and Rossman (1989) have proposed a set of guidelines for the conduct of qualitative research, and Rabinow and Sullivan (1987) have consolidated a number of perspectives on researching social and political phenomena which have been integrated into the design and conduct of the research for this study.

CHAPTER TWO

PEOPLE OF THE FLINT, SIGN OF THE CROSS

THE ORIGINS OF KAHNAWAKE'S POLITICAL CULTURE

A colony of Iroquois had lately been formed among the French, the peace which existed between the two nations having given these Indians an opportunity of coming to hunt on our lands. Many of them stopped near the prairie of the Madeleine, where the missionaries of our society who dwelt there met them, and at different times conversed with them on the necessity of salvation.

French Jesuit, 1715

Kahnawake's history has been shaped by waves of inter-cultural exchange and political adaptation. The Mohawks of Kahnawake inherited the rich legacy of the Mohawk Nation and the Iroquois Confederacy. But they are also descended from a group of people who rejected the political constraints of that tradition to stake out their own distinct place between the native society and the new European society. While Kahnawake as a cultural and political entity has thus always been unique, this did not exclude all external influence on the cultural and political foundations upon which the community was built.[1]

Syncretism is a term usually reserved for describing the merger of different, seemingly opposed, sets of beliefs into a new unified whole. With reference to the Mohawk experience and more specifically that of the Mohawks of Kahnawake, syncretism is not only a religious but a political, cultural, and ideological phenomenon as well. Kahnawake's history has evolved within the traditional pattern of Mohawk culture and the previous experience of the Iroquois people in general. New-found elements were integrated according to a pragmatic evaluation of Mohawk interests and needs. Yet they were nonetheless added to what already existed, creating a culture and politics that was wholly dominated by neither tradition nor innovation.

The Mohawks who moved to Kahnawake throughout this period were not divorced from the general experience of the Mohawk Nation or the Confederacy. In fact, in this early period all of the Iroquois societies were experiencing profound social, cultural, and political changes that would leave the Confederacy itself permanently transformed. The Mohawk northern movement that split the nation in the 1670s was the culmination of a transition started by the arrival of the White newcomers in 1609. Mohawks played a central role in forming the Iroquois Confederacy, and they were to have a pivotal role in its virtual dissolution and in the return to independent national and later village-level political principles.

The development of Kahnawake's political identity has been an effort to balance tradition and change. The need to root novel responses in the familiar ground of traditional Iroquois values is its most constant feature. From the beginning accommodating the push of shifting political and economic realities with the pull of valued links to the past has been the special talent of Kahnawake Mohawks. They were compelled to develop a fiercely independent ideology because of their precarious position on the geographic and cultural margin of both their traditional culture group and Euro-American society. As Christians they were different from other Mohawks. As Indians they were certainly not a part of Canadian society. And as *Kahnawakeró:non* (Mohawks from Kahnawake), both politically and spiritually, they formed a separate element from the mainstream of Iroquois culture. Thus almost by necessity, they have developed an identity of autonomy which incorporates all of these elements, retaining all the while a hard-headed pragmatism and unbreakable commitment to Kahnawake as a Mohawk community.

A detailed examination of Kahnawake's history reveals a number of persistent themes in the development of the community's ideology. The sources of an autonomous identity are found in the key events that have come to shape Kahnawake's politics and collective identity. The experience of the Mohawk people before contact with the newcomers, the introduction of Christianity, the re-organization of trade relations, the political marginalization of the community, and the resurgence of a political ideology have been major features of Kahnawake's history which have left a lasting impression on its politics. Each one of these major phases in the community's political development has added an element to the aggregate experience which now serves as the basis for political discussion and expression.

KANIENKE—ANCESTRAL MOHAWK HOMELAND

The Mohawk are descended from people who came to present-day New York and the St Lawrence valley around 1700 B.C. These early ancestors were culturally linked to the pre-historic Ohio River Valley mound-builder societies.[2] This large group, which included most of the other native nations that came to live in the eastern woodlands section of the continent, have a continuous presence in their present-day residence areas from around 700 A.D.

Certain groups gradually developed the unique features which made them Iroquois (Englebrecht 1985). For reasons not yet clear, it was also during this period of nation-building that the entire culture fell into a state of constant warfare. The first evidence of the ritualized torture and cannibalism associated with the historic Iroquois dates from this period (Snow 1984: 245). Strong evidence from oral traditions integrating these cultural features joins with the archaeological and scientific record at this point.

At the beginning of the 16th century, on the eve of contact with the Europeans, the Mohawks controlled a large corridor of territory. Kanienke included the area bounded by the St Lawrence River to the north from present-day Trois Rivières to the Oswegatchie river near Prescott, Ontario; to the east, by the Adirondacks west of the Hudson River-Lake Champlain-Lake George waterway all the way from present-day Albany, N.Y. to Sorel on the south shore of the St Lawrence; and above the Mohawk River from the Hudson River to Oneida Lake in central New York. Trade and warfare with other eastern nations brought them regularly into other Iroquois territories and as far north as Lac St Jean and the Saguenay River, sometimes even extending contacts along both shores of the St Lawrence to the Gulf (Trigger 1976: 796; Jenness 1955: 290).

The geographic territory in which the Mohawks lived had been inhabited by many different native nations for thousands of years, but every effort to determine fixed boundaries for the pre-contact period has been frustrated by a lack of scientific evidence of permanent occupation by any known group of Indian people. In fact, any attempt to determine permanent occupation areas and national boundaries marked in a European way is futile (Chapdelaine 1991; Trigger 1968: 430).

The most important fact in considering the area of pre-contact Kanienke is that all of the native nations of the northeast shared over time a large amount of territory. A recent study of Montreal's pre-history (Chapdelaine 1991: 45) points out that the lack of archaeological evidence supporting a permanent occupation of the area by Mohawks can be explained by the fact that they lived in a certain 'occupation

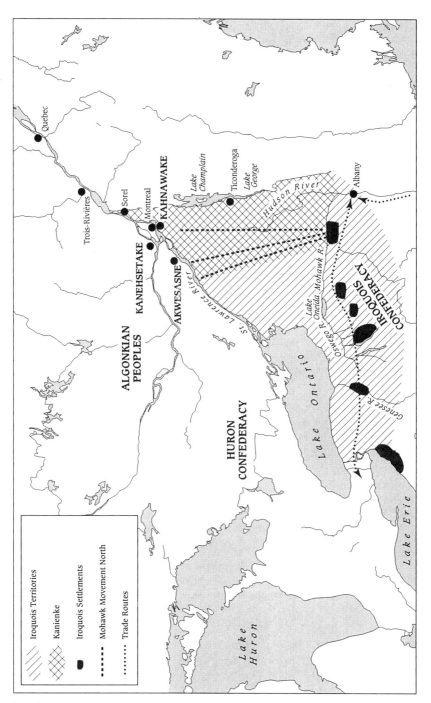

Kanienke and neighbouring territories

territory', and ranged widely over what may be termed an 'exploitation territory'. While villages may be situated at different locations at any one time within the larger area, Mohawk territory is best thought of in terms of the larger area that they hunted, fished, traded in, and defended as their own.

Support for this concept is provided by the oral traditions of at least three native nations concerning the pre-contact history of Montreal island, a city built around the French settlement of Ville Marie and over an abandoned Indian village. The most obvious indicator of a boundary at this site is the Mohawk name of the island where the village of Hochelaga was located: *Kawennote Tiohtià:ke*, meaning 'island where the people divide'. Early Mohawk oral accounts (Lafitau [1724] 1974: I, 86) of their own remote origins and migration to the Mohawk Valley settlements indicate a fairly recent move. It was said that after the creation, a female named *Kaihonariosk* led them from the west to Stadacona—present day Ville de Québec—and after some time to a better climate and land further south in the Mohawk Valley.

Some 18th-century Mohawks in Kahnawake also remembered stories of how at one time Mohawks and Algonkians lived together in the St Lawrence Valley, enjoying a trade relationship that provided the Algonkians with agricultural goods and the Mohawks with meat. A dispute later caused the Mohawks to abandon their settlements and move south. Since that time, the Mohawks believed that their relationships with the Algonkian and other Indian peoples had been adversarial because the Mohawks had to become warlike in order to guarantee favourable trade relations (Carse 1943: 34). Recorded Miqma'q oral traditions contain references to Stadacona as a settlement from which the Mohawks migrated south (Bailey 1933: 97–108). Also convincing is the oral tradition of the Mohawks' historical Algonkian enemies. They say that both Stadacona and Hochelaga were Mohawk settlements that Algonkians conquered and occupied for themselves (Grassman 1969: 77).

In the years immediately before the arrival of the European newcomers, the Mohawk people resided in a number of villages along the Mohawk River about two hundred miles south of *Kawennote Tiohtià:ke*. Again using contemporary reference points, the villages were located on the south side of the Mohawk River between Scoharie Creek and East Canada Creek a few miles west of Albany (Fenton and Tooker 1978: 467). There were eight villages that changed names and locations within the same general area every few years. The largest villages for three of these clans were *Tionontoguen* for the wolf clan, *Kantakaron* for the bear clan; and *Oshernenon* for the turtle clan (Trigger 1976: 645; Gehring and Starna 1988: 2). The turtle clan *Oshernenon*, later renamed *Kahnawake*, was the largest and the major village of the nation. Although centrally located one-quarter mile south of the Mohawk River at what is now Auriesville (Fenton and Tooker 1978: 467), it stood off to itself relative to the other villages.

All of this points to the conclusion that Kanienke before the arrival of the newcomers consisted of a broad area in which the Mohawk lived and interacted with the other native nations. Like the island *Hochelaga*,[3] most of the territory shifted hands over extended periods of time and the same site may have been the home of a number of nations during the entire period of its existence, keeping in mind the difference between the 'occupation' and 'exploitation' areas of the nations' territory. In the period immediately before the arrival of the French, the Mohawks were residing farther south in the Mohawk Valley, but by virtue of their exploitation of a much larger area as hunting grounds, they considered the area up to *Tiohtià:ke* as a part of Kanienke. When they referred to the island of Montreal as the 'place where the people divide', it was a recognition of a place where Kanienke and other native nations' territories began to divide.

THE MOHAWK NATION AND NEW FRANCE

> We return you [English] thanks for the powder and lead given us; but what shall we do without guns, shall we throw them at the enemy? . . . Before this we always had guns given us. It is no wonder the governor of Canada gains upon us, for he supplies his Indians with guns as well as powder; he supplies them plentifully with everything that can hurt us.
>
> Iroquois Chief, 1692

As the Iroquois, along with other Indians who lived in the St Lawrence Valley, encountered the growing European colonial presence within their territories, *Tiohtià:ke* was to become more than a place that separated Mohawks from the other native nations. On the south shore of the St Lawrence just across from the island was a place the Mohawks had called *Kentaké*, or 'the prairie'. This old hunting ground was to become the focal point for a political, economic, and ideological struggle that would split the Mohawk nation, causing one group to leave their Mohawk Valley villages and re-establish settlements to the north. New lives and a unique native community awaited them on the fringe of New France.

The Mohawks and the French first encountered each other in 1609 at Ticonderoga, on the western shore of what was later called Lake Champlain. Samuel de Champlain had joined a party of Algonkians challenging the Mohawks in battle. Unaware that they were part of a much larger and more powerful confederation of native nations which would seek retribution by nearly destroying New France over the next sixty years, Champlain unleashed his arquebus as the warriors approached, blasting through their wood-bone armour and killing many of them, including the war chiefs.

The hostility and misunderstanding engendered by this initial confrontation defined the Mohawk-French relationship at least until 1667. Although only 191 French were killed—38 in captivity—and another 143 were taken captive by the Mohawks and other Iroquois during this sixty-year period (Richter 1983: 540), far less loss than the Iroquois suffered through war and disease, the resolution of this problem was to become a French preoccupation for many years.

France's colonial rivals during these years, the Dutch until the 1640s and then the British, capitalized upon Mohawk-French enmity by creating a strong link with the Mohawk nation which would guarantee the Dutch and British colonies a stable trade relationship and consistent allies in the struggle to attain dominance of their new world. It was this English-French imperial presence, combined with the concurrent demands of military alliance and trade interests involving both powers, which framed Mohawk attitudes and actions toward the newcomers.

Mohawks initially came into sustained contact with Dutch colonialists moving up from New Amsterdam to build an outpost at the junction of the Mohawk and Hudson rivers. As the keepers of the eastern door of the Iroquois' longhouse,[4] the Mohawk people found themselves neighbours of a new settlement named Fort Orange. The two nations immediately established a trade relationship and military alliance which thrust the role of broker upon the Mohawk. The Dutch began to trade firearms with the Mohawks in the early 1640s, solidifying the relationship for the Mohawks and guaranteeing the Dutch a powerful Indian ally.

Until the middle of the 1650s, the Mohawks enjoyed the benefits of their relative proximity to the trading centre. Well-supplied with arms and ammunition, the Mohawks expanded their sphere of political influence and dominance through a middleman role in the fur trade. They were the contact through which other Iroquois nations traded with Fort Orange. They sought to consolidate their position through the elimination of Indian competitors in the fur trade by attacking and destroying numerous smaller native nations to the north (Fenton and Tooker 1978: 468).

Mohawk hostility toward the French was heightened by the fact that French missionaries were making gains in their efforts to create military allies of the Mohawks' traditional enemies. This, combined with the French economic threat of an alternative market for northern Indian fur suppliers, convinced the Mohawks to launch successful campaigns against the settlements of New France and into Huronia and other Great Lakes nations' territory.[5] Even when the British inherited the Dutch colonial empire, Mohawks continued to live and die by the strong trade links and military alliance that had been established through earlier experiences with the Dutch.

Things changed for the Mohawks in the mid-1660s. Their position of trade broker between the English and the other Iroquois nations had virtually guaranteed a dominant role in the overall Iroquois political-military scheme of alliances and policy-making with respect to European colonial powers. Their Iroquois cousins sought to counter that restrictive Mohawk-English monopoly by extending relations to the French (Fenton and Tooker 1978: 469). The Onondaga, left isolated in a Mohawk-dominated relationship, were particularly aggressive in attaining a peace with the French that would bring missionaries and trade to their country.[6]

The French had made numerous temporary agreements with the other Iroquois nations before this, causing a deterioration in intra-Iroquois relations to the point that a Jesuit among the Onondaga remarked in 1654:

> The lower Iroquois [Mohawk] who have become jealous of the upper Iroquois because of the treaty of peace which the latter were able to conclude with the French—will not lightly suffer these upper nations to come and trade with our French people. (Carse 1943: 16)

A decisive move was made on 13 December 1665, as the Seneca, Cayuga, Onondaga and Oneida formally allowed the Mohawks' French enemy to come into the longhouse 'through the chimney'. They made peace with the French despite the voiced objection of Mohawk leaders and despite the continued state of war between the Mohawk nation and New France. This amounted to a virtual invitation by the Confederacy to the French to bring the stubborn Mohawks into line with the new consensus policy of the other Iroquois (Fenton and Tooker 1978: 469; Grassman 1969: 84). This breach of Iroquois tradition and protocol forced the Mohawks to take on the French alone.

France seized this golden opportunity to eliminate a threat to their colonial empire without fear of immediate retaliation by the other nations of the Confederacy. Up to this point, New France's governor had been considering abandoning Montreal. The entire French colony was near bankruptcy and constant Mohawk raids had demoralized its people (Stanley 1960: 12). Now with the Mohawks politically isolated, French authorities renewed their commitment to saving the colony and launched a military campaign into the heart of Kanienke.[7]

While not a tactical masterpiece, the mission was nonetheless a victory for the French. They did not actually kill any Mohawks; in fact, returning to Montreal the regiment itself lost a number of men in a hurried crossing of Lake Champlain during a storm. Food taken from the

Mohawk villages was the only thing that saved the soldiers' lives during the arduous and logistically ill-planned march north (Stanley 1960: 17). Yet the Mohawk were impressed by the ability of the French to send two invading columns in such a short time span, and probably more important, they were convinced of the French will to remain in place and develop New France into a viable colony. The Mohawk nation sued for peace with France, and de Tracey thus achieved his primary objective of bringing the Mohawks to make peace with the colony.

This chain of events initiated a new era in French-Mohawk relations. In spite of the initial audacity displayed by de Tracey in claiming all of Kanienke after the victory,[8] the governor of New France was thereafter careful to cultivate a favourable and lasting relationship with the Mohawk nation. The peace was made official in 1667, and some indication of the terms are evident in the first speech given upon his arrival at Kahnawake by the Jesuit Frémin to the assembled nation. The Mohawks were promised two things by the French: Christianity and 'royal protection' (Grassman 1969: 276). While the Mohawks were at this point still quite unfamiliar with the necessity of the former, the latter's benefit could not have escaped them.

Royal protection was actually a code word for alliance with New France, and a challenge to the Mohawks' traditional English allies. But apparently the governors of New York saw no need to initiate what would be a costly conflict with France over the allegiance and friendship of the Mohawk nation. The English would only go so far as to provide counter-incentives to the French offers while attempting to impress upon the Mohawk leadership a sense of British military and cultural superiority.[9] The French recognized this fact and sought to draw the Mohawks away from Albany and into Montreal's sphere of influence.

French efforts to lure Mohawks north were intense, and the New Yorkers were simply not up to the task of matching offers with New France. Soon, there was a noticeable number of Mohawks leaving the Mohawk Valley to take advantage of the opportunity the new location just outside of Montreal presented. The relationship at this point is characterized in a remark by a contemporary historian:

> three considerable men of the Praying Indians [Mohawks of Kahnawake] came to Albany . . . and were invited to return to their country. They answered, that they were young men, and had not the skill to make a suitable answer, and had not their ancient men to consult with; but promised to communicate the proposals to their old men, and would bring back an answer in the fall. I find nothing more of this in the [New York] Register of Indian Affairs, though it might

have been of great consequence had it been pursued to purpose; but such matters, where there is not an immediate private profit, are seldom pursued by the English with care and assiduity, with which they are by the French. (Colden [1727–47] 1958: 176)

The English neglected their relationship with the Mohawks and then wondered aloud why the French were so successful in attracting so many to the new settlement outside of Montreal. *Teoniahikarawe*, or King Hendrick, commented to the English after the migration to Canada was nearly complete:

> Brethren, you have asked us the reason of our living in this dispersed manner. The reason is your neglecting us [Mohawks] for these three years past. You have thrown us behind your backs and disregarded us; whereas the French are a subtile and vigilant people, ever using their utmost endeavors to seduce and bring our people over to them . . . (Armstrong 1971: 17–18).

The only serious English effort to counter the French policy was initiated by New York governor Donegan between the years 1682 and 1686. Donegan was himself a Catholic and established a policy of offering Kahnawake Mohawks the services of English Jesuits and land for a new settlement at Saratoga. He also promised the Canadian Jesuit Superior protection in the colony if he would consent to relocate the mission (Devine 1922: 65; Leder 1956: 104). But by this time, a growing number of Mohawks had discovered the advantages of life at *Kentaké* across from *Tiohtià:ke*, between the French, the English, and the Iroquois Confederacy.

MOTIVATIONS FOR THE MOHAWK MOVEMENT

A complete understanding of the motivation behind the mass movement of Mohawks from their Mohawk Valley villages to the new northern settlement requires an appreciation of the traditional pattern of Mohawk factional politics. The introduction of Christianity and shifting economic realities combined with this characteristic dynamic of Mohawk political life to divide the nation. The result was the formation of a new Mohawk community supported by a different set of beliefs and re-interpretation of Mohawk national interests.

By the time Kanienke had suffered de Tracey's invasion in 1666, the Mohawks themselves were consolidating a series of victories against other native nations in which they had achieved this primary goal of boosting their own population through the integration of huge numbers of war captives. The mourning war, where captivity led to assimilation from one nation to the other, was the norm among all of the Iroquoian

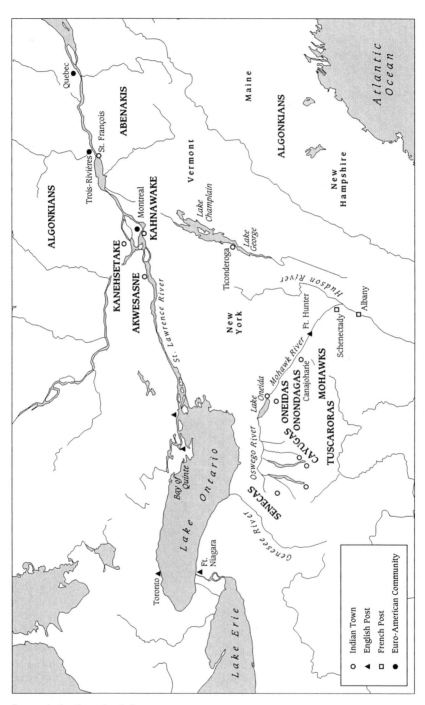

Iroquois in the colonial era

peoples (Richter 1983: 532). The effects of the captivity-assimilation process upon the host nation radically altered the Mohawk nation starting in the 1650s. Previously, the Mohawk policy of building 'one family and one people' (Walworth 1926: 303) by integrating their culturally and racially similar captives was practised without any noticeable modification of Mohawk society itself. But the sheer increase in the number of captives living among the Mohawk and the previous introduction of many of these Indians to Christianity ended this pattern. The introduction of firearms among the Mohawk in the 1640s had led to the expansion of Mohawk power throughout the region. The Mohawks moved against their traditional enemies and were largely successful because of superior firepower and newly developed skills in using the weapons. They quickly defeated their weaker enemies and terrorized many of the larger native nations allied with the French.

With this success came an increasing number of captives. From the 1640s to the 1670s, the Mohawks and the other Iroquois completely destroyed and captured the remnants of the Neutral, Erie, and *Khionontateronon* nations. They also consistently defeated and made captive members of the Susquehannock, Abenaki, and other Algonkian nations, as well as some of the Siouian nations in the Mississippi River Valley and other nations in the mid-Atlantic region (Richter 1983: 537). But, because of their numbers and ideological influence, no group of captives had more impact upon Mohawk society, and on Iroquois society in general, than the members of the Huron Confederacy when they were absorbed.

The Hurons were traditional rivals of the Iroquois and the gradual defeat of these French-allied natives by the Iroquois culminated in the dispersal of the various Huron nations from their traditional territory around Lake Ontario. Some of the Huron nations fled southwest to the Great Lakes region, but most of them sought the protection of the French at Quebec. After sheltering them for a few seasons, the French responded to the dangerous demands that their vanquished Huron enemies be released into the hands of the Iroquois.

In 1654, the French governor betrayed his Huron allies and appeased the Iroquois for a time by promising that the Huron refugees could be taken. In 1656 after much Mohawk-Onondaga fighting over the spoils of victory, the *Attignawan* nation, or the Huron Bear clan, was taken in by the Mohawk nation, and the Rock clan was taken in by the Onondaga (Trigger 1976: 809–11). Various other Hurons were taken in by the rest of the Iroquois. The Seneca, for example, had a village called *Gandagarae* made up entirely of Huron adoptees. The influx was so great that after 1656, out of a total population of around 10,000, there were more than 1000 Huron-born people living among the Iroquois (Trigger 1976: 826–30; Richter 1983: 537).

A Jesuit living among the Iroquois during the time of the influx commented:

> If anyone should compute the number of pure-blooded Iroquois, he would have difficulty in finding more than twelve hundred of them in all the Five Nations, since these are, for the most part, only aggregations of different tribes whom they have conquered. (Béchard 1976: viii)

This may be an exaggeration, but the observation that the Iroquois' make-up had been altered through this process was valid. The Iroquois were a radically different society after the 1660s, and in the Mohawk case the influx of Huron refugees added fuel to factional fires that were already burning among the Mohawks. Christianity became a political issue for the first time. As many of the Huron that were adopted were sincere converts, Mohawk leaders now had to deal with the problem of satisfying the additional pressure from them to allow Jesuit missionaries into Kanienke.

Religion in this period became a major line of cleavage among the Mohawk, although political cleavages were always a prominent feature of Iroquois society. The different bases of leaders' authority in traditional society had led to conflicts among the Peace Chiefs' traditional authority, the War Chiefs' military power, and the Pine Tree Chiefs' secular wisdom even before the newcomers had introduced additional pressures (Fenton 1955: 335). Yet the Iroquois's *Kaienerekowa*—Great Law of Peace—had created a system to manage that conflict through a rigid condolence ritual and procedural protocol geared toward achieving consensus-based decisions. The newcomers as Christians introduced lines of cleavage which were outside the traditional framework and which made consensus on any issue involving religion impossible.

Historians recounting the migration of Kanienkehaka from the Mohawk valley to Kentaké have always had to deal with the issue of religion's role in motivating that movement. The first students of the Kahnawakeró:non were Jesuit scholars who tended to highlight religion as the central motivating force (Béchard 1976; Devine 1922). Recent works, influenced by the contemporary Mohawk interpretation of their own history, have almost completely de-emphasized religion's importance in this formative period of Kahnawake's political development (Blanchard 1982a; York and Pindera 1991: 85). As is usually the case, the best explanation of religion's role in driving the Kanienkehaka migration lies somewhere between the two. Religion was in fact one of two important reasons Mohawk people left their villages to create a new Mohawk settlement in the northern part of Kanienke. Along with opportunities to capitalize on the strategic location of Kentaké relative to Montreal and Albany, religious motivations brought the factional divisions within the community into bold relief, leading to the formation of a distinct community.

The Kanienkehaka's spiritual life before Christianity centred on the reality of two worlds, between which man's existence shuttled in the form of temporal reality and dreams. Man was Onkwehonwe, and the spirits of the Sky World were Onkweshona; although inhabiting different realms, both forms of existence were real. Religious practice was focused on communicating with the spirits to receive guidance and on travelling in various forms between the two worlds. The Iroquois system of religious rituals contained two essential elements: specific rituals for giving thanks to the Creator through prayer, and non-specific means of communicating with the spirit world through dream interpretations. These non-specific religious practices included rituals such as sweat lodges, fasting (vision quests), trances and self-mutilation, and later, alcohol inebriation (Blanchard 1982b: 82).

Perhaps the most important feature of the pre-Christian Kanienkehaka's belief system was the absence of a theological doctrine. James Smith, an 18th-century English captive, studiously observed the pre-Christian beliefs:

> Those of them who reject the Roman-Catholic religion, hold that there is one great first cause, whom they call Owaneeyo, that rules and governs the universe . . . but they differ widely in what is pleasing or displeasing to this great being. Some hold that following [the] nature of their own propensities is the way to happiness, and cannot be displeasing to the deity . . . Others reject this opinion altogether, and say that following their own propensities in this manner, is neither the means to happiness nor the way to please the deity. (Smith [1780] 1978: 156)

Aside from illustrating the high level of philosophical debate engaged by the Kanienkehaka, this passage demonstrates that the non-Christian Iroquois belief system was absolutely democratic in terms of interpreting the nature of God and man's obligations to the Creator.

The type of Christian message first introduced to these people by adopted Huron converts, and later reinforced by Jesuit missionaries among them, was a Catholicism designed to allow a synthesis of these native beliefs and the newcomers' message of Christ as the saviour of man. There were three central aspects of the native system: thanksgiving prayer; spirit world communication; and an absence of theological doctrine. The newcomers' Christian message was accepted insofar as it did not contradict these essential elements. With some compromise on the part of both the Mohawk and the Jesuit missionary, they were able to create a unique form of Catholicism which would satisfy the Kanienkehaka's intense spiritual appetite and the Jesuits' overpowering drive to gain at least nominal converts to their religion.

The Jesuits who preached among the Kanienkehaka were guided by 'probalism', a Catholic doctrine developed by St Thomas Aquinas.

Probalism has been an official doctrine of the Jesuit order, indeed of the Roman Catholic Church, since the beginning of the 19th century. In essence, it states that when the licitness or unlawfulness of an action is in doubt, 'it is lawful to follow a solidly probable opinion favoring liberty, even though the opposing opinion, favoring the law, be more probable' (Cross and Livingstone 1983: 1128). This doctrine allowed the Jesuits to develop Christian Indian communities without necessitating the complete destruction of native belief systems or institutions before beginning instruction or baptism, and to compromise on issues of faith and work toward their goal of furthering the absorption of Christianity among the Indians without necessarily disrupting those native institutions which were compatible with a liberal interpretation of Catholic doctrine. One analyst of the cultural conflict between French and Indian has confirmed this conclusion:

> With due deference to Governor de Frontenac, whose policy aimed at converting the Indians into French Catholics, the missionaries . . . simply sought to develop a Christian Indian civilization . . . Instead of rejecting the entire social fabric, they hoped to improve on local customs and approximate a Christian ideal of sanctified conduct. (Bowden 1981: 81–3)

For the Christianized Indians' part, most of the Jesuits teachings were wholly integrated into the pre-existing belief system. The teachings did not clash with the Mohawks' religious beliefs, and the black-robed missionaries were viewed as new and powerful shamans in a very traditional sense (Béchard 1976: 30; Bowden 1981: 81).

The integration of Rotinohshonni and Christian beliefs in ritual and ceremony was accomplished by simply combining the two traditions. Thus the Christian Mohawk would come to merge the Corpus Christi procession and tree-planting ceremonies in their Saonteneratonniate, or 'planting of the trees' ritual. The feast of St Jean the Baptist was marked by a Teksienhoiaks, or 'firing into the fire' ritual in which weapons were discharged into a ceremonial fire built at the base of a flagpole. The Jesuits ministering to the Mohawks received a special dispensation allowing them to say mass in the Mohawks' own language (Carse 1943: 39). If the intellectual and spiritual conversion to Christianity was smooth, the social effects of that process were of a dramatically different character.

Depopulating the Mohawk Valley
Beginning in 1667, the Mohawk River country was largely abandoned by Mohawk people, so much so that by the end of the American Revolution, every Mohawk community would have moved north and been transplanted in Canada. This mass migration was precipitated by

the founding of a small French Jesuit settlement, named La Prairie, across from Montreal on the plain called *Kentaké* by the Mohawk. In 1668, some Mohawk captives being held at Quebec and other Christian Indians or those seeking to become Catholic converts—mainly Oneida, Huron and Onondaga—came to live outside the White settlement (Campeau 1988: 468; Stanley 1950: 199). At this point, the Jesuits decided to establish a permanent mission settlement here and attract other Indians who were inclined to embrace Christianity. The settlement during this early period remained a haven for persecuted Christian Indians, and its population was limited.[10]

Alcohol-induced violence was a major factor in motivating some Mohawks, particularly women, to move to Kentaké away from its English source in the Mohawk Valley. Among the Kanienkehaka, alcohol had taken on a religious significance in communicating with the spirit world through the achievement of *Kannontiouaratonseri*, or a state of complete inebriation. But its use inevitably led to terrible bouts of fratricidal violence, and over the long term, social disruption and cultural disintegration. Evidence of this process is given early on by the Jesuit historian and proto-anthropologist Lafitau in 1724, as he describes the corruption of an ancient religious practice called *Ieouinnon*, the virgin cult, and traditional moral restraints by the widespread use of alcohol (Blanchard 1982b: 90):

> the arrival of the Europeans . . . made foolish virgins of them by giving them brandy . . . [the virgins] came out of their retreat intoxicated and did a thousand extravagant things . . . At Agnie [Kanienke] . . . when some of them had too conspicuously dishonored their profession, the elders were so much ashamed of them that they resolved in the council to secularize these irregular girls whose scandalous conduct had dishonored the tribe. (Blanchard 1982b: 94)

Alcohol was barred from the Kentaké settlement for many years, even though by 1671 it had again become a problem because Frenchmen were opening taverns and selling liquor immediately outside the Mohawk settlement (Stanley 1950: 199). Nonetheless, the settlement was known as a refuge from alcohol in its early days, inspiring an Iroquois proverb which translates: 'I'm off to Laprairie,' meaning in effect 'I give up drink and polygamy' (Thwaites 1959: v. 63, 167).

After the 1666 French victory over the Mohawk, and the subsequent peace which brought missionaries to Kanienke, the population of Kentaké exploded. From its original beginnings as a refuge for various converts escaping persecution by their traditional brethren, with the heavy influx of Mohawks fleeing the Mohawk Valley's desperate times the village came to take on an entirely Mohawk face. By 1673, the Christian Hurons and most other Iroquois had left Kentaké to form another community in Montreal under the sponsorship of the Sulpicians of the Grand Séminaire (Campeau 1988: 468). In 1682, the pastor at La Prairie commented that 'we think that in two or three years all of the Agnie [Mohawk] will be in this place, more than eighty have settled here recently' (Thwaites 1959: v. 62, 183). The growth in population, increased contacts with neighbouring whites, and soil depletion caused the settlement to move four times up the river until, in 1718, the village of Kahnawake was established at its present location, about twenty miles from the original Kentaké-La Prairie settlement.

Throughout the period from 1667 to the 1730s, the Catholic community continued to attract a large number of Mohawks from the Mohawk Valley. In the early 1670s, the community contained five longhouses and about twenty families from various backgrounds and tribal affiliations (Béchard 1976: 29; Fenton and Tooker 1978: 468–9). But by 1677 Mohawks dominated the community. The Mohawks, still allied to their southern kin and seeking more than religion at Kentaké, came into political conflict with the other peoples represented in the community:

> under the leadership of Achinwanet, many [Huron] departed to start a new village at the foot of Mt Royal . . . While the agitation was at its height, another Huron chief was drawn into it . . . Sad to say he sharply disparaged the village. His unseemly language highly offended a large number of the Christian Indians, particularly the Mohawk and Onondaga chiefs. (Béchard 1976: 51)

With the emigration of other Indian groups, the character of the community changed from strict religious devotion to a mélange of traditional Mohawk culture, devout Christianity, and the atmosphere of a trading and diplomatic centre. By 1677, the ban on alcohol was a thing of the past; the Mohawks had even brought in gunsmiths and a tavern ministering to their secular needs (Thwaites 1959: v. 63, 215).

In 1679, the entire settlement was forced to move to the Island of Montreal when hostilities erupted between the other nations of the Iroquois Confederacy, principally the Seneca, and the French. In 1680, the Jesuits were granted the Seigneury du Sault Saint Louis, for the explicit purpose of encouraging a Christian Iroquois settlement of the area. When the Indians were free to leave Montreal to re-establish the settlement a year later, some Mohawks and the other Iroquois remained in the city and joined with the Indians at the Sulpician Sault-au-Récollet (Campeau 1988: 469).

With this division, the people returning to the south shore from their year-long sojourn in Montreal were mainly Mohawk. This grant made by the French Crown on behalf of the Mohawks was the first formal recognition of the 'Iroquois' character of the settlement.

The villagers quickly turned the place into a Mohawk village by erecting the distinctive Mohawk-style defensive wooden triple-palisades (Thwaites 1959: 245). They also actively recruited those Mohawks who remained in the Mohawk Valley. Catholic Mohawks were especially successful in convincing others that life at Kentaké was preferable to life in the Mohawk Valley.

Even with a major smallpox outbreak in 1680, the Mohawk population continued to increase rapidly. In 1679, before the move to Montreal, there were 100 warriors and approximately 400–500 people living at the settlement. By 1716 there were 200 warriors and about 800–1000 people, and by 1736, 300 warriors for a total population around 1200 people. These figures are for Kahnawake alone exclusive of the Mohawk populations at the Sulpician Montreal mountain settlement, which later combined with Christian Algonkian and other Indians and moved to the northern part of the island at Sault-au-Récollet, and finally in 1721, 30 miles west to Oka or Kanehsatake. This large and growing population was compared to the 160 warriors and a total of 600 Mohawks remaining in the Mohawk Valley in 1736 (Fenton and Tooker 1978: 469; Thwaites 1959: v. 62, 245; Carse 1943: 11).

The community's formation was also aided by Jesuit programs designed to protect new converts from retrogressive influences by physically isolating them as a group. The goal of segregating the Christians from the non-Christian Indians, and from non-exemplary Europeans, led to the formation of a number of missionary settlements populated solely by Christian Indians and Jesuit missionaries (Bowden 1981: 83; Stanley 1949: 347). In the case of the Mohawk nation, the social conflict and cultural disruption caused by the conversion of large numbers of Mohawks to the new religion made necessary an exodus from their home villages. The coincidental Jesuit policy of encouraging Christian converts to resettle away from the Mohawk Valley convinced them to make the move north.

The point that the Jesuit settlement policy was coincidental deserves emphasis, for there is every indication that even if the Jesuits had not founded the Christian village at Kentaké, the Christian Mohawks and their followers would have left their homes to form a new political community. The traditional pattern of Iroquois political development revolved around the continual formation of new political units. The basis of Iroquois governance was complete consensus on every issue or decision brought before the community as a whole. Failure to achieve consensus had a paralysing effect on governance. Political disputes traditionally played themselves out as polarizing arguments, and the problem was resolved through the fractionalization of larger units and the formation of smaller, more homogeneous communities, usually on the village level. Duality of interest was in fact common even among the pre-contact Mohawk (Fenton 1955: 335), and it gave rise to the Iroquois system as the prototype for later decentralized federal systems.

The Christian-traditional division arising from the influx of converted Indians and Catholic missionaries into Kanienke brought about a factional conflict which was familiar to the Mohawks who were involved. There was, for example, intense factional infighting to determine Mohawk policy toward the French in the 1640s. War with New France was of course the immediate policy decision, but the factional dispute over the issue continued for years as the clans argued over the treatment of captives and later whether or not to accept Jesuit missionaries (Trigger 1976: 645–6). This clan-based factionalism centred on disputes between villages, the female residents of villages all being of the same clan. There is some indication that the people of the large Turtle clan village of *Oshernenon* were instrumental in leading the Mohawk effort to reconcile with the French.

It was at Kahnawake that the first mission was established by Frs Frémin and Pierron when they entered Kanienke in 1667. It was there that the majority of people who would later migrate north as Christians were living:[11]

> After his Majesty's arms had conquered the lower Iroquois, it was at
> [Kahnawake] that the faith was embraced with more constancy than in
> any other district of Agnie . . . [although] I admit that considerable evil
> conduct and infidelity still prevail . . . (Grassman 1969: 291)

The seeds of a new Mohawk community were thus planted, and within five years, the community of Catholic converts at Kahnawake included more than 30 baptized adults.

The Mohawk 'believers' constituting the Christian community were drawn to Catholicism for a variety of reasons.[12] Just as the imported Christian message and rituals fitted into the native belief system with some modification, the idea of capitalizing upon the Jesuits' presence in Kanienke appealed to those recognizing the power of the missionaries, both spiritual and temporal.

> The religious sincerity of many of these conversions is questionable,
> but in nearly every case—even the most wholehearted—the first open-
> ing came from symbiotic efforts of headmen and missionary to gain
> influence from the relationship. (Richter 1985: 5)

The fact is that Mohawks became Christians for a number of reasons, not the least of which was political. The attraction of the Catholic rituals, the Jesuits' medical utility as healing shamans, and the evident power of the French war gods all played important roles in convincing Mohawks to become Christians. But most important was the partnership between leading Mohawk chiefs who initially sponsored the missionaries to gain prestige and material benefits, and the Jesuits who recognized the value of recruiting key Mohawk players to the French side (Richter 1985: 7).

With the injection of prestige and material benefit into the conversion process, the missionaries came to symbolize not only a religious difference among individuals, but also real political cleavages among various leaders and the factions they represented. The new beliefs, burdened now as they were with political significance, undercut the traditional means of social and political organization of the community. For every Christian convert, in most cases influential persons who had hosted the missionaries, there were many more people who were followers. Although perhaps not all were sincere converts themselves, they constituted a 'Christian' faction at odds with the traditional leaders of the community (Richter 1985: 9).

The Christians were known as *Onkwehonwe Tehatiisontha*, or 'real men [Iroquois] who make the sign of the cross'. The best example of leadership's role in influencing Mohawks to become *Onkwehonwe Tehatiisontha* is the story of the Mohawk chief *Togouiroui*, alternatively known as Joseph, Kryn, or The Great Mohawk. *Togouiroui* became a Christian in 1673, sometime after leading the defence of Kanienke and a subsequent Mohawk victory over their ancient Adirondack enemies, the Mohicans. In the years that followed, *Togouiroui* himself moved to Kentaké and made several trips back to the Mohawk Valley, bringing with him hundreds of followers (Béchard 1976: 83). This accomplishment was no doubt aided by the conditions left in the wake of de Tracey's Kanienke expedition.

With their villages burned and food stores destroyed, the Mohawk people embarked on a period of rebuilding. But the reconstruction of their villages was interrupted by constant and devastating attacks by the Mohicans. European diseases such as smallpox were still making their rounds among the Mohawk and presented a constant menace. Add to this the debilitating effects of large-scale alcohol abuse already permeating Mohawk society (Blanchard 1982b: 90), and many Mohawks were understandably disenchanted by their lives in the Mohawk Valley. Those who were looking for a change undoubtedly found the means to achieve it in a new identity as a Christian, or 'Praying Indian', complete with a new village at Kentaké which promised shelter from the scourges of disease and alcohol.

THE MOHAWK NATION AND TRADE

The formation of a distinct Christian Mohawk identity cannot by itself account for the migration out of the Mohawk Valley. For while it was certainly within the traditional pattern of Iroquois political development for the new group to form a village of its own, the choice of such a distant and isolated place as Kentaké demands further explanation. At least one historian of the period concludes that the motives for the migration were related not to religion, but to military strategy and politics:

> The Christian Iroquois migration appeared to be a division that weakened the League, but much more so its success appears as a unified strategy of diversification in the face of a common European enemy. (Delâge 1991a: 61, author's translation)

But this conclusion neglects the attraction Kentaké had as a site for conducting trade with both the French and English. The move to Kentaké was in fact calculated to take advantage of the Mohawk nation's position as coveted allies of both New France and New England. By establishing themselves at Kentaké, the Mohawk could take advantage of the Catholic religious atmosphere to which they were drawn. But just as important, the Mohawks used this location to make themselves the intermediaries in the lucrative Albany-Montreal trade route. They were able to generate a profit out of their individual political immunity and special legal status as Mohawk people in the colonial balance of power.

In all of their relations with European imperial powers during the colonial period, the Kahnawake Mohawks consistently staked out a position of autonomy based mainly on their advantageous location and their ties with the Iroquois Confederacy. Trade and Catholicism constituted the initial magnets attracting Mohawk migration. Even more than Christianity, for which zealousness diminished over time, their role in the Montreal-Albany trade link came to characterize the Kahnawake Mohawks. By the end of the 18th century, their actions and thought were oriented to guaranteeing their political status and role as vital links in this trade relationship.

In almost every instance where Kahnawake Mohawks were parties to negotiations or treaties, the discussion of trade and the Mohawks' role in it was central (Jennings 1984: 177; Blanchard 1982a: 131–2). In one example from 1735, Massachusetts' Governor Jonathan Belcher attempted to guarantee Mohawk neutrality with this statement:

> . . . if there should happen a war between King George and the French King . . . I shall have a good opinion of your fidelity . . . there is no question but your justice and faith, as well as your interest, will hold you to peace with us. You will always be honestly dealt with by Capt. Kellogg at the Truck House, where you may have such things as you need, at a cheaper rate than any others can or will let you have them. (Indian Treaties 1856: 132)

The most thorough study of the illicit trade in New York during this period boldly concludes that the Kahnawake Mohawks' primary reason for
living in Kahnawake revolved solely around their role in the trade:

> To a great extent the livelihood of the [Kahnawake Mohawks] depend-
> ed on the money that many of them earned as porters in the illegal
> trade. Without this incentive most members of the tribe would have
> returned to their homelands in New York . . . (Norton 1974: 126)

Even discounting this speculative conclusion on the Kahnawake
Mohawks' commitment to their new home, the Montreal-Albany trade
was in fact a flourishing business for all involved. French-Canadian
traders in Montreal could make high profits selling their furs to Albany
merchants during the winter when the St Lawrence River was frozen
and the Hudson River remained an open waterway to Europe. The huge
disparity in efficiency of transportation and in quality between English
and French manufactured goods—mainly woollens—allowed Albany
merchants to sell their goods in Montreal at half the French price and
still make twice the French profit (Jennings 1984: 284). The only problem was that this entire enterprise was illegal under both French and
British law. Even when the two empires were not at war, imperial policy forbade free trade between the two colonies. But with the vital participation of the Mohawk, local merchants in both Montreal and Albany
nonetheless managed to conduct £12,000 worth of trade in 1720.

The Mohawks would either bring goods directly from Montreal to
Albany, or circumvent colonial forces during times of heightened
enforcement by bringing goods from Montreal to Fort Oswego on Lake
Ontario, then through their former Mohawk Valley villages into Albany.
This role merged perfectly with the Mohawks' political position as an
autonomous community. Recognition of their special status by both
colonial governments was key if the Mohawks were to fulfil their role in
this enterprise. The Kahnawake Mohawks gained that special status
among Indians and Europeans by a constant assertion of independence
and persistent reminders to all parties of their strategic value as an ally
(Green 1991: 259).

This special status was recognized by one student of the era as an
'understanding' between those involved:

> [The Mohawk] presence at the head of the Mahican Channel created a
> very special situation on that vital artery of transportation. Conscious
> of kinship, [Valley] Mohawk and Caughnawaga rarely and reluctantly
> fought each other even when their patrons warred most bitterly . . .
> trade could be carried securely along the Montreal-Albany axis
> because of the understandings between the dominant Indians at its
> ends. (Jennings 1984: 176)

The impression given by this statement is that the Indians were not merely beasts of burden, but in fact defined a crucial role for themselves as sponsors and agents of trade. The Kahnawake Mohawks' power to influence colonial policy as a result of this role is illustrated in the French governor's appeasement of their anger when individual French entrepreneurs attempted to siphon profits by establishing a trading house of their own among the Jesuits serving the Mohawk community. This was the first of two documented instances in which the Mohawks used their political leverage with the French authorities to guarantee their special trade status (Norton 1974: 127).

At the beginning of the 18th century, the Kahnawake Mohawks were successfully operating their end of the enterprise at near maximum capacity (Green 1991: 271–2). One non-Mohawk Iroquois commented on the trade route that 'there is an open road from this place to Canada as of late, yea, a beaten path knee deep' (Norton 1974: 126). An Albany merchant, Robert Sanders, employed so many porters that he had three sub-contracting Mohawk agents, named in his logs as Joseph Harris, Agness and Marie Magdelaine.

A second instance of Mohawk political leverage occurred in the 1720s. A French woman named Marie Anne Desaulnier and her sister came to reside with the Jesuits at Kahnawake in 1720. Within a short time the sisters had established a trading house for Montreal merchants which contracted Mohawks to porter goods to Albany. By the mid-1720s, the sisters were garnering the profits formerly earned by Mohawks. When the French military commander complained of the illicit operation to the Governor and threatened to reinforce the garrison stationed at the mission to stop it, the Mohawks joined in protest of the Desaulnier-Jesuit enterprise by threatening to withdraw their military allegiance and return to New York. The Kahnawake Mohawks were successful in gaining a secret licence from the Governor to carry on the trade, and forced the sisters' eviction from their village (Jennings 1984: 159, 284; Norton 1974: 126–7; Hamilton 1963: 155; Green 1991: 271–5).

From the beginning, colonial governments had realized the interdependent relationship they shared with the Mohawks. This economic relationship in turn reinforced the political status of the Mohawk. During Queen Anne's War, New York and Canada secretly negotiated the 1701 Schuyler-Callières Agreement, which guaranteed the *Kahnawakeró:non* free passage into New York. The special relationship and the Mohawks' attachment to their specific interests in and around Albany were further demonstrated by the fact that New York was unable to obtain peace for the New England colonies further to the east (Norton 1974: 128-9). Until a separate peace was negotiated, Massachusetts and Connecticut suffered many Kahnawake Mohawk raids. During King George's War, the citizens of Albany complained about French-allied *Kahnawakeró:non* openly trading in the city. Again the colonial government passed secret measures allowing the Mohawks to travel freely (Norton 1974: 196–7).

Shifting Goals and Strategies

Having carved a place for themselves between the colonial empires of England and France, the Kahnawake Mohawks also redefined their relationship with their former Confederacy and Iroquois cousins. Despite a strong assertion of village-level autonomy and sovereignty from the start, as evidenced in their diplomacy and treaty-making (Indian Treaties 1856; Surtees 1985), the Mohawks of Kahnawake maintained strong cultural and kinship ties to their Iroquois brethren (Lafitau 1974). The history of relations between the Mohawks in Kahnawake and others during this formative period is crowded with examples of how they forged their new political identity in the diplomatic arena.[13] Prior to this period, their goals had synchronized with those of the Mohawk Nation as a whole. But now the Kahnawake Mohawks had redefined their political ends to reflect their new character as a self-reliant community bent on maintaining its territorial and political position.

The most interesting example of this new thinking is the creation of an alliance to counteract their loss of formal status within the Iroquois Confederacy (Tehanetorens 1972: 71). The Christian Mohawk sought to replace the 'relative force' lost by their exclusion from the Iroquois Confederacy in a rapidly shifting colonial power balance by the formation during the 1750s of a Mohawk-led association of Christian Indians formerly allied with France (Blanchard 1982a: 202):

> The French force's ouster completely changed the colonial balance of power. First Nations lost the power which they held during the period of imperial conflict, and from this point on, their relative strength was considerably reduced. The British victory made a pan-Indian alliance against the invader a necessity. (Delâge 1991b: 45; author's translation)

As Iroquois, the Kahnawake Mohawk were no strangers to 'pan-Indian' political unions. The formation of the Seven Fires[14] accomplished the goal of replacing their League role with a new national-level form of power centred in Kahnawake.

Even before this overt expression of autonomy, the Kahnawake Mohawks had developed a political position utilizing their links to both native and newcomer societies. An historian has remarked of their role in colonial politics:

> [the French Governor] found peace with the [Five Nations] so necessary to Canada, that he pursued it by all the means in his power. For this purpose the Praying Indians (who, as I observed before, are

> Mohawks, and have always kept a correspondence with their own
> Nation) were employed to bring it about . . . (Colden 1958: 123)

This observation points out two important facts: 1) the Kahnawake
Mohawks had established themselves as an autonomous political entity
from the earliest period of their history by re-aligning their political
goals and devising novel diplomatic strategies; and 2) they maintained
their cultural and kinship ties as Mohawks despite the political break
from the Iroquois Confederacy.

An indication of the degree to which Kahnawake remained
Mohawk and resisted incorporation into French-Canadian society is
the consistent conflict between French authorities and the Mohawk
leadership during this period. French colonial administrators could not
appreciate the Mohawk position, nor its value to their own leadership.
While the high-level political authorities knew better, local governments and military officials constantly complained of the Mohawks'
special status. In 1741, Governor Beauharnois of the district surrounding Kahnawake wrote to his superiors in Quebec of a terrible trend
developing under his very nose: 'Sault Saint-Louis has become,
Monseigneur, a type of republic' (Delâge 1991a: 66; author's translation). This resistance was matched by the Kahnawake commitment to
their kinship ties and other links which bound them to the Mohawks as
a people and a nation.

There are many examples in the historical record where
Kahnawake and other Mohawks refused to engage in battle, even
though they were staunch allies of warring parties who threatened
reprisals. But the links transcend a simple refusal to kill each other.
There was consistent communication among all of the Mohawks and
the maintenance of a community ideal which persisted throughout the
tempestuous colonial era (Béchard 1976: 95; Devine 1922; 102–5). When
a group of Kahnawake Mohawks travelling with some Christian Ojibwa
and Ottawas in the Ohio Valley during 1756 came across what they
assumed was a British-allied Mohawk war party, an English captive was
told by the Kahnawake chief:

> . . . he whispered for me to not be afraid, for he would speak to the
> Mohawks, and as they spoke the same tongue as we did, they would
> not hurt the Caughnawagas, or me: but they would kill all the Jibewas
> and Ottawas that they could, and take us along with them. (Smith
> 1978: 84)

Even the one instance in 1693 when Kahnawake Mohawks were forced
to prove their loyalty to the French by participating in a raid on the five
remaining Mohawk villages in the south, they saw it mainly as an opportunity to reunite separated families and increase their own population

by bringing more than 300 Mohawks back with them to the Catholic settlement (Grassman 1969: 292).

The autonomy practised in politics soon translated into a cultural distinctiveness for Kahnawake. Even aside from the Catholic foundations of the community and its special economic role, their politics infused the Kahnawake Mohawks with an identity which blended all of their experiences. A speech made in 1755 by *Tekarehtanego* during White captive James Smith's adoption ceremony is indicative of the synthesis of autonomy and tradition in the formation of Kahnawake's identity at that time. Tradition is evident in the fact that the Kahnawake Mohawks were continuing the captive-adoption ritual, and were using traditional ritualistic language in their ceremonies. But rather than being adopted into the Mohawk Nation per se, Smith is told that as a result of the ceremony 'every drop of White blood was washed out of your veins; you are taken into the Caughnewago nation, and initiated into a warlike tribe' (Smith [1780] 1978: 31). Clearly, the foundation of a new community not wholly divorced from the other Iroquois, but unique in many important ways, had been completed.

The American Revolution tested the strength of Kahnawake's autonomous political identity by creating pressures on Kahnawake to abandon its independence and throw its lot in with either the British or the rebels. The pull was strong, but the Kahnawake Mohawks realized that siding with a losing imperial power would be fatal, and they decided to protect their own interests as a community by adopting a policy of neutrality. When approached by Governor Carleton for service on the British side, Kahnawake leaders used the wonderfully ambiguous language of Iroquois diplomacy to defer participation. Feigning ignorance, the Mohawks replied to Carleton that they 'did not know or understand the origin or nature of this quarrel between the King and his Children,' and that they were 'at a loss [to know] how to act' (Stanley 1964: 222).

They were, in fact, fully aware of the conflict and its implications. The British agent in Kahnawake, J.D. de Lorimier, supported Carleton and tried to persuade the Mohawks that they should follow the example of their brethren in the south led by Joseph Brant and join the fight against the rebellious American 'children'. But pressures to join the American side were equally great. Many Kahnawake captive-adoptees had been taken from the former British colonies, especially Massachusetts and Connecticut but also from New York. These individuals may have chosen to remain and make their lives among the Mohawk, but as with the Mohawk themselves, kinship ties were strong. These captives and their Mohawk offspring pushed for siding with the Americans. Moreover, the Mohawks' Oneida cousins had sided with the Americans and during their visits to Kahnawake were strong persuaders to end the Mohawks' neutrality.

Kahnawake nonetheless remained officially neutral throughout the Revolution, although some individual Mohawks may have fought for the Americans. In the next British-American conflict, the War of 1812, the Mohawks were secure in their judgement that supporting the British defence of Canada against American aggression was a political and military necessity. Close kinship ties to the American side were overridden by concerns that the American invasion would put their lands in jeopardy. Consequently, the Mohawks battled with the British to repel American invaders in numerous engagements around Montreal, such as Châteauguay and Les Cèdres. Most notably, at the Battle of Beaver Dam in June of 1813, de Lormier led 180 Catholic Mohawks in a British victory over the Americans. This was a significant event for the Mohawk. It was the first time the entire Mohawk Nation had been re-united as a military force since 1667. The Catholic Mohawks and those under Tyendenaga's son John Brant and John Deseronto had combined as allies of the British (Stanley 1963: 225).

The end of the War of 1812 ushered in a new era for the Mohawk. Hostilities between the British-Canadians and the Americans ceased and, soon after, the fur trade began a general steep decline and eventual evaporation as Kahnawake's economic base. Thus Kahnawake entered the modern era with a loss of political and economic significance. The political power of the Iroquois Confederacy was in shambles as a result of the Revolutionary War. And even though practically the entire Mohawk nation was now resident in Canada, the significance of that fact was dampened by the dismal forecast and cold calculations of power politics in this new era: without any significant economic or military meaning to the new empire being built by the British in Canada, the Mohawk nation was politically irrelevant to the Euro-Americans.

The concept of the Mohawk nation as a sovereign entity lost its relevance to all but the Mohawk people themselves. The Mohawks of Kahnawake turned inward and braced themselves as a community for the long struggle to adapt in a changing political reality. Just as they had separated from the other Iroquois during the early 18th century and defined a place for themselves in the north, now the Mohawks had to take stock of their situation entering the middle of the 19th century and redefine themselves. Only two things were sure about in their future: the commitment to remain within the Mohawk cultural sphere, and the knowledge that such a commitment would entail a constant fight to defend the land and political rights which were their only guarantees of that identity's perseverance.

Considering Kahnawake's early history and the evolution of the community from an element completely embedded within the traditional Mohawk nation and Iroquois Confederacy structures to a related yet discrete entity, it is clear that origins have influenced subsequent developments in its political culture and ideological orientation. Kahnawake's was a mainly localized development as an independent entity. Despite the maintenance of strong cultural and social ties to the traditional Iroquois communities, more important economic and political linkages with Euro-American society were institutionalized. Kahnawake had become a community between two worlds.

Contained in the analysis of motivations for Mohawk migration from the Mohawk Valley to the St Lawrence Valley settlements, and the creation of a new native society, are issues which continue to be salient in the modern era. Christianity and trade were the main reasons people chose to leave their Mohawk Valley homes for the St Lawrence Valley. The particular character of the religious movement and trade relationship which developed led to autonomy and a commitment to maintain the distinctiveness of their culture and political status. These same issues continued to shape the setting for politics in the community well after the move north. Chapter Three will examine the ideology of autonomy in Kahnawake's modern era.

CHAPTER THREE

THE DRAGON OF DISCORD

KAHNAWAKE IN THE MODERN ERA

You are all of equal standing and of equal power, and if you seriously disagree the consequences will be most serious and this disagreement will cause you to disregard each other, and while you are quarrelling with each other, the white panther (the fire dragon of discord) will come and take your rights and privileges away. Then your grandchildren will suffer and be reduced to poverty and disgrace.

Iroquois prophecy, 15th century

Kahnawake's modern era began in earnest with the arrival of the Lake St Louis and Province Line railway in August, 1852. The British government expropriated a large amount of Kahnawake territory to facilitate the construction of a direct rail link between Montreal and the American border town of Malone, New York. With the building of piers, docks, and ancillary structures in Kahnawake to accommodate the railway and its passengers, the western section of the Mohawk village was effectively transformed into a free-traffic and trade zone. Kahnawake Mohawks saw the end of the community's physical isolation as an unwelcome and even ominous development. To their firm opposition the Governor General, Lord Elgin, responded that 'no one, whether white man or Indian, is permitted to stand in the way of improvements' (Devine 1922: 393).

With the construction of the rail line, Kahnawake was pulled from its position as an isolated community on the periphery of North American industrial society and thrust directly into the new reality of the 19th century. In Mohawk minds, this transition was like a storm long brewing, but still its arrival was a shock. Many abandoned their Kahnawake homes in the face of the transformation: twenty families left for Manitoulin Island in Ontario rather than live with the changes (Devine 1922: 393).

Mohawk aversion to living sedentary lives on their reserved parcel of land ran deep. Perhaps recognizing the type of changes forthcoming in their community, more than half the population seriously considered abandoning the settlement in favour of a new location far from the intrusions of the growing industrial and commercial centre across the river. Following a referendum which had been held on 25 January 1860 and subsequent instructions by the Department of the Interior to submit a formal request to cede the land to the government, on 17 June 1875 four Kahnawake Chiefs representing 800 Mohawks (out of a total seven Chiefs to a population of 1557) presented a petition to the Minister offering to sell the whole of the Reserve lands at $25/acre (PAC-RG10: v. 1963, #5029).

The petition was indicative of the growing tensions within the community, with some people trying to profit privately from outsiders by illegally using or renting lands. This new attitude stood in direct contrast to the collective values which had traditionally characterized Mohawk culture. Many members of the community apparently recognized an erosion of their traditional values and so demanded of the Canadian government an opportunity to relocate Kahnawake elsewhere. The Minister responded that:

> the best means of putting an end to these complaints . . . would be a Public sale of the Reserve of Sault St Louis . . . a cession, by the said tribe, of the Reserve to the government, in order to emigrate into another place in Canada, or to the United States. (PAC-RG10: v. 1963, #5029)

It was made clear that those who wished to remain could be provided with farmland at a price comparable to their stake in the cession.

For reasons that are not specified in the documentary record nor clear in the oral tradition within Kahnawake, the move by most of its population to relocate Kahnawake was itself abandoned in short order. In fact, by the turn of the century, the Kahnawake Mohawks as a group had recommitted themselves to protecting the community's existing land base, perhaps realizing that their future was in the territory now designated as their 'reserve' lands by the Canadian government, however unreflective it was of their traditional existence. Efforts were made to solidify Kahnawake's hold on that land base through legal and political means.

The issue of rents due to the Mohawks from lands leased to settlers by the Jesuits within the boundaries of the old Seigneurie de Sault St Louis was pressed. As well, the Mohawks reasserted ownership and possession of an acquired territory about 60 miles north of Kahnawake in the Laurentian Range near Ste Agathe-des-Monts, the Doncaster Reserve. Canada had set aside 16,000 acres of mountainous land at that location for the 'Iroquois of Caughnawaga and Two Mountains

[Kanesatake]' in 1851 as part of the Land Transfers Act and Order in Council (P.C. 1851–1415). This was to compensate Indians in general for lands that had previously been taken. The Mohawks' commitment to remaining in the area is demonstrated in their shift in attitude towards Doncaster; whereas before 1900 there was little knowledge of or interest in the territory, soon after that date they sought to establish control and limited occupation there.

By 1901, the Canadian government wanted back the reserve it had set aside in 1851. The government's own research had determined that the land was essentially useless as a location for settlement or agricultural exploitation. Given that the land was 'of no value' and the Mohawks would not accept relocation from prime land on the south shore of Montreal to adopt a sedentary rural agricultural lifestyle in Doncaster, the Interior Department offered to buy it back at the 'generous' price of 30 cents per acre (Chief Surveyor: 1901).

But the Mohawk attitude had obviously shifted in the generation since they had considered a relocation. In his meetings with Mohawk leaders, the government agent encountered stiff resistance to the idea of giving up any territory, finding that the government's offer to buy would 'not be an inducement to surrender'. The Mohawks instead received consent to travel to Doncaster and survey the territory themselves, upon which they decided that if the government would not make an offer for additional compensatory lands in exchange for Doncaster, the territory would be 'retained for the use of their children' (Chief Surveyor: 1901).

The entire period from the end of the fur trade to the middle of the 19th century had been an uneven accommodation by the Mohawks. The Jesuit stationed in Kahnawake in 1843 remarked somewhat wryly on the Mohawks' reluctant adaptation to new lives as a sedentary people restricted to agriculture and prevented from asserting any degree of political or economic power: 'farming was slow game for them' (Devine 1922: 379).

Indeed, the transition was arduous. In 1870, there were 1300 Mohawks living in Kahnawake—the village population had been substantially reduced by around 15% by a cholera epidemic in 1832 (Devine 1922: 393, 409). For the first time, the Mohawks were forced to abandon their traditional roles in politics and warfare to take up occupations adapted to the post-colonial era. During this period approximately 50 Mohawks were farmers, while the majority of people supported their families by producing arts and crafts for sale in Montreal, by piloting river boats down the dangerous series of rapids on the St Lawrence River from Long Sault through Lachine to Montreal, or by enlisting as showmen in the various travelling circuses and Wild West Shows popular throughout North America.

Despite their relative success at integrating into the general market economy, the Mohawks were beginning to feel the effects of marginalization in the political sphere.[1]

In the latter half of the 19th century, the Mohawks of Kahnawake began to forge a new role for themselves. It was no longer possible to base themselves on the material context of the previous centuries. As a result of shifting global economies and the consolidation of the North American nation-states' territorial, economic, and coercive hegemony, Mohawks faced the challenge of reconciling traditional roles with the limitations imposed upon them by the dominant and expanding industrial Canadian and American states. The Mohawks adjusted to the inevitability of the Euro-American tidal wave, yet managed to preserve the essential distinctive characteristics of their traditional society. Their political strategies were by necessity re-oriented to reflect integration into the 19th-century market economy.

Basically, the Mohawks sought to perpetuate their nationhood and distinct culture and protect their land base by adapting traditional social and economic roles to the structure of the newly established Canadian political regime and economic system. Instead of being fur traders, Kahnawake men became wilderness guides and boatmen. Precluded from acting as independent or mercenary warriors, they volunteered as regular soldiers in the Canadian and American armed forces. And in 1890, as a community, they accepted the Canadian federal government's legislation redefining the Canada-Kahnawake relationship: the Indian Act.

The effort to preserve valued Mohawk mobility and individual economic independence is typified in their eagerness to escape the uneventful sedentary existence of the village. Kahnawake men figured prominently in various wars and British imperial adventures around the world. For example, a number of them took part in the 1855 Land Arctic Search Expedition as guides and expert canoemen (Frisch 1975: 27–30). Some served as infantrymen with the Union army during the American Civil War.[2] They were also an important element in the forces of the 1884–85 Gordon Relief Expedition in Egypt.[3]

Between these adventures, the village economy revolved around river-rafting and the craft trade, with some supplemental income derived from a stone quarry operated by the community. An American visitor to the village in 1883 observed a thriving cottage industry in bead-work and ornamental native-style crafts. The volume was remarkable; at one location over 10,000 pounds of beads were stored (Smith 1883: 398).

By the end of the century, the Mohawks integrated further into the North American economy by developing particular roles in the construction industry. Specifically, they joined in specialty occupations conveying and installing the 'high steel' used in bridge-building and the erection of the new American 'skyscrapers' (Katzer 1972). This integration led them not only to the local Montreal marketplace, but to the regional industrial centres of the United States.

THE INDIAN ACT

The gradual modernization of individual roles and the economy as a whole parallels an ascendence of the system of governance in Kahnawake established by the Euro-American Indian Act. This political process reflected the same compromise between tradition and modernity on the part of the Mohawks as did the modernization of the economy. For quite a while after the passage of federal legislation authorizing various ministries to take control over Indian Affairs, the Canadian government did not even attempt to impose itself upon or alter Kahnawake's political structure. An Indian Affairs historian has remarked that:

> Although the Caughnawaga Indians, now recognized as a Band, had become subject to the provisions of the [Indian Act], the Department seemed to content itself in keeping touch only through a part-time agent . . . visiting the four Chiefs once a week or less . . . It was not until 1934 that a full-time Indian Agent with a constituted Agency Office on the Reserve was authorized. (Taggart 1948: 12)

An elected system of government nominally succeeded the traditional government in 1890, when the community accepted the provisions of the Indian Act (Villeneuve 1984). The establishment of the Indian Act system brought with it an administrative link to the federal government through an Indian Agency located near, and later within, the reserve. The Indian Act also established an electoral system and put in place a 'band council' of locally elected men to form the political leadership of the community. The Canadian government had previously made an intense effort to assert some degree of control over the territory. In 1882, a government-sponsored land survey was conducted with the explicit purpose of imposing a land tenure regime based on individual allotments rather than common ownership. The Walbank Land Survey for the first time enumerated land parcels and created a membership list of persons eligible for government recognition as Mohawks of Kahnawake (Taggart 1948: 15–17). Thus, the inception in 1890 of Kahnawake's modern political institutions—the band council, the Land Allotment system, and the Membership List—represented the government's successful effort to replace the local control inherent in a traditional system with a Euro-American system of governance.

Acceptance of this regime was hindered from the start by its derivation from Canadian law and its specific purpose of controlling land tenure and membership for the Canadian government. It was strictly an administrative application of the Indian Act, and it introduced a foreign institution with no real claim to authority in Mohawk lives. In fact, its limited validity and utility was openly affirmed and the traditional community government co-existed with the Indian Act regime for some time, with traditional chiefs sometimes serving as nominal band council administrators (Taggart 1943: 22).

Differing Kahnawake and Department views on the role of the Agency within the community were the most common source of conflict in the early stages of accommodation. Whereas the Mohawks saw the Agency as a means of maintaining a relationship with the Canadian government, the government itself clearly saw the Agency as an instrument of control. Inasmuch as the Department restricted its own activities to maintaining essential political links, Kahnawake was accommodating and even enthusiastic at times in its support of the system. The Mohawks adapted smoothly, for example, to requirements for selecting band council members to represent the community to the Department. Almost immediately, Kahnawake established a system of elections in accordance with the provisions of the Indian Act. A Department report on the election of band councillors in 1893 details the process by which leaders were elected by consensus at a meeting of representatives elected in each of the reserve's six sections. The system apparently enjoyed a great deal of support—even with only men eligible to participate, there were just over 300 votes cast (PAC-RG10: v.2681, #137,015).

The Department's records for this period are also rife with examples of discord between the Department and the local Kahnawake government. A 1904 Annual Report on Kahnawake by the Inspector of Indian Agencies and Reserves, for example, notes the band council's persistent criticism of an unsatisfactory state of affairs and mismanagement by the assigned Agent. A number of complaints related to the Agent's failure to fulfil his legal responsibility to guard against trespass, specifically for encouraging White settlement in the territory by giving permission to local people to live within the Reserve, prompted the Inspector to recommend acceding to the Mohawks' demands for action:

> The Council is not unreasonable; but it can easily be understood, in view of the Iroquois character, that complaint and dissatisfaction will never cease until the matter is conclusively dealt with. I do not think the matter should be left in the hands of the local Agent. (PAC-RG10: v.3048, # 237,660, pt.8)

The 'Iroquois character' referred to by the Inspector was actually an emerging culture of politics in Kahnawake which allowed for the accommodation of the Indian Act system based on a perception that the Canadian government shared the Mohawk commitment to an ideal of mutual co-existence between nations. In the Mohawks' view, both the Department and the local Mohawk government had responsibilities in different realms of authority. The Mohawks were willing to accept the Indian Act system as a framework which relegated the Department to an intermediary role between their seat of government and the seat of Canadian government. But when the Department attempted to assert any degree of influence over internal affairs, or to restrict Kahnawake's political autonomy, the Mohawks reacted strongly. The Mohawks and the Canadian government held two different views on the same legislation and institutions. This permitted the Act and those institutions to survive as long as it has in the vacuum between the two views—with minimum conflict. When the nature of the Act as perceived and imposed by the Canadian government became clear, Mohawk resistance emerged fuelled by a feeling that the Canadian government betrayed the 'true' meaning of the Act in Mohawk eyes. Misunderstanding (dual understanding) thus contributed to peace for a while, but eventually formed the crux of the Mohawks' resistance to integration in the Canadian system.

Both this perception and the definition of the relationship, as the 1904 example demonstrates, were flawed. The Canadian government created the Indian Act not as a means of co-existing peacefully with native nations and autonomous Indian communities, but as an instrument of internal colonial domination over what Canada saw as marginal minority communities.[4] While on the surface portraying a purposeful protection of Indian lands and status, the Indian Act and associated legislation were really the means by which Canada sought eventually to usurp all Indian lands in the name of the Crown and to abrogate Indian rights and special status by assimilating all Indians into the general population and culture. As time wore on, the Mohawks became more aware of the true purposes of the Indian Act.

REACTION: THE FIRST TRADITIONALIST REVIVAL

In 1926, the Mohawks of Kahnawake had been politically distinct from the Iroquois Confederacy for 250 years. While kinship and other social and cultural ties remained strong, the community's autonomy in the political sphere was an established fact. But just as a 17th-century shift in the Mohawks' political and economic environment made imperative a redefinition of goals in the form of a break from the Confederacy, in the face of 20th-century pressures a reunion with the ideology and institutions of the ancient League was an appealing option.

The key event which precipitated a Kahnawake commitment to recreating its political link to the Confederacy was a threat to the established Iroquois right of free passage between the United States and Canada. In March, 1926, a Kahnawake Mohawk named Paul Diabo was arrested in Philadelphia as an illegal alien. Immediately, the entire Iroquois community including the Grand Councils at both Onondaga and Six Nations was galvanized in support of Diabo. The arrest was a direct challenge to the concept of Iroquois sovereignty and indeed to the very idea that the various nations making up the Confederacy still existed apart from the United States and Canada.

Charging Diabo with being an illegal alien, the Iroquois argued, was a violation of the Jay Treaty of 1794, which included provisions recognizing the Indians' existence as nations and guaranteeing their peoples' right to travel freely between the territories. On 8 July a federal judge in Trenton, N.J. agreed with the Iroquois, and the Iroquois free-passage right was reaffirmed. It survived two later appeals by the US Department of Immigration (Blanchard 1982a: 284–5).

The significance and power of Iroquois unity in support of a common cause was not lost upon the Kahnawake Mohawks or the people of the other Iroquois communities. As an unprecedented show of solidarity in celebration of their victory, a Grand Council of the Iroquois Confederacy was scheduled to be held at Kahnawake. Despite the many sources of potential conflict between the various communities since their physical separation hundreds of years before, a pervasive sense of re-emerging unity had come over the people. During a planning session at the Catholic church hall, an Onondaga speaker discounted the possibility of real or imagined differences interfering with Iroquois unity with this statement:

> [He said that] we were all [Onkwehonwe] and that is why we were meeting. He said that when anybody came in that door he should take his religion off like a coat, and hang it up. (Blanchard 1982a: 285)

Permission to use the church hall property as a meeting place was denied by the Jesuit pastor. So instead, a Longhouse structure was constructed to house the Grand Council. With the physical resurrection of a Longhouse in Kahnawake, the community began its partial re-alignment with traditional Iroquois political institutions.

Re-creating the Confederacy link gave to Kahnawake politics an entirely different tone and focus. Hundreds of years of political isolation and complete village autonomy had left Kahnawake alone to deal with the pressures for integration into the general landscape of Canadian society. Despite the ease with which they had assimilated into the greater North American market economy, complete political and social assimilation into Canada was viewed as equivalent to a cultural death sentence. Rediscovering the power of their membership in the Confederacy gave the Mohawks in Kahnawake a renewed source of authority and influence in defending their land and rights from a growing assimilationist effort on the part of non-Indian governments.

In a sense, re-creating the political ideology of the Iroquois was a natural response in searching for a means of protecting the distinctiveness and territorial integrity of their community. Since the coming of the modern era, Kahnawake territory had become open to expropriation by the Canadian government in support of business interests. Roads, bridges, and rights-of-way were carved out of Kahnawake to provide favourable transportation routes for Canadian commerce. The community was saturated with non-Indian residents who found Kahnawake an attractive tax-free alternative to living and doing business in Montreal. There was a very real fear on the part of some Kahnawake leaders that they had lost control of the community's future development as a Mohawk community, and that their people were well on their way to cultural assimilation.

Choosing Sides—Revival and Reaction

Nowhere was this justifiable fear reflected more than in the opposing programs of the two assertive political factions of the 1940s. On one side of the argument were those who favoured a deeper integration into Canadian society. Generally, this group represented Mohawk entrepreneurs and those who had chosen to live outside the community. Known officially as the 'Intelligent Party', its members consisted mainly of educated and 'off-reserve' progressive Mohawks favouring a further institutionalization of the Indian Act system. Closely allied with the Catholic church, this group favoured an expansion of the scope of the Indian Act in Kahnawake, an elimination of the traditional Longhouse as a form of government and as a source of religion, and increased funding for economic development in the community (Blanchard 1982a: 296–9).

Opposing the Intelligent Party were the traditional Longhouse people. Ironically, joining with the Longhouse in opposition to the business program were the band council Chiefs serving under the Indian Act. Both the traditional leaders and the elected band councillors advocated a return to a traditional government and an abolition of the Indian Act's application in Kahnawake (Blanchard 1982a: 292–5). In alliance with the leadership of the Confederacy, the band council pushed for a rejection of the assimilationist Intelligent Party policy, both internally and externally.

Convincing Mohawks living within the community that their land, rights, and culture needed to be protected by rejecting further assimilation was easy. All one had to do was look around to see the results of assimilation in the inability of most young Mohawks to speak their own language, and in the ever-growing manifestations of non-Indian behaviour and values in the community. Yet non-Indian society continued to attract some. Many Mohawks had in fact left the community and saw Kahnawake as nothing more than a base of operations or a retreat from the summer heat of places like New York City or Detroit. Others saw Kahnawake primarily as a tax- and regulation-free locale for economic ventures. The value of Kahnawake for these people did not lie in the preservation of its Mohawk character or territorial integrity.

In testimony presented before the Indian Act parliamentary review committee in June, 1947, the contrast between the assimilationist and traditionalist ideologies was laid bare. Speaking for the elected band council, the Longhouse, and the Six Nations Confederacy, Matthew Lazare described the Kahnawake position on reform in the community. He listed a six-point program that included: 1) a return to traditional Iroquois-style government; 2) control over membership; 3) a rejection of taxation in any form, especially of taxing individual Mohawks; 4) a rejection of Canadian citizenship; 5) a demand that all non-Indian residents be removed from Kahnawake; and 6) a demand that the physically abusive Sisters of Ste Anne nuns be removed from teaching positions in government-run schools (Blanchard 1982a: 295).

Speaking for the Intelligent Party, Ed Beauvais stated in response that the traditionalist revival was nothing more than an embittered attack on the church, and portrayed the band council and the Longhouse people as misguided reactionaries. Prosperity, according to the Intelligent Party, could only be achieved if the Canadian government supported a complete modernization of the electoral system in Kahnawake. He called for three major reforms: 1) moving the bi-annual election date from February to July, so as to allow non-resident Mohawks to vote in the community elections; 2) imposing a literacy test for political participation; and 3) requiring a qualifying exam for potential officeholders (Blanchard 1982a: 299).

When it came time for the federal government to choose a side in this dispute—Kahnawake was in this case only the most advanced case and representative of tensions existing in many other Native groups—it naturally supported that which reaffirmed Canada's existing role and authority in the various Indian communities. Implementing one program or the other would signal its attitude toward reform of the Indian Act. The federal government's policies and legislation were eventually revised, and most of the Intelligent Party's program was reflected in the new 1951 Indian Act. Within Kahnawake, the revisions temporarily satisfied an influential group, but the restructuring had the effect of creating two solid and opposing political factions.

The division of the community into traditionalist and modernizing blocs after World War II set the basic foundation for contemporary politics in Kahnawake. A long history of accommodating to change as a single unit had come to an end. This period, according to a historian of the Iroquois, was a critical juncture:

> World War II had shifted the communities' attention in an outward direction, had ended the vestiges of the remaining barter economy, and had begun to undermine community cohesiveness. (Hauptman 1986: 135)

The division can be viewed as being a natural part of the Iroquois factional differentiation process which led to the formation of Kahnawake in the first place. After all, the Mohawks had lost the commonality of interest previously ensured by a single culture, religious orientation, and occupation. In another era the traditionalists and modernists might have decided to form their distinct communities in separate parts of Kanienke. But this was the mid-20th century, and Kanienke was limited to small, fully occupied 'reservations' within the vast expanse of their former lands. Rather than being able to relieve the pressure of political conflict by out-migrating to new villages, Mohawk leaders were forced to choose sides within their community, and to live with the divisions.

A Crisis of Faith

Living with this division in the community was initially manageable only because the cleavage was along political lines. Before the late 1950s, issues of culture and religion were untouched by the growing split. Active Longhouse adherents remained a small minority among the Catholic majority of Kahnawake, and given the limited impact of government on the daily life of the community, politics in general were a secondary concern compared to more important economic and social issues.

Both of these pre-conditions for stability evaporated at the end of the 1950s. The Longhouse movement began to attract large numbers of adherents, creating friction between those who remained Catholic and the new traditionalists seeking to supplant the church with a native belief system. The choice between the political programs promoted by the traditionalist and the Indian Act factions became a personal issue for every community member. The scope of government activity in the community also increased drastically with the construction of the St Lawrence Seaway toward the end of the decade. This major assault on the Mohawk land base and sovereignty highlighted the very real differences between the two programs. In the end all Mohawks were to come away with a clear sense of what further integration into Canadian society meant, and what the promise of a return to the Iroquois tradition held.

The impact of integration on their legal rights had become apparent during the Second World War. Just as in the Diabo case of 1926, the United States government sought to capitalize on heavy Mohawk migrations to find work in American cities and to deny the existence of Iroquois sovereignty. The American government decided that all World War II era legislation applied to the Mohawks, including the military draft:

> In two later draft cases[5] . . . involving Mohawk Indians from the Six Nations and Caughnawaga reserves, the federal courts went even further, holding that the Selective Service Act was applicable to Indian non-citizen aliens from Canada residing in the United States . . . The Court dismissed the Mohawks' contentions that the Jay Treaty . . . exempted them from being drafted into military service in the United States. (Hauptman 1986: 6)

Much closer to home, the Canadian government was similarly attacking the principle of Mohawk sovereignty by again attempting to again expropriate large amounts of land in Kahnawake. This time, the Canadians planned to run the St Lawrence Seaway straight through the riverfront settlements occupied by the Mohawks for almost 250 years, even though averting expropriation and constructing the Seaway trench farther out into the river would have added only two million dollars to the final cost of the project. The Conservative Party parliamentary opposition, including future Prime Minister John Diefenbaker, decried the Kahnawake expropriation as unnecessary and illegal (Mabee 1961: 208). The Premier of Quebec, Duplessis, would have nothing to do with the expropriation of Mohawk land. He criticized the Canadian federal government for impinging upon what he viewed as a provincial jurisdiction, and saw the construction of the Seaway through Kahnawake as a 'monumental mess' (Chevrier 1959: 105; Mabee 1961: 50; see Chapter Seven).

Over the political protests and legal actions initiated by Kahnawake's band council, the Seaway Authority enticed individual Mohawks directly affected by the expropriation with cash settlements. Once most of the individual challenges had been settled, the Authority received a writ to evict the remaining Mohawks who had refused to abandon their land for cash settlement. In a final attempt, the band council petitioned the United Nations for assistance in combating the Canadian violation of due process and deprivation of the Mohawks' 'inherent rights of possession of their land and property' (Villeneuve 1984: 66).

The Liberal government disregarded the protests of the Mohawk band council and concerned Canadians. The government official charged with implementing the seaway project in the Montreal area,

Lionel Chevrier of Cornwall, Ontario, could not understand the Mohawk government's resistance to this seizure of their territory. In his memoirs, Chevrier wrote of Kahnawake's opposition:

> The Indians, perhaps with some prompting, took the position that there was a chance to make some money out of the seaway . . . The Indians were certainly led to believe that the more fuss and trouble they made the more money they would get . . . sometimes I felt that the Indians were just having a lot of fun at the expense of the seaway. (Chevrier 1959: 104)

The Mohawks were certainly not averse to 'having a lot of fun' at the expense of Chevrier. In one memorable incident, the Mohawks had a peace-pipe smoking ceremony in which Chevrier smoked the calumet upside down. The ridiculous image was featured in the Montreal press the next day, causing Chevrier to comment: 'I endured a great ribbing from my colleagues in the seaway the following morning . . . one colleague said, "100 years ago, we would never have left that meeting alive!"' (Chevrier 1959: 104). Unfortunately for the Mohawks, it was not one hundred years earlier, and all their efforts to halt the construction failed. The band council had been appealing to the Canadian government to honour its agreements with the Mohawks. It also sought a guarantee from the British government that when devolving to Canada control of the Indian relationship, it had stipulated that prior treaties would be respected. In 1952 the band council wrote to the Home Secretary in London regarding Anglo-Indian treaties. The reply was forwarded to Ottawa and given to the Indian Agent on 4 April 1952. The band was told: 'they may rest assured that the new Indian Act does not alter in any way such rights as Indians have under their treaties' (Ghobashy 1961: 114). This reaffirmation of the Mohawks' rights as clarified in the Royal Proclamation and the Gage Decision[6] gave credence to the strategy of working within the context of British-Canadian law to stop the expropriation.

Community strategy at this point was stated clearly by the Mohawks' lawyer:

> The Caughnawaga Band Council has not advocated secession from Canada or independence, but their policy is inter-dependence within the Dominion, with safeguards for minority rights, and respect for treaties and royal proclamations. (Ghobashy 1961: 117)

Officially committed to working within the framework of the federal structure, the band council was soon disillusioned by the callous disregard displayed in the eventual full expropriation by Order in Council (P.C. 1955–1416) and the forced relocation of homes in Kahnawake. There was a growing sense among Kahnawake Mohawks that the rules of the game were skewed against them; even with treaties in hand and armed with rational legal arguments, the community was ignored by the federal government and their village was overrun and destroyed by bulldozers and earth-movers.

Faith in the Canadian government and in the British Crown as reliable protectors of Mohawk land rights was shattered by the Seaway debacle. It was clear that the non-Indian governments were not going to honour commitments made hundreds of years before in a completely different context. It was also easy to see how the community's strategy of legal action within the Canadian federation had failed miserably. A new answer was needed, one which did not depend upon the honour of non-Indian governments to guarantee Mohawk rights.

PROMISE OF THE PAST: THE SECOND TRADITIONALIST REVIVAL

In stark contrast to the cooperative strategy of the band council, a different group of Mohawks from various communities were taking direct action to confront the injustice of the Seaway expropriation. In August 1957, 200 Mohawks led by Francis Johnson of Akwesasne repossessed the site of an ancient Mohawk village near Fort Hunter, N.Y. in response to the upcoming seizure of Mohawk lands in Kahnawake and Akwesasne by the Seaway Authority (Hauptman 1986: 149). In what became known as the Standing Arrow movement, a new Mohawk strategy was born:

> Although Standing Arrow's leadership was short-lived, he did predict
> . . . the strategy that the Iroquois and other Indians nationwide would
> use in their fight to save their lands and their way of life: more renewed
> assertions of sovereignty and treaty rights; more vocal calls for land
> claims; more careful manipulation of the press to gain attention for
> Indian concerns; and more organized demonstrations and protests.
> (Hauptman 1986: 150)

The significance of this new strategy consisted not in the tactics used, but in its links to a parallel traditionalist movement. The band council was not precluded from undertaking bold action and voicing pressure in support of Mohawk rights. But it was the people drawn to the traditionalist movement who embraced these tactics wholeheartedly, and political action became the hallmark of the Longhouse.

Just as in the 1920s, a political crisis fuelled the resurgence of the Longhouse in Kahnawake. The difference between the 1920s and the 1950s was that the latter movement was an explicit rejection of non-Indian society and European-style government. In the 1920s, the political link to the Confederacy was reaffirmed without any specific religious or cultural content for the union. In the 1950s, the Longhouse people sought to complete that link to the historical Iroquois by recreating a traditional society in total. It was no longer a matter of choosing between political programs or strategies: now people had to choose between opposite lifestyles. Disillusionment with the teachings of the Catholic church and the Seaway betrayal by the Canadian government brought about a severe crisis of faith. The answer to Kahnawake's problems, for an increasing number of Mohawks, consisted in the resurrection of a traditional society and an explicit assertion of nationalist objectives.

Corresponding to the two major sources of discontent in the community, the traditionalist revival of the 1950s had two faces. The ceremonial and ritualistic focus for the spiritually oriented contrasted with the explicitly political agenda for others. Two individuals represented the dual nature of the movement. Key players in the revival, Louis Hall and Joe Phillips, were responsible for rebuilding the Kahnawake Longhouse in response to the crisis of faith. Each had experienced his own personal crisis of belief—both had been baptized Catholic and had considered spiritual vocations in the Church before rejecting Christianity (Blanchard 1982a: 301).

Phillips and those he represented concentrated on preserving the culture of the Iroquois by immersing themselves in the rituals and ceremonies of the Longhouse. Hall and his followers developed an increasingly militant strategy for asserting Mohawk political sovereignty *vis-à-vis* non-Indian society. Despite the different foci, the two were united in a commitment to replace the band council government with a traditional Iroquois-style government.

Thus by the end of the 1950s Kahnawake was divided into factions. In the decade since the emergence of distinct strategies in the late 1940s, the disparity between those 'Intelligent Party' Mohawks who favoured cooperation with Canadian authorities and who had gained control of the band council, and those 'Traditionalist' Mohawks who favoured increased autonomy and a confrontationist strategy grew very wide. The band council and the majority of Mohawks were still not convinced of the Longhouse program's long-term viability as an effective strategy to guarantee the community's security, and an internal debate raged. The legacy of that debate is the division and factional cleavage that characterizes the contemporary politics of Kahnawake.

The divisions and factionalization now evident within the community were direct results of the loss of control inherent in the Indian Act's implementation in Kahnawake. In the 19th and early 20th centuries the community suffered a gradual erosion of its power with a subsequent loss of autonomy and further integration into the Canadian economic and political superstructure as a marginal element. The most obvious manifestations of this were territorial intrusions in the form of land expropriation in the interest of Canadian commercial and industrial development. The Mohawks were also forced to recognize the economic necessity of acquiescing in the revision of their political status with respect to Canada. With their traditional sources of income no longer viable, and in the midst of an economic and occupational adjustment, even the paltry protection and economic incentives offered by the Indian Act in return for surrendering political autonomy must have seemed worthwhile to many.

Nevertheless, most Kahnawake Mohawks maintained a consistent ideological position, refusing to accede to the Canadian government's demands for a surrender of identity or the idea of a distinct national status. The Indian Act is an inherently assimilationist document which seeks to coopt Indian nationhood by placing Native peoples within Canadian society—but to be sure, by creating a lower status and maintaining racially segregated political institutions. Despite their minimal cooperation in the administration of the Indian Act, the Mohawks managed to maintain their traditionally sovereigntist political culture. They accomplished this by reforming the culture in the modern era to reflect an acceptance of the political framework imposed upon them by the Canadian government, while insisting upon their independence and autonomy with respect to the arbitrary rules established on the authority of Indian Act legislation.

In the latter half of the 20th century, a number of key events have caused attitudes to shift. Even as early as the border crossing case during the 1920s, basic political and legal inconsistencies within the relationship's framework were laid bare. The crisis of faith in the Catholic church, the implementation of an elected system of government, the growth of an internal Indian Act bureaucracy, and the coming of the St Lawrence Seaway all contributed to another shift in political culture.

The Seaway in particular, because of the destruction and dislocation brought on by massive land expropriation, was a clear sign that the relationship embodied in the Indian Act was no longer sufficient to protect Kahnawake from the very real threats presented by Canadian society. Previous transgressions by Canada had involved more abstract rights, and the community had at least maintained its historical land base and territorial integrity. The Seaway drove Kahnawake away from a position of trust in the Canadian government—'back to the woods', in words contained in their oral tradition. Back to a much older alternative ideology predicated on basic and consistent assertions of independent nationhood.

CHAPTER FOUR

BACK TO THE WOODS

TRADITIONALISM IN KAHNAWAKE

Brother! We have borne everything patiently for this long time past; we have done everything we could consistently do with the welfare of our nations in general—notwithstanding the many advantages that have been taken of us . . . our patience is now entirely worn out.

Thayendenega, Mohawk, 1794

When the Mohawks of Kahnawake went 'back to the woods' in search of guiding principles, they revisited a political tradition uniquely suited to the purpose of re-establishing their community on a solid foundation. The institutions and political thought of their Iroquois forefathers had survived into the modern era. More than a memory or cultural remnant, they were operational concepts in a number of Iroquois communities. The Onondaga nation in upstate New York was still governed by a traditional Iroquois council, as were segments of various other Iroquois communities in New York and Ontario. In the minds of many Iroquois the traditional Iroquois political philosophy remained a salient idea and powerful alternative to Euro-American values. With this living tradition so accessible, the Mohawks of Kahnawake embarked upon an intensive immersion into the culture in a conscious effort to re-learn and re-implement traditional ways in their own community.

It was soon discovered that the path leading 'back to the woods' contained an obstacle making the wholesale adoption or easy implementation of traditional ways impossible. In the years since Kahnawake had been distanced from the other Iroquois communities, that culture had been modified in response to shifts in the political and economic environment. These shifts were largely particular to the circumstances within the other communities. The most important was the integration of the teachings of the 19th-century prophet *Skaniatariio*, or Handsome Lake, into the political message contained in the

Kaienerekowa's much older set of ideas. The Mohawks of Kahnawake saw Handsome Lake's synthesis of indigenous thought with Christian morality as a corruption of the original concepts. The Mohawks, who through a return to traditionalism were rejecting their own Christian background, were dismayed to find that most of their Iroquois brothers and sisters had adopted a religion based in part on Christian teachings!

There were, however, other sources of traditional knowledge within the communities unaffected by Handsome Lake, and the few Mohawks who had preserved the traditional ways became important resources in the transformation of the community. The Mohawks began to participate in the political process within the wider traditional Iroquois community. Exposed to the mechanisms and procedures of Iroquois governance, the Mohawks found they did not share the values underpinning the contemporary Confederacy's formal structures. Alone again, the Mohawks of Kahnawake, joined by most Mohawks in the nation's other communities at Akwesasne (near Cornwall, Ontario) and Kanehsatake (northwest of Montreal), began to develop an ideology which attempted to replicate the 'authentic' Confederacy before it had been altered by the influence of Handsome Lake.

The cultural and political duality of the traditional revival in Kahnawake has already been discussed, but it is worth emphasizing that both the spiritually and politically oriented traditionalist Mohawk groups in Kahnawake and the nation's other communities had divorced themselves from the main body of the Iroquois Confederacy, and embarked on an independent path toward the re-establishment of traditional values in Mohawk country. Previous chapters in this study have shown how Kahnawake retained a basically Iroquois political culture in spite of the cultural and political difference between the community and the source of that tradition.

Having made a commitment to revive traditionalism within the community, the Mohawks of Kahnawake were engaged in a re-orientation of outward political structures and symbols to make them conform to the inward values and principles which had continued to live on in the local political culture. Traditional re-orientation in Kahnawake results in an ideology which recognizes the power and significance of Iroquois structures and symbolism, but which at the same time modifies the Iroquois values and principles where they conflict with those contained in the established local culture as it has evolved since the distancing of Kahnawake from the main body of the Iroquois Confederacy. Understanding ideology in Kahnawake demands a knowledge of an objective representation of the historic Iroquois political thought and an understanding of how that objective tradition has been modified in the process of re-creating traditionalism in Kahnawake itself.

VIEWS ON REFORMATION

Scholarly work dealing with the modernization of culture in Kahnawake was previously limited to the field of anthropology. From the 1950s through to the 1970s, anthropologists were concerned with the process of acculturation among North American Indians; Kahnawake provided a fertile laboratory for their investigation of the 'fact', which they alone perceived, that Indian people were increasingly distanced from their indigenous roots. Despite their focus on forms of social organization and religion, the studies conducted under this rubric are valuable in that they point to the political manifestations of contrasting paths taken by Mohawks in the modernization of their culture.

These studies represent an attempt to fit the Kahnawake experience into a theoretical structure predicated on the belief that the process of cultural change consisted in the displacement, within individuals, of characteristics from one culture by those of another. The central premise was another unchallenged belief that cultures themselves were stable blocs of attitudes and patterns of organization. Thus in the Kahnawake case, anthropologists focused on instances where Indian individuals, or groups of individuals, displayed attitudes or characteristics representative of White culture, and this was seen as a process whereby Indians were becoming less Indian and more White. Archetypal Indian and monolithic White cultures were paired off as poles between which individuals navigated in constructing their identities. Within this framework, a number of concepts emerged to explain the multitude of variations in culture within communities like Kahnawake.

Nativism

In the aftermath of the internal battle over the Indian Act revision, the late 1940s saw the bifurcation of Kahnawake's traditionalist and modernist political blocs. Anthropologists studying Kahnawake culture at the time were struck by the intensity of political differences within the supposedly homogeneous Indian community. Voget remarked that 'The contemporary scene . . . is characterized by political dissensions of high intensity, which are also linked with religious differences' (Voget 1951: 221). As evidence for this remark, Voget mistakenly equated Longhouse affiliation with an exclusively religious sentiment. The tangential 'linkage' he observed between politics and religion had in fact by that time become inextricable. In spite of this, he was prescient in observing nascent cleavages and creating a matrix to explain them.

Voget explained the development of blocs within the community in terms of differential levels of 'nativism'—where individuals had re-integrated elements of traditional Iroquois culture to the extent that the re-integration caused a noticeable modification or abandonment of

European cultural characteristics. He did not examine the connection between differentials in the re-integration of native culture and political differences, but in hindsight the research is useful in illuminating the early formation of different branches of traditionalism as discrete political ideologies. According to Voget, there were 300 Longhouse people— 10% of the population—in Kahnawake in 1950. These 300⁻ were described as former Christians who had adopted the religion of Handsome Lake and who formed three separate traditional groupings: the Grand River Longhouse, the Onondaga Longhouse, and an unaffiliated Longhouse (Voget 1951: 222).

With respect to the three Longhouse groupings, and between the Longhouses and the majority of the community, Voget observed that 'Inter-group interaction is minimal and wholly political in nature. Cooperation occurs for the most part when the security of the whole is threatened' (Voget 1951: 222). While this broad assertion is unsubstantiated speculation on the intensity and motivation of group interaction, it does indicate that there were noticeable differences rooted in traditionalism, some of which manifested themselves in politics as early as 1950. Voget noticed a basic similarity in the core beliefs of all those he would term 'native-modified'. Members of all three Longhouse groups were separated from the majority of the community, Voget believed, by a 'nativism' consisting of five key elements (Voget 1951: 222):

1. Destruction of the Indian Act
2. Re-establishing traditional Mohawk government
3. Distinct peoplehood
4. Focus on ancestry
5. Historical view: dispossession.

Revitalization

In contrast to the static view of culture undergirding Voget's studies, later anthropological work on Kahnawake moved from a concern with change in individuals to a focus on cultural systems as a whole. In the 1960s, Postal examined the community as an example of what was termed 'revitalization' in Indian communities (Postal 1965). A more appropriate conception of the work done under this framework would centre on a process of re-invention rather than revitalization. Postal saw in Kahnawake the reconstruction of Iroquois social and political structures in a traditional cultural vacuum divested of any real connection to traditional values, and revitalized for a modern reality. The salient connection, in her view, was how social and economic deprivation lead to a pragmatic recreation of the cultural-political framework better suited to accommodating this environment.

Postal integrated two examples of cultural change in Kahnawake into her argument. She investigated a case of what she termed 'Hoax Nativism' during the years 1916-1920, during which a charlatan, snake-oil type, traveller came to Kahnawake selling salvation in the form of pan-Indianism and a return to the old ways (Postal 1965: 271). The charlatan eventually gained a great deal of support in the community and succeeded in bilking many Mohawks. The Thunderwater Movement was only halted upon the intervention of a Mohawk who exposed the traveller as a fraud.[1] Postal concluded that Mohawks in Kahnawake did not know enough of their own traditions during this era to recognize even such an obvious hoax.

Postal coupled this case with the emergence in the 1920s of what she viewed as real nativism in the form of the Handsome Lake religion. The advent of Six Nations Chief George Thomas in 1923 was the beginning of a revitalization which was consolidated in 1947 with the condolence[2] of two Kahnawake chiefs in the Six Nations Confederacy (Postal 1965: 273). Postal believed that embarrassment over the Thunderwater hoax pre-disposed the Mohawks to re-orient their culture along more authentically traditional lines represented by the Longhouse. At the time, she did not see a base within the community for resurrecting Iroquois forms of social and political organization. The absence of all traditional forms in Kahnawake previous to the 1920s allowed those who would reject the European religion and culture to re-integrate key elements of the Iroquois traditional culture as a coherent and unified whole.

Thus Postal explained the emergence of traditionalism during the 1920s in terms of the community's reflection of three key factors: 1) traditional culture in Kahnawake had been sufficiently disintegrated to respond to nativism; 2) Kahnawake Mohawks were not much accepted by or integrated in the wider non-Indian society; and 3) Kahnawake Mohawks displayed a continuing faith in the primacy of native values and principles. Postal's explanation is flawed only by her strict adherence to the revitalization model. Clearly, she should have collapsed the first two factors to describe the retention of sufficient cultural linkages to tradition to allow the re-emergence of a traditional culture when called for by shifts in the wider environment. The strength of the Longhouse revival versus the flash of Thunderwater is evidence that the former's authenticity was recognized and continued to resonate strongly within the community. Postal mistook the Kahnawake Mohawks' empathy for the native cause represented by Thunderwater's pan-Indianism—which in fact re-emerged as a strong and persistent theme in native politics during the 1970s—as evidence of the superficiality of their culture, as if only those Indians who did not possess a culture of their own could be party to a broader Indian movement.

The development of a political component within the revival of a traditional culture is a general feature in Indian revitalization movements, but most often the emergent political program represents a 'modernization' in the sense that the indigenous political elements are abandoned or subsumed in favour of a Euro-American framework (Voget 1956: 256). This view has pre-disposed researchers such as Postal to see the revival of tradition in Kahnawake as occurring in an environment devoid of authentic traditional culture. Her theory led to the conclusion that only acculturated peoples could argue for political goals conceived of in European terms—goals such as sovereignty and civil rights. But this conclusion is undermined by the fact that more often than not it is a case of Indian people using—or misusing— 'European' terminology to express what remain essentially indigenous concepts. As we shall see in the chapters to follow, it does not automatically follow that because an Indian expresses himself in European terms, that his perspective is European.

Persistence

The theory that Indian societies have maintained key elements of their traditional culture while accommodating modernity in other, more superficial ways has been another focus of anthropological research in Kahnawake. Voget's study during the early 1950s of kinship changes since the traditional period—reflected in the clan system, family systems, and marriage rules—led him to conclude that 'certain principles have been accorded a new importance, and others, formerly of great importance, have been restricted in their application or are completely lost' (Voget 1953: 392). Voget did not link his conclusion concerning kinship to politics but, on its own or as a counterpoint to Postal's theory of a traditional cultural vacuum, the extension of the idea of persistence to the political realm is important. That certain principles of tradition have been consciously elevated in importance, while others have been subsumed in the process of accommodating a new reality, can be extended to the political realm in the Kahnawake case particularly, given that in the Iroquois tradition the family is the primary unit of political as well as social organization.

In the 1960s, Freilich put forward an argument in favour of the Kahnawake Mohawks representing a case of cultural persistence. In his work on the Mohawk High Steel trade and the transient Mohawk community in Brooklyn, NY, he compared contemporary Mohawk culture with that of traditional Mohawk society (Freilich 1963). His conclusion was that the defining features of traditional Mohawk society with respect to gender roles and group interaction were also present in contemporary Mohawk society. He saw in both the traditional and contemporary cases a 'warrior ethic' which manifested itself in clearly recognizable ways.

In Freilich's view, whether the pre-occupation was warfare or High Steel, the structure of Mohawk society had remained the same. He saw a pattern of seven persistent cultural characteristics. With respect to the men: 1) a 'conquering hero mentality' which pushed the men to prove themselves away from Kahnawake and return home to glory; 2) a rejection of hierarchical, formal, or 'lineal' authority; and 3) the necessity of danger or excitement inherent in whatever endeavour the men had chosen to pursue. The women had two persistent characteristics: 4) the necessity of close contact with the matrilineal family or other Mohawk women; and 5) child rearing. And as a group: 6) the maintenance of an 'adoption complex' which allowed non-Mohawks to be easily integrated into the community; and 7) a disinterest in the accumulation of property (Freilich 1963: 180).

The major problem with Freilich's work is that the comparison focuses only on the most superficial aspects of culture in both the traditional and contemporary examples. Beyond this, as is the case with most studies which contrast contemporary with traditional Indian societies, the model posited as 'traditional' is in fact no such thing. The society used as a traditional reference is drawn from historical accounts during the colonial era, perhaps the period of greatest change in the entire history of Indian peoples. Indian life during this era was only slightly more representative of traditional ideals than the contemporary society. The contemporary example used by Freilich is also unsuitable because it represents to a large degree an expatriate group which never did consolidate into a community away from Kahnawake. His group did not represent contemporary Mohawk society so much as it did a segment of the Mohawk population living in an urban context for extended periods of time.[3]

The entire concept of a 'warrior ethic' is problematic if it is conceived of as a special feature of Mohawk or even Indian society—as Freilich asserts in his study. It seems that the male bravado which forms the basis of Freilich's thesis is evident as well in the non-Mohawk men involved in High Steel or other construction occupations. The traditional traits ascribed to the Mohawk women too seem to be traditional gender roles present in many ethnic groups. Thus Freilich's work is flawed in that it is not particularly well-constructed methodologically, nor is it informative regarding traditionalism in Kahnawake. Yet there is some value in the fact that Freilich sensed in modern Mohawks a degree of consistency with their forebears. He was not able to discern the link, but in looking at overt manifestations of an old social order, perhaps he was concerned with the wrong part of contemporary Mohawk society?

Mathur is another anthropologist who has examined the Kahnawake Mohawks as a community and come away with the view that they exhibit strong similarities to traditional Iroquois society.

Like Freilich, Mathur saw persistence, but her theme was that contemporary Mohawks had abstracted the essence of the Iroquois tradition and realized that essence in a very modern fashion (Mathur 1973; Mathur 1975). Mathur focuses on the 'body polity' as the essence of traditional Iroquois society, drawing on these early 18th-century observations of the Jesuit ethnographer Lafitau:

> The affairs of state are those which hold their principal attention. The continual state of defiance in which they are with their neighbours, makes them always alert to profit from all the favourable odds or of putting their neighbours into disorder . . . They are always occupied at home, in reflecting on all that has passed to observe and to deliberate without ceasing on the slightest event, to train their young people in these affairs, to teach them the style of their councils, the oral tradition in which they preserve their history of their land; of the virtue of their ancestors, and to retain among them this martial spirit, which makes their tranquillity in peace and their superiority in war. (Mathur 1975: 40)

Mathur's theme was the continuation of the preoccupation with activities described in Lafitau. She was unconcerned with the lack of a pattern of maintenance with respect to social organization or other cultural traits and focused exclusively on the persistence of traditional Iroquois culture in the modern militant political ideology of the Kahnawake Mohawks (Mathur 1973: 14).

Mathur described a process of 'rational revitalization' leading to the creation of 'self-conscious traditionalists'. Her theory, 'Third Generation Tribal Nationalism', avoids the faults of the previous theoretical models by offering an explanation of how a society could reactivate in an authentic way elements of a tradition not present in immediately preceding generations. Acknowledging that there is no direct and unbroken pattern of development, the self-conscious traditionalist seeks to operationalize dormant values and principles located within the history and memory of his people. Traditionalism in this view is a process of re-learning and exposing what has been subsumed within the culture. This is opposed to strict revitalization theory which sees the process as one of re-invention. With Mathur's theory, static representations of culture are abandoned in favour of an approach which sees culture as a dynamic process, and traditionalism as a constant referencing back and forth between what is remembered of the past and what is demanded by the exigencies of the present.

Mathur's general theory on Indian traditionalism holds special significance for Kahnawake. She argues that the particular content of the Iroquois tradition makes communities like Kahnawake ideally suited for the assertion of 'tribal nationalism' in the contemporary context.

The two keys to the Great Law tradition, which forms the basis of Iroquois traditional culture, are its political sophistication and the fact that it demanded active proselytizing (Mathur 1973: 16–17). Mathur argues that contemporary Iroquois retain the political sophistication and energy observed by Lafitau in their 18th-century ancestors. Bringing the analysis into the 20th century, she believes the persistence of key traits from their traditional political culture has given contemporary Mohawks a powerful advantage in this age of mass communication. Bequeathed a complex and powerful political philosophy as well as a living tradition of oratorical skill, Mathur sees Mohawks as fortunate in possessing both the message and the means for advancing their goals in the contemporary era:

> The persistence of oratory for the political man from the basic culture described by Lafitau remains a functional tool today when TV has become the weapon of post-literacy. True cultural persistence appears to occur if the traits are desirable or valued, not merely by the subordinate society, but also by the dominant society . . . Thus, doubly reinforced, the value of the political man and the speaker in Iroquois society becomes clear. (Mathur 1973: 17)

The external political environment plays a key role in the development of traditionalism as an ideology, Mathur points out, by demanding certain tools and techniques. But in their drive to create an effective cultural vehicle *vis-à-vis* external powers, the self-conscious traditionalists initiate an internally-driven and introspective selection from a grab-bag of symbols, principles, and values. This process of elimination or refinement results in the persistence of elements which, in Kahnawake, have come to define the contemporary Mohawk political culture.

Along with re-invigoration of certain means—the Great Law system, and communication skills—Kahnawake Mohawks have shaped a consistent message out of the various elements previously identified (Voget 1951: 222) as the characteristics of a nascent 'nativism' during the 1950s. These have been modernized and consolidated into three core principles: the achievement of sovereignty through the re-implementation of a traditional form of government; the strengthening of an identity of distinct peoplehood through a focus on ancestry; and the redress of historical injustices surrounding the dispossession of Mohawks from their traditional lands.

There is a special significance to the land issue in the Iroquois case. That land conflicts have become the primary legal battlefield is a result of the failure of Canada to safeguard substantive Iroquois land rights derived from treaties and domestic legal contracts. With particular reference to the Mohawks of Kahnawake, the St Lawrence Seaway during the 1950s and the 1990 crisis at Oka are clear examples. With the land issue providing the spark which has ignited Mohawk nationalism in the contemporary era, the Mohawks of Kahnawake typify what Mathur called the 'New Indian' challenging non-native society on a 'New Battlefield' during the 1970s. To Mathur, the Iroquois traditionalists were unique in their drive to 'propagandize' their ideas and strategies to all Indians. This active assertion led to the recognition of a singular level of intensity and militancy in Mohawk traditionalism, manifested in what she called at the time a 'tribal nationalism' (Mathur 1973: 17).

The gradual refinement of an ideology based on the principles identified above reached its present stage by the mid-1970s. The interplay of land issues, sovereignty, and identity was evident throughout the steadily increasing number of confrontations between Mohawks and the United States and Canadian governments. The set of ideas had crystallized into an action plan by 1974, when Kahnawake Mohawks occupied and attempted to re-settle an area of their traditional territory in the Adirondack Mountains near Utica, NY. In the midst of the ensuing confrontation with New York State authorities, a Federal negotiator observed that 'Sovereignty is a key word to the Mohawks. They insist without wavering that the Mohawk Nation is an independent sovereign government' (Kwartler 1980: 17). Clearly by this time the Mohawks who were in the forefront of political activism had gone through the process described by Mathur and had in fact consolidated a set of principles which underlie contemporary politics in Kahnawake.

This discussion has set the framework for a detailed analysis of the content of the adaptive process in Kahnawake and of the creation, in response to a functional demand, of a thoroughly modernized political ideology derived from a solid base of Iroquois traditions which had been subsumed for years. Kahnawake Mohawks realized that in the new political reality a successful assertion of nationhood and the safeguarding of their land base demanded the reformulation of their strategy toward a more steadfast reliance upon the traditional elements in their political culture.

IROQUOIS POLITICAL TRADITION— KAIENEREKOWA, THE GREAT LAW[4]

What are the key elements of the Kaienerekowa—the Great Law—the text of which forms the basic reference point for all traditional Iroquois values on government and social organization?

The Iroquois Confederacy was originally composed of five nations—Mohawk, Seneca, Onondaga, Oneida, and Cayuga. Iroquois oral traditions tell of how the nations were brought together by a Peacemaker after a long period of internecine wars. The Peacemaker's message of power-sharing, compromise, and unified purpose was received by the five nations as a solution to the problem of incessant competition and hostility. The *Kaienerekowa*, or the Great Law of Peace, remains a masterpiece of political theory. Through a blend of symbolism and specificity, this oral law stemming from the 14th century detailed the formation of a truly democratic system of political organization and the first genuine North American federal system.[5]

The *Kaienerekowa* was specific regarding the operation of the Confederacy's federal system. Complex strictures of proportional representation of nations, veto powers, rules of order, and precedence in debate were interwoven with the aforementioned symbolism. Iroquois society was characterized by an extensive democracy. The central concern of the federal system was to ensure the perpetuation of this popular sovereignty, and the entire mechanism was organized so that chiefs directly represented the will of their people. The Iroquois system was truly democratic in that all legitimacy flowed directly from the people. While chiefs were selected to represent the people in the Grand Council and to foreign bodies, they determined the interests of the nation through a process of public discussion and consultation. The *Kaienerekowa* instructs that:

> Whenever a very important matter . . . is presented to the Council of the League and that matter affects the entire [Confederacy], the Sachems of the League must submit the matter to the decision of the people and the decision of the people shall affect the decision of the Council . . . This decision shall be a confirmation of the voice of the people. (NAITC 1984: 57)

Iroquois democracy had two main features: consensual decision-making, and a participatory political process. All members of the community participated at some level in the political process. All of the cleavages in the society were represented by some sort of mechanism; gender and clan were the two main bases upon which political roles were differentiated. Both through these special mechanisms, which usually took the form of small councils with advisory functions *vis-à-vis* the chiefs, and through public debate of all issues concerning the nation, community members were assured of some influence on the chiefs' decisions.

The differentiation of political roles based on gender illustrates both principles. No decision could be taken without the unanimous consent of all representative groups, and women were guaranteed a special role in the process leading up to the achievement of a political consensus. In the Iroquois view, women were by nature responsible for the perpetuation of the community, in terms of both physically giving birth and preserving the culture through child-rearing and education. They were innately concerned with stability and the common weal. Consequently, through numerous formal mechanisms, Iroquois women were assigned political responsibilities for selecting and recalling nominal leaders and effectively vetoing any decision which they deemed to be against the interests of the community as a whole. Nominal leadership positions were limited to men because the Iroquois judged men generally more qualified for the demands of leadership offices; that is, the more overtly aggressive and egoistic psychological make-up of men makes them more suited to oratory, debate, and military leadership. Yet traditional Iroquois chiefs merely represent the will of their community, a community effectively controlled by its women.

The political role of a chief was to be a representative in the most literal sense of the word. His essential function was to determine the general will of his people and represent their interests to the League. But an Iroquois chief was more than that; he was also a moral and spiritual leader. If political power in general was derived from the community, then the chief's status derived not from an effort to consolidate the support of various factions or groups, but from the people's respect for the moral worth of the man. The Mohawk word for chief, *Royaner*, in fact translates to 'he who is of the good'. The chiefs' spiritual and political roles are succinctly summarized in the *Kaienerekowa*:

> The thickness of [the chiefs'] skins shall be seven spans . . . their hearts shall be filled with peace and goodwill. Their spirits want for the good of their people . . . the spirits of anger and fury shall not find place in them, and in everything they say and do they will think only of the [people] and not of themselves, thinking ahead not only of the present but also of the generations of unborn yet to come. (NAITC 1984: 40)

Chieftainship, then, was a sacred trust between the people of the nation and those men selected by virtue of their character to represent the people in both the spiritual and political realm.

Iroquois society was matrilineal and organized into sub-tribal units called clans. All social and political functions were centred around the clans at the local level, and around nations at the League level. Representation also followed this scheme. Each nation's chiefs were chosen from among a specific clan by its women as representatives of that particular family group. At the League's Grand Council, the nation's chiefs joined to speak as one. The actual mechanisms of representation and social organization are vital to understanding Iroquois society as a whole, but concern us here less than the implications that these mechanisms had for Iroquois ideas defining the polity and leadership roles.

The *Kaienerekowa* pervaded the five nations in all aspects of their society, and it specified that each nation remained distinct yet a part of the larger whole. For the Iroquois, there was no differentiation of the mode of government or the spirit of the polity between village and

League. The Iroquois' conception of the polity may be discerned by examining their views on the interrelation of social structure, representation, and the government's source of legitimacy.

The linkage of politics to morality in the *Kaienerekowa* is further underscored in Iroquois ideas of the purpose and origin of government. The Iroquois believed that the transition from insulated tribal existences to the establishment of a formal government was initiated by a Huron Peacemaker, *Deganawida*, who came across Lake Ontario into the land of the Iroquois. Bringing his ideas of peace and justice first to the Mohawk and then to the others, *Deganawida* succeeded in unifying the Iroquois under his system of religion and government. Though the story of his coming is now thoroughly infused with symbolism and mythology, the nature of the Peacemaker's message and political ideas remains clear; to a wicked woman who symbolized all those initially resisting the message, he said:

> The message I bring is that all people shall love one another and live together in peace. This message has three parts: peace, righteousness and power, and each part has two branches. Health means soundness of mind and body. It also means Peace, for that is what comes when minds are sane and bodies cared for. Righteousness means justice practised between men and nations. It means a desire to see justice prevail. It also means religion, for justice enforced is the will of the Creator and has his sanction. (NAITC 1984: 18)

The purpose of government in this tradition is to govern all aspects of the peoples' lives. This was only possible because of the non-differentiated and homogeneous nature of Iroquois society and the fact that the instrument of government was not a state in the modern sense at all, but essentially the moral force of the community itself. It was government by the people based upon a principle of consensual agreement regarding the interests of the nation in the political sphere. And it was government by the people based upon a shared conception of morality in the social and religious spheres.

Thus far 'the people' have been referred to throughout the discussion both as the polity and as instrument of government in the Iroquois system. What exactly is meant by this phrase? On one level, 'the people' referred to the *Onkwehonwe*, or the original people inhabiting the land of the Iroquois. But at another level of analysis, references to 'the people' in effect reveal Iroquois views on human nature which establishes their need for a formal system of government. The creation story illustrates the purely humanistic and pragmatic view of human nature which guided the formation of the Iroquois' philosophy. The story is replete with passages describing the dichotomy between good and evil as it exists in human beings, and it also contains a section describing the

creation of equal but inescapably different peoples. These two elements, the primordial struggle between good and evil, and the incom-
patibility of racial groups or 'nations', are the basis for the Iroquois' formation of nation-oriented government structures. They believed each
race, or 'nation', should determine its own separate existence in harmony with the different but equally valid existences of the other 'nations'.

Thus the Iroquois conception of human nature is one that accepts
differences between men as natural and inescapable facts of life.
Acceptance is the key word, for the Iroquois believed that peace was
possible only if each nation governed itself by the rules which the
Creator gave each of them. This is a relativistic view. The *Kaienerekowa*
was given to the *Onkwehonwe* by *Sonkwaiatison* through his messenger in the personage of *Deganawida*. It is also a view remarkably
sensitive to the psychology of inter-group dynamics and the politics of
diversity. At its core is a belief that self-determination and national
autonomy provide the only guarantees of peaceful co-existence.

The views on human nature expressed in the *Kaienerekowa* are no
doubt the product of centuries of observation on the part of the Iroquois
people who transmitted the message through the ages, yet the immediate historical circumstances surrounding the founding of the League
also confirm the symbolism of the creation story. The fact that the
Peacemaker delivered his message in the midst of war and degradation
gives context to the purpose of the message itself. The Iroquois prophecy was that the Creator told the Iroquois:

> You were created from the earth of this island. I now realize that you
> would not survive very long among the others . . . you will need time
> before you come into contact with the other beings. You will also be
> given a sacred way by a messenger who will visit you and your descen-
> dants. (NAITC 1984: 8)

The creation story's intuition of an evil side to man's nature and the
difficulty this posed to peaceful co-existence were realized in the years
leading up to the formation of the League. The Iroquois had forgotten
the instructions of the Creator and had degenerated into barbarians
who could not live with each other, much less with the other nations
inhabiting the earth. It was a time in which the Iroquois had no moral
values and fought viciously both among themselves and with other
nations. The vision corresponds to an actual historical period in which
the five nations were isolated, poor, and in danger of losing their independence to other more powerful groups of Indians. It was the lowest
point in their existence, and the time was right for the messenger to
appear with the Creator's reminder through the *Kaienerekowa* of how
to live a good life by following the principles of peace, righteousness,
and power. The reconstitution and revitalization of the Iroquois under

the principles of the *Kaienerekowa* initiated an era that lasted up until European contact, an era in which the Iroquois League prospered and in fact dominated within their traditional territories.

Symbolism has already been seen as a major feature of the Iroquois political philosophy. The two dominant instances of Iroquois symbolism revolve around the League's formation. The Peacemaker's mission to the Iroquois characterizes good and evil as basic human traits kept in check by the existence of a proper government. Armed only with the supernaturally-inspired message of peace, the Peacemaker ventured into the violent world of the Iroquois. He encountered man's good side in the person of *Haiawatha*, whom the Peacemaker convinced to join him in spreading the good message. Soon after, he encountered man's bad side represented by *Atotarhoh*—a fearsome cannibal sorcerer with a mane of snakes—who rejected the message of peace. The formation of the League was possible only after *Atotarhoh* was persuaded to accept the message and become an integral part of the new confederacy. The symbolism involved in this story conveys all of the *Kaienerekowa*'s basic meaning. First and foremost it confirms the message of peace's validity; second, it demonstrates that only through unity can the people survive; and finally it shows that conciliation can overcome any obstacle to achieving the necessary consensus.

The most pervasive Iroquois symbol by far is the Great Tree of Peace. In it one sees the essence of the Iroquois' political philosophy. A great tree planted on the shores of Onondaga Lake represents the federalist principles of the *Kaienerekowa*—voluntary confederation of autonomous nations, self-determination, and peaceful coexistence— and the democratic spirit of the people themselves. Underneath the tree lies a war club, symbolizing the obsolescence of conflict among those who accept the Law. From the base of the tree grows the Great White Root, symbolizing peace and charity for any nation that wishes to trace the root back to the Iroquois and take shelter beneath the principles of the *Kaienerekowa*. And above the tree is an eagle, eternally watchful of any danger or threat to the peace and security of the people. The symbol of the Great Tree of Peace is a powerful reminder of the ideas contained within the system of traditional Iroquois thought. But appreciating the beauty of pure-form ideas is one thing, and thinking of ways to make the ideas transcend the boundary between philosophy and politics is another.

THE TRADITIONALIST VANGUARD IN KAHNAWAKE

The Iroquois ideology's transition from the realm of ideas into a doctrine of political practice has not been smooth. Within Kahnawake, the re-learning process has proceeded at a different pace and with different foci for various segments in the community. Overall, the Mohawks have made a commitment to re-implementing traditional values into their political lives, and the three tenets of Mohawk nationalism (p. 19) continue to unify the community. But those who have taken a lead role in re-educating themselves and spreading traditionalism among other Mohawks in Kahnawake have split along a number of axes. There are those who would abstract principles from the traditional teachings and realign the mechanism of government to reflect modern reality. There are those who decry the synthesis of tradition and modernity and insist upon the literal interpretation of traditional law. It must be realized that in terms of their individual intellectual development, most Kahnawake Mohawks are newcomers to traditionalism. And it is sometimes the case that those who have led the way in the move to traditionalism have done so with the blind fervour of the newly converted, setting themselves out as the vanguard and attempting to impose their particular interpretation of Iroquois tradition upon the community.

There has been no unified movement toward or interpretation of Iroquois tradition in Kahnawake. Beyond the consensus that the Indian Act and Western political values are inappropriate, there has been no singularly acceptable framework established within which a standard interpretation of the *Kaienerekowa*'s principles could be achieved. This lack of a consensus has manifested itself in mainly negative ways and has led to serious confrontations within the community (Alfred 1991; Hornung 1991; Johansen 1993). Aside from their utility as explanatory factors, the differing interpretations are instructive because they each focus on a different aspect of the holistic message presented in the *Kaienerekowa*. It is as if different groups within Kahnawake have taken to building disparate interpretations each based on a single disembodied part of the *Kaienerekowa*'s rich text, which itself contains three unified principles: Peace, Power, and Righteousness.

Incongruity has been a consistent theme in the revitalization of the Iroquois tradition, and throughout the classical era of the Iroquois Confederacy a certain degree of tension between seemingly contrary aspects of the tradition had been present. Noon, for example, described how the Iroquois value system was inherently dualistic and led to a manifest dichotomy between the idealized 'female' values stressing peace and health and the more often realized destructive 'male' values (Noon 1949: 22–40). He also examined the impact of a shifting political environment upon the operation of the traditional system among the Grand River Iroquois and found that modernity led to the erosion of the tradition's integrity and value among the Mohawks at the Grand River. Noon observed that 'The intrusion of the Dominion [Canada] into the affairs of the Six Nations prevented the decision of the [Confederacy] Council from possessing the attribute of finality which is necessary for effective governmental coordination' (Noon 1949: 112). Specifically, the Confederacy at Grand River was unable to reconcile the traditional authority of the hereditary chiefs with the emerging social and political status of an educated élite, which led to divisions within the community. In Kahnawake, the nature of the reform process is reflected in the fact that cleavages have formed not along class or clan lines, but on the basis of opposing strategic visions toward the achievement of shared goals offered in the general ideology.

The different approaches were clearly evident when different groups within Kahnawake responded to questions from Canada's Royal Commission on Aboriginal Peoples (RCAP) during a forum in May, 1993 concerning their views on the issue of 'governance' or the achievement of Mohawk sovereignty (RCAP 1993: 80–1). Grand Chief Joe Norton of the Mohawk Council of Kahnawake (MCK) expressed his desire for a transition period to traditional government in which his Indian Act-elected band council would work itself out of a job. Charlie Patton of the Mohawk Trail Longhouse expressed the view that traditional government should be achieved through the efforts of the External Relations Committee of the Six Nations Confederacy. Stuart Myiow Sr stated that the Governor General of Canada should strike an accord with the 'true traditional people' of Kahnawake and exclude anyone who had accepted foreign laws or the MCK. Finally, Dale Diom and Kahn-Tineta Horn of the Mohawk Nation Office argued for sovereignty within the established norms of international law as a right of self-determination.

It seems every Mohawk would share the sentiment expressed by Charlie Patton in his statement to the RCAP Commissioners:

> You have to clear out that thinking that you are our father and we are your children . . . You have to look at this and say that we are equals, we are nations . . . We have to look at making a relationship where peace, living together and respecting each other is at the forefront. (RCAP 1993: 82)

But beyond this, there are three major divisions within the community on the best way to achieve the ideal relationship described by Patton.

Those Mohawks who associate with what is commonly referred to as the 'Mohawk Trail' Longhouse represent a view entirely consistent with that of the formal structure of the Iroquois Confederacy. In terms of its spiritual and cultural focus, the Longhouse is an eclectic mixture but identifies most consistently with the beliefs espoused by the majority of other Iroquois traditionalists. This group can trace its lineage back to the original revival of the Longhouse religion during the 1920s, when links to Six Nations Reserve traditionalists and teachers were established in the community. Within Kahnawake, the group is viewed as having accepted the Handsome Lake Code—the most obvious indication of the group's affinity to other non-Mohawk Iroquois communities—but in fact it combines a reverence for the *Kaienerekowa*, the teachings of Handsome Lake, and stories and ceremonies adopted from other native traditions. With respect to spirituality and ceremony, it is perhaps the most vital expression of innovative application of cultural symbols.

Politically, the group favours a strong alliance with the present Grand Council of the Iroquois Confederacy and a further integration of Kahnawake into the political structure of the Confederacy. Its political activism tends to take place within the defined framework of the Confederacy, with a consistent dialogue between its leaders and the Confederacy chiefs. The group's members participate in the affairs of the Grand Council and constitute the officially recognized traditional institution in the sense that the Grand Council considers the group's leaders to be its legitimate representatives in the community. Because of this simple view on the achievement of sovereignty within the Iroquois Confederacy structure, the group tends to defer to the Confederacy chiefs in political matters and relies upon an interpretation of the Great Law which stresses almost exclusively those sections which describe how the peace was achieved and how the Peacemaker told the Iroquois to spread the great peace among all nations.

The Warrior Longhouse has consistently been the institution most representative of Kahnawake's traditionalists as a whole.[6] The group has taken from the *Kaienerekowa* a completely political interpretation focused on the assertion of Mohawk power *vis-à-vis* the state. In their view, the *Kaienerekowa* is seen in purely political purposes. Divested of its spiritual and cultural meaning, the *Kaienerekowa* is interpreted by this group as a type of revolutionary manifesto for the creation of a Mohawk state. This legislative formulation of Mohawk sovereignty, consciously explained in terms familiar to non-natives, represents an abandonment of the uniquely indigenous conceptual framework to the embrace of a European perspective. One of the group's leaders, Kenneth Deer, provided a clear illustration of the Warrior Longhouse's interpretation in an editorial: 'The Mohawks have their own Constitution, a land base, a population, the ability to make and enforce laws, and the ability to make agreements with other nations. These are all the components of a nation-state' (*Eastern Door* 1, 10:2).

This conceptualization of sovereignty has nothing to do with ideas contained in Great Law and is drawn directly from European thought on the pre-requisites of statehood. Not surprisingly, in contrast to the Six Nations Longhouse, the strategy which has evolved from this interpretation is focused on the trappings of statehood and the creation of power measured in European terms. The Warrior Longhouse promotes a strategy of staking out and defending territorial, economic, and political boundaries in the drive toward the realization of a Mohawk state. A 1987 document from the Warrior Longhouse entitled 'Statement on War Chiefs, Warriors, Warrior Society and Warfare' is typical of the group's elevation of the power aspect of the Great Law's message over others:

> Peace is the absent [*sic*] of abuse, of aggression and the absent [*sic*] of injustice. In order for Peace to exist you must establish a moral society with righteousness and with just and moral minds prevailing to keep this peace safe. Once it has been established, then you must have the third and most often forgotten part of this trilogy. Power—the power to protect the peace, to ensure that peace can survive with all the injustices about us . . . Peace cannot exist without the Power to defend it and protect it.

Another Longhouse group in Kahnawake takes what may be termed a purist approach to the message contained in the Great Law. The group asserts that sovereignty can be achieved only through a fundamentalist reading and wholesale re-implementation of the structures described in the ancient text. The Five Nations Longhouse focuses its attack on the injustices perpetrated by White society and deprecates those Mohawks who cooperate with non-native authorities or who work within established institutions. The Five Nations Longhouse interpretation of the *Kaienerekowa* is divested of all spiritual meaning and even more so than the Warrior Longhouse concentrates on the structural aspects of the text.

Devoid of any consideration of the other two elements of the Peacemaker's message, the Five Nations Longhouse group emphasizes righteousness in every aspect of its political strategy by setting itself apart from and above others. Its members have launched a sort of moral crusade against the enemy, perceived as anyone who does not share their interpretation. The view is fundamentalist, that Mohawks should apply historic concepts to the modern situation without modification in any way. This applies to the minutiae of the *Kaienerekowa*'s stipulations concerning governing forms, process, and social organization, as well as to the framework of relationships deriving from historic treaties between the Confederacy and non-native polities in North America.

The Iroquois political tradition in its true form as represented by a holistic reading of the *Kaienerekowa* contains key elements which are crucial to the integrity of the system, such as a differentiation of gender roles, clan representation, direct participation, and consensus-based decision-making. But more important, the Kaienerekowa contains values and principles which must be integrated into the practice of politics within the community for the system to function properly. For the most part, the traditionalist movement in Kahnawake has focused on superficial structural aspects of the *Kaienerekowa* and has neglected the importance of embedding the values undergirding the Iroquois philosophy. No one traditionalist interpretation within the community has become hegemonic in the minds of Mohawks because each has focused on superficial aspects and has failed to re-implement the system which would allow traditionalism to advance beyond its utility as a means of asserting power *vis-à-vis* external forces, to become a unifying social and political movement within the community itself. Each Longhouse has parcelled up the holistic message and concentrated on a single part of the value system. As a means and message in opposition to external forces, the community remains powerful. In any confrontation the Mohawks unite, and the full force of the *Kaienerekowa*'s message and the energy of all Mohawks is brought together.

Still, internally, in the process of creating a consensus on a spiritual, cultural, and structural basis for co-existence among Mohawks, the traditionalist movement has faltered. Those who stress peace ignore the political nature of the Mohawk relationship with non-native society and the real conflicts existing in the social and cultural arena between Mohawks and other communities. Those who fixate on power ignore the basis of strength in the *Kaienerekowa*—soundness of mind, body, and relationships—and focus on a corrupted European notion of power, a mistaken abstraction of the indigenous notion. They surge toward the achievement of power without the balancing influence of the other two principles to limit or counsel their efforts. And the righteous ones, who blame White society for all the community's ills, focus only on the injustice inherent in the imposition of a history not chosen by Mohawks. They ignore the complex nature of the present-day relationship and the importance of harmony and cooperation in the achievement of the stated goals.

MAINSTREAM NATIONALIST IDEOLOGY IN KAHNAWAKE[7]

Traditional ideas and the philosophy of the Great Law are not the sole monopoly of the Longhouse traditionalists. In recent years, the general political ideology in Kahnawake has developed features of the Great Law into modern principles beyond the abstract values contained in the *Kaienerekowa*. Most of the general population have managed to integrate rediscovered traditional principles into a modern interpretation capable serving as a philosophy of government in the modern age. Still maintaining the key foci of sovereignty, identity, and land, what will be termed the nationalist ideology—as opposed to the traditionalist ideology—has emerged as the overall interpretation of Iroquois tradition which serves to orient politics in Kahnawake.

In contrast to the Longhouse movement which refers constantly to static interpretations of tradition, mainstream nationalism in

Kahnawake exhibits a flexible interpretation which jealously guards only the basic principles and values contained in the *Kaienerekowa* and allows for a modification of strategy dependent upon the demands of the political environment. Most Mohawks seek the abstraction of values from the *Kaienerekowa*, not the re-implementation of an ancient social and political order in the community. The material in the following section attempts to identify a consolidated position within the community on key issues, a consensus community position on the translation of Iroquois tradition into a viable set of guiding principles for the future development of the community's institutions and relationships with other people. A characterization of nationalist ideology in Kahnawake in its present form is discussed in terms of the previously identified set of goals—the achievement of what is generally understood as self-government.

Progress in the Mohawk mind means movement toward the re-alignment of political relationships, with the objective of recreating a balanced and respectful sharing of powers and resources. For all of its historical underpinnings, Kahnawake's political ideology is in essence future-oriented. It is obsessed with independence and the freedom to choose the terms of the community's collective associations.

The Mohawk political objective is essentially one of maintaining control. The distinguishing feature of Kahnawake's conception is its synthesis of principle and practicality. Rooted in the Iroquois tradition, and patterned according to Kahnawake's particular historical experience, Kahnawake Mohawk decision-makers nonetheless clearly demonstrate a willingness to adapt to changing political realities. The adaptive instinct is freely acknowledged. A distinction is made between the virtue inherent in a willingness to adapt and the inherent weakness in allowing someone else to dictate the terms of the adaptation.

Restoring respect and balance among Mohawks is the primary internal objective in Kahnawake. For the majority of Mohawks, the first step toward reconciliation is the reformation of existing internal governmental institutions. The MCK's efforts to create an institutional framework for self-government are still perceived as having been only marginally successful. The view is that concrete progress towards sovereignty has been achieved in spite of, rather than because of, the existence of a band council institution linked to the Indian Act and the Canadian government. The MCK is seen as problematic in terms of process and representation. The problem lies in its charter as an administrative organ of the Canadian government and creature of the Indian Act. It is simply unacceptable to Mohawks to have a government based on Euro-American laws and principles.

The key to the reformation of Kahnawake's internal organization is the reintegration of traditional Mohawk values in the political system.

Opinions are divided on the structure and format of government, but there is near-unanimity on the necessity of reorienting decision-making and leadership selection to reflect Mohawk political culture rather than Western values. The perception of a uniquely Mohawk or Iroquois set of political values is widespread in Kahnawake. Here the power and influence of the *Kaienerekowa* runs deep, and represents the only alternative to Western politics in the minds of most Kahnawake Mohawks. The modifications made by their ancestors to the ideals of the *Kaienerekowa* have little impact in the face of a resurgence of the Peacemaker's message.

Segments of the Mohawk public revere the principles established in the *Kaienerekowa*; the majority feel that the principles established in the *Kaienerekowa* can be abstracted to form new rules adapted to the modern age.

Mohawk values in politics revolve around two axes: accountability and leadership.[8] The concept of accountability in Kahnawake is embedded in the simple rule that all power and legitimacy flows from the collective will of the people. Institutions and the actions of leaders are alike held to the standard that near-unanimous consent must be obtained for legitimacy to be granted. It is generally accepted that whatever form of government emerges from the reformation of Kahnawake's institutions, it must be one which incorporates all of the community's diverse viewpoints and political orientations. This conception may not be radically different from the Western concept of consent, but Mohawks demand accountability at every stage in the political process. There is no parallel to the Western concept of tacit consent; the public must be constantly consulted and the collective will perpetually gauged to successfully practise government in Kahnawake.

The concept of leadership in Kahnawake again reflects the *Kaienerekowa*. The assumption of a leadership role does not imply elevated status or privilege. On the contrary, leaders are seen as servants of the collective will. Leaders are not so much respected as tolerated by the Mohawk public. Leadership is in every sense of the word a burden, stemming from the mediation function which is the primary occupation of a Mohawk leader. The primacy placed on accountability dictates that leaders spend most of their time developing a consensus, and leaders take on the role of conciliators between various interests and factions within the community.

Within the framework created by the intersection of these two major elements, there are a number of other values which are evident in Kahnawake, but which are accorded varying degrees of importance by segments of the Mohawk population. Oratorical skills, intelligence, aggressiveness, and demonstrated respect for others figure high in the calculation of a leader's worth, for example. But the primacy of accountability and leadership by consensus is well established.

Mohawk views on the legitimacy of the Indian Act are illustrative of two salient points in Kahnawake's political ideology. First, the Indian Act regime as it currently exists is clearly unworkable as a framework of government for Kahnawake. But does this require a complete redesign of the mechanism used by Canada to relate with the community? Most Mohawks think not. While denying the legitimacy of the Indian Act in its current form, there is confidence that the federal government can reform the orientation of its Indian Affairs bureaucracy to reflect the terms of a new relationship. Among those Mohawks who remain most accepting of the Indian Act's authority within the community—administrators and directors of the various institutions—there is general agreement that the Indian Act must be replaced by a better legislative instrument.

At the same time there is a hint of caution at the suggestion of a radical disruption to the existing system. These views are evident in comparing the following statement by a key administrator: 'The only positive aspect is the [exemption from] taxation aspect, and land preservation. Overall, it is a very outdated document.' And by another that:

> The Indian Act has had a profound effect on us in terms of identity, actual and for membership—and this effect can't be annulled by dismissing the Indian Act. It's like it is 'in us' and we have consented to elements of it.

The latter statement represents a rare moment of candour with respect to the internalization of an 'Indian Act mentality' among the general population in Kahnawake. Where there is a general consensus on the need to make such a move away from the formal institutions of the Indian Act system, it is based more on an intellectual understanding of the problems of Canada's colonial relationship with Kahnawake than on a complete psychological and moral rejection of the Indian Act. While there is consensus that the basic premise of the Indian Act is flawed and that its application is uneven, some of its constituent institutions and rules are valued.

Over time, most Mohawks have come to integrate various elements of the Indian Act system into their political culture. Significant efforts have been made by segments of the community to recognize and address this fact, and an attempt has been made to re-orient values to a more traditional Mohawk ideal. Yet the imposition of this very particular set of Western values and institutions has been internalized to the degree that it now presents an obstacle to the re-implementation of a traditional form of government, or even to the reform of Indian Act-mandated institutions currently existing within the community, to reflect a more traditional orientation. The key to overcoming this obstacle seems to lie in the recognition of the fact of internalization, and in taking steps to reverse the Indian Act's erosion of traditional values. Yet the majority of the community is unable to recognize, or unwilling to counteract, the internalization process.

Even among those who have come to recognize the internalization of the Indian Act, there is disagreement on the nature of the Act's effect on contemporary Mohawks. The starting assumption is that the imposition of the Indian Act must be necessarily and absolutely viewed as a negative. Those holding this view see the Indian Act as responsible for the destruction of a society and a culture, and for the creation of an oppressive system of colonial domination. Others see a somewhat more complex interaction between the community and the Indian Act. They agree that the net effect of the Indian Act's application has been negative, although the Indian Act itself in their view constitutes only one of many factors responsible for the erosion of traditional values and Mohawk institutions. Further, they argue that there are indeed positive elements in the design and application of the Indian Act which may be appropriated for use by a Mohawk government in the future.

These others recognize that the Indian Act did partially achieve its initial goal of protecting Indian lands from encroachment, and still serves as a barrier to the erosion of the Mohawk land base by preventing individual sales and enforcing a jealous Federal interest in the Territory. Furthermore, they see the administrative structures and procedures developed to implement the Indian Act system as useful tools for the administration of a post-Indian Act Mohawk government. They consider the basic design of the Indian Act system valid, in that it created a Federal responsibility for relating with Indian nations, and a structure for managing that Federal responsibility. Only as it evolved did the managers of the Federal responsibility corrupt the initial instinct to relate on a respectful basis into a self-serving drive for jurisdictional control and political domination. Essentially, this view rejects the assertion that it is necessary to jettison everything and reinvent government; rather it recognizes that the internalization is to some degree a fact of life and seeks to build on the acceptable tools within the Indian Act.

As for the band council system of government currently existing within Kahnawake, which is a creature of the Indian Act but which has made strides toward independence, there is a stronger commitment to the goal of reformation rather than elimination or replacement. Mohawks view the current band council administrative apparatus as essentially their own creation, taking into account the modifications which have been made in its structure and philosophy. There is a clear distinction between the two major functions the band council performs. On one hand, Mohawks see much potential in the further improvement of the administrative institution housed in the council office. At the same time they reject the legitimacy of the political institution centred around the council table.

In a recent survey,[10] 62% of the respondents answered 'no' to the question, 'Do you consider Kahnawake's existing band council structure (MCK) to be an appropriate and workable form of government for the community?' But 71% answered 'yes' to the question, 'Do you think it is possible to reform Kahnawake's existing band council structure (MCK) to make it an appropriate and workable form of government for the community?'

That Mohawks make a clear distinction between the administrative and political with regard to the band council is supported by their stated views on the strengths and weaknesses of the current system, according to a survey conducted in 1992 (see Table 4.1).

As Table 4.1 illustrates, most Mohawks consider the band council to be effective in its role as a service provider and administrative centre, but in the political realm, the perception of the band council shifts toward a negative evaluation. Mohawks evaluate three key elements of the band council's political role negatively: in the decision-making process; in leadership and leadership selection process; and in representation.[9]

It is generally believed that the major obstacles preventing the resurrection of a Longhouse government for Kahnawake have been disagreements in the interpretation of the *Kaienerekowa*, and personality

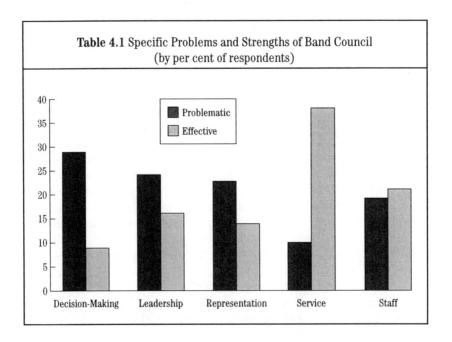

Table 4.1 Specific Problems and Strengths of Band Council (by per cent of respondents)

conflicts among the leadership of the various Longhouse groups. Divisions among the Longhouse groups may have allowed the MCK to maintain its status as community government by default. While these divisions may have been important obstacles to political conciliation in the past (this too is debatable; all political factions have disagreement and personality conflict), the simple fact is that the purist approach to reviving a traditional form of government does not today hold mass appeal in Kahnawake.

Most Mohawks recognize that traditionalism means more than erecting structures which imitate old ways of doing things. Here again, political values are important. Mohawks clearly distinguish between form and content, and in their evaluation of the Longhouse alternative to the Indian Act system, they recognize a familiar format vacant of any truly traditional values. Thus for the majority of Mohawks in Kahnawake, the Longhouse structures are inauthentic attempts at traditionalism, and they represent poles of division rather than unifying and constructive forces within the community.

The alternative of implementing a wholesale replacement of the Indian Act with a traditional system is being questioned. The idea of abstracting values from traditional knowledge and integrating them within existing structures has gained increasing credence. Very few people in Kahnawake deny that 'traditional Mohawk laws and structures need to be modified to make them appropriate to our modern situation.' Indeed, a minority of respondents to the survey answered 'yes' to the question, 'Do you believe that traditional Mohawk laws and structures provide a sound basis for a system of government in Kahnawake?'

One certain indication of the shift in thinking since the process of revitalization began in the 1970s is the current view of the MCK's commitment to re-introduce a traditional form of government. In 1979, a public forum, further confirmed by referenda, challenged the MCK to 'work itself out of a job' and replace the band council system with a Longhouse government. Whereas the mandate has for years been accepted as a public consensus, many younger Mohawks who did not participate in those original discussions are now questioning the mandate. The events of the 1990 crisis have also shaken the confidence of Kahnawake Mohawks with respect to the capability of a traditional body to govern the community effectively. There is substantial disagreement as to whether the mandate is still valid. In the survey, 56% of respondents answered 'no' to the question describing the original mandate and asking, 'Do you agree that the 1979 mandate authorizing the Mohawk Council of Kahnawake to make such a change is still valid?'

Still other Mohawks view the wholesale structural reformation as subordinate to the revitalization of the community's traditional values and spiritual health. Many Mohawks concur with the young woman who stated that:

> . . . moving from a Band Council system would require a lot of work and input. The community must be prepared. First work on healing ourselves in order to work together . . . The 1979 MCK mandate is not valid . . . The primary mandate is reconciliation, the move to a traditional form is secondary.

What exists in Kahnawake is a unique combination of a rock-solid commitment to the removal of a foreign system and a very diverse set of responses to the question, 'What are we going to do about it?' In the survey, over 75% of the respondents view Canadian laws as illegitimate in Kahnawake. At the same time a full 70% were unable to explain the specific reasons the Indian Act was illegitimate.

All of these reactions to Kahnawake's effort to reform the political system reflect an ambiguous criticism and impatience. Mohawks are generally critical of efforts undertaken by both the MCK and the Longhouse groups. At the same time, they are impatient for the emergence of authentically Mohawk and truly representative institutions. Two conclusions can be drawn: 1) Mohawks are demanding a new system of internal organization which synthesizes the best of existing administrative institutions and integrates traditional Mohawk values; and 2) despite the perception that it is a flawed institution, the MCK is still seen as an appropriate structural framework for a new renewed community government.

Whatever form of internal organization the Mohawks of Kahnawake eventually choose to implement, the replacement of Canadian authority will necessitate a re-evaluation of the community's capacity to supply the financial and human resources for self-government. Reassuming political control will place a large burden of administrative and political control on the community's governing institution. Thus, the Mohawks must consider Kahnawake's jurisdictional capacity—the ability of their community to manage the various aspects of self-government—on a financial, administrative, and political basis.

Mohawk confidence in the capability of Kahnawake to assume control and manage all aspects of self-government is more important than tallying figures on available resources, for it details the framework for cooperation that Mohawks are considering. In their move toward reassuming control, what do Mohawks see as a desirable power-sharing arrangement between themselves and Canadian governments?

There is general trepidation in Kahnawake with regard to the community's existing jurisdictional capacity. In four key sectoral areas, Mohawks identified some deficiency in either the natural or human resource potential of the community to become self-sustaining.

Considering the four sectors—economy and finance, culture and education, health and social welfare, justice and security—40% of the respondents to the survey selected 'none' in answer to the question, 'If Kahnawake received no outside assistance or federal government funding, in which specific areas, if any, do you think the community would be self-sustaining?' Of the four sectors, Culture and Education received the highest positive response with a total of only 24%. Moreover, only 31% of the respondents selected 'yes' in answer to the question, 'Do you think that Kahnawake today possesses the human and financial resources to sustain its own government and manage its own affairs?'

Mohawks clearly see the need for cooperation with Canadian authorities in a transition to control over community affairs. It is a nearly unanimous view that the move to a restructured form of government should take place gradually rather than as immediately and wholesale. The key to this issue is that Mohawks recognize the limits to autonomy imposed by a dearth of resources. Within the community full independence is commonly understood to be the ideal state of affairs for Kahnawake. But completely Mohawk institutions and state-like autonomy are goals whose prospects of achievement must be considered in conjunction with the development of an independent resource base.

There is no contradiction in the majority of Mohawk minds between working toward the ideal of independence and working with Canadian authorities to provide for an interim solution. Although there is some disagreement on the nature and implications of consciously working toward independent state-like sovereignty in the future, most Mohawks answered 'yes' to the question, 'Do you think that Kahnawake can be considered sovereign if it relies upon outside governments for the funding of basic services?' That is, most Mohawks consider government funding to be reparations for previous wrongs committed against the Mohawk people.

The term 'reparations' is appropriate because of the international law implications it carries. In Kahnawake, government transfer payments and funding of social programs are viewed as a form of inter-state foreign aid program rather than social assistance. Whether as payment for lands stolen and still illegally occupied, or as reparations for the destructive Canadian assimilation policies, Mohawks see the funds transferred from Ottawa to Kahnawake as small efforts toward the repayment of a huge debt. In the same spirit, there is no gratitude or sense of accountability to Ottawa.

On this issue, a Mohawk man put it bluntly, 'We are still sovereign if we rely on government funding because it's owed to us as rent.' Another man explained that: 'Kahnawake could still be considered sovereign if it relies on funding, but it depends on what guise it comes to us. Rent, not welfare, is what we should get.' Yet despite consensus at the conceptual level for reliance upon external sources of funding, there is recognition of the need to establish an economic basis for self-government assertions in the political arena. This recognition is more pronounced among the Mohawk administrators working within the community's institutions. They recognize the limitations placed on their freedom of action by external economic control.

In evaluating the funding options usually available for local aboriginal governments, a self-governing Kahnawake institution is faced with three existing or foreseeable funding sources: federal transfer pay-ments, local taxes, and the sale or lease of lands. The irony contained in the Mohawk rejection of the Indian Act's legitimacy while failing to agree on an alternative legal or philosophical foundation is reflected in the funding issue. Mohawks clearly reject all but federal transfer payments as a fiscal basis for government. It is paradoxical that most Mohawks demand complete autonomy while failing to realize the financial responsibility inherent in the assumption of control.

As stated earlier, most Mohawks view federal transfer payments as a legitimate means of economic self-sufficiency, whether conceived of as transition support or as a permanent element of their fiscal plan. They also almost universally reject the idea of local taxes as a potential source of revenue for a future Kahnawake government.[11] As could be expected given the community's recent history, not a single survey respondent stated that selling land was an appropriate means of generating revenue. But a large number of Mohawks express their disapproval of even leasing lands to non-Indians in the interest of economic development. Thus the options available for the emerging community government are limited.

There is one other potential source of revenue generation available to leaders in Kahnawake. Collective business enterprises form the basis of many successful tribal economies in the United States. Admittedly, tribal governments in the United States have much more flexibility in developing their economies, but Kahnawake has itself had the opportunity to generate revenue through large-scale collectively controlled business enterprises. The attractiveness of this option would seem to be obvious in Kahnawake. But Mohawks have consistently rejected any form of organization within the community to implement a collective enterprise on a scale sufficient to provide a resource base for government. There is support in principle for the concept, but in reality every endeavour has been derailed at either the grass-roots, administrative, or political level.[12]

The lack of an existing resource base has not deterred Mohawks from developing clear ideas on the proper division of powers between a future self-governing Mohawk institution and external authorities. In eight key areas of jurisdiction, Mohawks have expressed priorities for

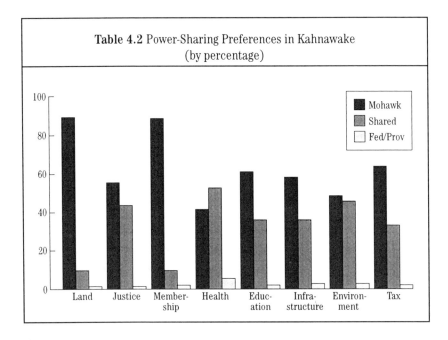

Table 4.2 Power-Sharing Preferences in Kahnawake
(by percentage)

retaining control and dividing control between the local Mohawk government and other agencies representing the authority of external governments. Table 4.2 illustrates the primacy Mohawks place on exclusive control over two areas: land management and membership. It also indicates the level of support for power sharing with other governments in other areas.

The preference in all but one sector (health) is for exclusive Mohawk control, but realizing the deficit Kahnawake faces in terms of professional expertise and skilled labour, most Mohawks are willing to accommodate the idea of shared responsibilities for all but the most critical jurisdictions. Land and membership are singled out because of their significance to the protection of Kahnawake's distinctiveness. Mohawks recognize the protection of Kahnawake's land base and distinct identity to be the community's primary political goals. These two jurisdictions therefore transcend considerations of financial or administrative expediency. But with respect to the other areas, Kahnawake is open to cooperating with external governments in the provision of basic services and administering the institutions of government. In the survey conducted for this study, less than 10% of the respondents stated that it was unacceptable to use non-Indian expertise in administering Mohawk institutions.

In terms of jurisdictional capacity, the view in Kahnawake is that the level of autonomy and self-control achieved need not necessarily reflect the community's level of economic self-sufficiency. Indeed, most Mohawks consider the continuance of federal transfer payments to be a right. Even those Mohawks who recognize the problems inherent in tying the community's government to the economy and fiscal health of a foreign government see no contradiction in using federal moneys as an interim solution to the problem of a resource deficit in Kahnawake. Having rejected most other means of revenue generation, and relying on an unspecified but implied federal funding obligation, the Mohawks of Kahnawake will obligate their future government to develop a fiscal plan integrating two possible elements: unanimously supported collective business enterprises, and taxation of non-Indian interests and individuals in Kahnawake.

As with their views in the area of jurisdictional capacity, there is some disparity between the ideal and the practical in the Mohawks' views on relationships with other governments. The ideal in Kahnawake is rooted in the concept of the *Kahswentha*, where the Mohawk nation would relate with others on an equal footing. This 'nation to nation' concept is generally accepted to be the ideal relationship also between Kahnawake as a community and other governing authorities having an impact on its affairs.

If the entire self-government process is viewed as a gradual progression toward complete community control over all aspects of its public affairs, then solidifying political links with other communities is the final step to the achievement of self-government. With its internal organization consolidated, and with the issues surrounding jurisdictional capacity resolved, Kahnawake sees the freedom to structure its relations according to its own priorities and interests as the final element in the exercise of its sovereignty.

The vast majority of Mohawks see their future associations as a collectivity within the framework of the Iroquois Confederacy. The old image of an Iroquois people united by the *Kaienerekowa* and guided in their external relationships by a common Iroquois purpose remains a powerful ideal in Kahnawake. Yet the Iroquois Confederacy has never held widespread political sway in Kahnawake, and except for a minority of the community represented by one of the Longhouses, the Mohawks recognize that political reality demands that they focus on Kahnawake as an independent political entity at least during the transition to the ideal. So the traditional ideas drawn from the *Kahswentha* and *Kaienerekowa* concerning the nature of the political community and international relations have been recast as guiding principles for Kahnawake rather than for the Mohawk nation. This is not to say that the Mohawks have preempted all issues of nationhood with respect to the *Kaienerekowa* and traditional Iroquois structures, but political necessity has forced them to shift the level of analysis down to the village from the nation. The common view is that until the Iroquois Confederacy and all other Iroquois communities can agree on a plan to reunite under the traditional institutions, Kahnawake will appropriate for itself those elements of tradition which are valuable in its own effort to reconstruct a self-governing community.

The central element of the Iroquois tradition in this view is political independence. People in Kahnawake look to their history as Iroquois and as Mohawks specifically for justification of the assertion that political cooperation does not necessarily place limits on the sovereignty of parties to the association facilitating that cooperation. This idea is an Iroquois invention and has inspired the creation of subsequent political associations based on what became known as the federalist model.[13] In this way, the Mohawks of Kahnawake evaluate the political landscape and look to advance their interests as a community by creating associations with whatever other political entity exists.

Thus for the Mohawks, cooperating with Canada at the present time to maintain their community implies no surrender of sovereignty. And the prospect of Canada continuing to occupy a prominent place on that political landscape means only that they will have to continue relating with Canada in the future. There is no internalization of the idea of Canada, no supplanting Kahnawake's sovereignty caused by participating in an administrative association with Canadian authorities. This is why the distinction between administrative and political linkages is so important. Throughout its long history as a community—one which began three centuries before Canada's—Kahnawake has never explicitly consented to a surrender of land or any other aspect of its sovereignty. Mohawks take the long view of history and see their current predicament as a phase in the evolution of their nation, with the only constant being the continuing existence of Kahnawake amidst a succession of larger, more powerful, but shorter-lived political entities.

Kahnawake's relationship with the Province of Quebec is illustrative of this concept. There is a persistent concern among students of the relationship about the response of Kahnawake Mohawks in the event of the Province's secession from Canada. The first and most obvious Mohawk response is to question the basic assumption that it is possible for the Province to secede from the federation. If there is no legal mechanism within the Canadian Constitution or the body of common law allowing a secession, is a separation possible? More importantly, the Province is a constituent element of a federal structure which represents the sovereignty of the Canadian state. It is not a sovereign in itself and thus does not possess title to any of the territory currently administered by its institutions. This is even more pronounced with respect to Indian and Inuit lands within the boundaries of Quebec; as with these other sovereign territories, Kahnawake is not a part of Quebec. Thus a movement among the people of Quebec to secede from the federation must not be based upon the creation of a new territorial unit which includes Mohawk lands. Likewise, a movement to create a new form of administering the territory within the Province must consider the Mohawks' prior relationship with the Government of Canada and their unwillingness to forego this relationship without substantial reconsideration of their interests and the potential for a better relationship in the future.

Intellectually, the prospect of a new relationship with Quebec does not pose a challenge to the principles which have guided the Mohawks throughout their long interaction with other European societies in North America. In the abstract, the Mohawks would implement the principle of the *Kahswentha* in their relationship with a new neighbouring sovereignty just as they always have. There is no difference in this respect between their position toward the Dutch in the 16th century, the English in the 17th century, the French in the 18th century, the British in the 19th century, or Canada in the 20th century. Their historicism is clear in the opposition generally evident among the Mohawks of Kahnawake to participating in any form of constitutional entrenchment of collective Native rights. There is an apparent aversion to creating a formal bond between Euro-American and indigenous societies on either a legal or ideological level.

On a practical level, the Mohawks discount the idea of secession and are concerned with the impact of the Province's drive for increased power within the federation. Especially in the wake of the 1990 crisis, the added factor of Quebec's misplaced obsession with 'law and order' on Indian lands coupled with a striking ignorance of Mohawk values and principles has led to a breakdown in cooperative relations. As the Mohawks of Kahnawake continue to gain small measures of success in rectifying their relations with the Government of Canada, these gains are offset by consistent efforts on the part of the Province to usurp Federal and Mohawk authorities and gain jurisdictional control of Mohawk lands and people. The Mohawks are aware of the Province's objective of recentralizing the control of Mohawk communities in Quebec City in response to the Federal government's projected decentralization and Ottawa's divestiture from Mohawk jurisdictions in favour of Mohawk self-government.

As Table 4.3 illustrates, the Mohawks of Kahnawake have clear preferences on the type of political linkages their community government should enter into with other governments.

Most Mohawks recognize the utility of establishing external relationships with every government sharing the political space occupied by Kahnawake. None of the entities listed as options in the survey conducted as part of this study were rejected outright as a candidate for

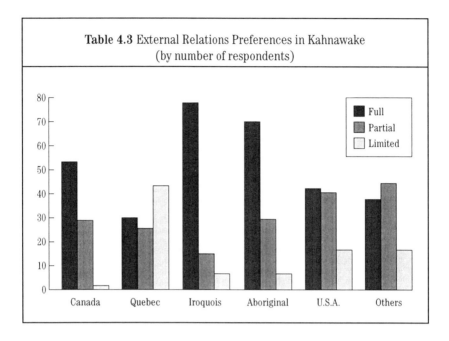

Table 4.3 External Relations Preferences in Kahnawake
(by number of respondents)

political linkage with Kahnawake.[14] Given the background to the issue described above, it is not surprising that there is no special allegiance to Canada in Kahnawake. In fact, despite the existence of a federal fiduciary responsibility, close social and cultural associations between Mohawks and Canadians on an individual level, and the shared historical relationship with Britain, Canada figured no higher than the United States, Britain, or any other nation-state.

As part of our survey, respondents were asked to rate their preference for establishing external relationships with various political entities. They were also asked to indicate whether or not the relationship should be a 'full', 'partial', or 'limited' linkage. Most respondents stated a preference for either full or partial linkage with Canada, the United States, and other nation-states. In considering the stated preference for full linkage only, Canada (54%) registered only slightly higher than the United States (43%), and other nation-states (38%).

This is in clear contrast to the Mohawk view on relationships with other aboriginal nations and the Iroquois Confederacy. The Mohawk view of their own sovereignty is obviously transferred to other aboriginal communities. A full 93% of respondents to the survey indicated that there should be full or partial linkages with both the Iroquois Confederacy and other aboriginal communities. The Iroquois Confederacy and other aboriginal communities are the clear choice in Kahnawake as the linchpins of a network of future external relations.

The prevailing view on external relationships is expressed in the comment offered by a Longhouse leader that Kahnawake 'should establish relationships with whoever we wish. A full relationship does not means a loss of jurisdiction or sovereignty but can enhance both.'

Re-Conceptualizing Sovereignty in Kahnawake

In Kahnawake, progress is movement towards the ideal of complete autonomy and the realization of the Mohawk right to self-determination. Mohawks see the consideration of self-government arrangements as part of the inevitable process of divesting themselves from colonized status and regaining the status of an independent sovereign nation. Thus self-government means simply regaining control over the processes and powers of governance as an interim measure to the eventual objective of autonomy.

The Kahnawake Mohawks' reformulation of the concept of sovereignty is a manifestation of their belief that Indian and Inuit peoples should not be saddled with the burden of conforming to a Euro-American institutional and legal model to justify their assertions of nationhood. The Euro-American conception of sovereignty is predicated on the achievement of what Blackstone referred to as 'a supreme, irresistible, absolute, and uncontrolled authority' over territory (Scruton 1982: 440). In Kahnawake, the conventional usage of the term 'sovereignty' has been abandoned in favour of an indigenous reformulation. It is based instead upon a mutual respect among communities for the political and cultural imperatives of nationhood—a flexible sharing of resources and responsibilities in the act of maintaining the distinctiveness of each community. While the English word is maintained, the content of the definition is being replaced by Mohawk ideas which move beyond 'sovereignty', using the word as just the closest approximation of an indigenous idea. The indigenous idea itself is being expressed, and 'sovereignty' is being redefined in the process. Sovereignty for the Mohawks of Kahnawake is represented by the Mohawk language word *Tewatatowie*, which translates to English as 'we help ourselves'.

There is a strong sense of self-sufficiency and independence in the political usage of *Tewatatowie*, particularly as it relates to group interactions with other communities. The word itself is used in Mohawk philosophical rhetoric and is linked to concepts contained in the *Kaienerekowa*. Thus Mohawk sovereignty is conceived of not only in terms of interests and boundaries, but in terms of land, relationships and spirituality. In this context, it is easier to discern the essence of the Mohawk definition of sovereignty. The idea of balance among people and communities is pervasive in Mohawk culture and spirituality; the achievement of a balanced relationship based upon respect for differences, whether among individuals or communities, is valued as the achievement of a harmonious ideal state of affairs. The essence of Mohawk sovereignty is harmony. Through its linkage to the *Kaienerekowa*, the concept is endowed with a spiritual power which precludes the compromise of the ideal in the interest of political expediency or power calculations. A balanced and respectful relationship among others (the people), between the Mohawk people and the earth (land), and between the Mohawk people and other communities forms the ideal represented in the Mohawk use of the term 'sovereignty'.

There is a keen sense of history in Kahnawake, and most Mohawks are aware of the path their community has taken from autonomous nationhood to wardship under Canadian institutions. This history reflects consistent rebuttals of their attempts to operationalize the ideal of harmonious co-existence within the framework of the Canada-Kahnawake relationship. Canadians are also aware of the history of the relationship between native and non-native societies. But while the majority of Canadians wish to see native societies integrated within the social and political framework they have created, Mohawks reject the idea of buying into what are essentially foreign institutions. They have recognized the political realities and the necessity of cooperating with Canadian authorities to create institutions and arrangements which will afford the community control over its internal organization, expanded jurisdictional powers, and more flexible external relationships. Canadians perceive these as ultimate objectives; Mohawks assuredly do not.

Having a clear sense of their goals does not cause the Mohawks of Kahnawake to develop tunnel vision with respect to interim measures. Without prejudice to the nationalistic goals, Kahnawake is aggressive in pursuing pragmatic arrangements to ensure that in the meantime the community achieves a level of security and prosperity. Despite some fears within and beyond the community, Kahnawake's short- and mid-term solutions do not include a radical re-implementation of an ancient social or political order. The vast majority of Mohawks feel unprepared culturally to take on the task of recreating a purely traditional society at this point. The consensus interim goal is a synthesis of the familiar with elements of the traditional into a workable and appropriate institutional framework to confront the current political reality facing the community.

Self-government as a long-term goal in Kahnawake is based explicitly on traditional concepts reflected in its political culture. In the short and mid-term the principles contained in the *Kaienerekowa* and *Kahswentha* are implemented as much as possible. On the continuum from short- to long-term goals, Kahnawake Mohawks insist on the maintenance of a position of sovereignty. Whether agreeing to a funding arrangement to build a hospital in 1985, or entering into formal self-government negotiations in 1991, Mohawks have consistently maintained that their efforts to improve life in Kahnawake should in no way be interpreted as consent to the legitimacy of Canadian institutions.

The major political obstacle Mohawks and Canadians face is essentially conceptual: they hold radically different ideas of Canada. Conceptually, Canada may be a nation, or it may be a political framework for cooperation between nations. For most Canadians it is both. For most Mohawks it is at best only the latter. The people of Kahnawake have allegiance solely to the Mohawk nation, and their view of the Mohawk nation is one in the fullest sense of the term as it is used in international law. This is in contrast to the illogical current usage among Native and non-Native politicians—'First Nations' in reference to Indian communities—which in fact refers to bands within the meaning of the Indian Act. The difference in usage highlights the hegemonic influence of Canada-as-Nation thinking even in aboriginal circles. By accepting the label, the so-called First Nations have in fact consented to being an integral element of the Canadian nation. But the Mohawks' nationality is rooted in their distinctive concept of sovereignty.

With this fact well established within the community, Kahnawake is limited in how far it can proceed in a partnership with Canada. Canadians would seek to bring Mohawks as full members into the nation they have created, while Kahnawake must as citizens of another nation resist the attempt to erode their Mohawk institutions and identity. From the Mohawk perspective the problem is a lack of respect for the sovereignty of the Mohawk nation. They hope for a partnership with Canada that recognizes the limits of their alliance rooted in their political philosophy, while still allowing both Canadians and Mohawks to benefit from the association.

Again from the Mohawk perspective, there is plenty of room for manoeuvre within the Canada-Kahnawake relationship without compromising Mohawk sovereignty. Kahnawake as a community of the Mohawk nation is vested with considerable local autonomy. This allows substantial progress without prejudice to larger issues of sovereignty and broader political associations. Current and future progress is expected to feed into an expanded conception of self-government in the long term which would respect Mohawk national sovereignty and the right to self-determination. The expanded concept would not preclude further cooperation between Canada and the Mohawks. It may in fact promote cooperation by forcing a negotiated power-sharing agreement and mutual recognition of jurisdictional control and delegated responsibility.

CHAPTER FIVE

THREE MOHAWK CHIEFS

Right now Indian people are sitting on the fence, damning the
Indian Act but afraid to abolish it. Our people are reluctant to
change the Indian Act for fear that the purse-strings of the fed-
eral government are going to be tightened or treaty and abo-
riginal rights will be abrogated. But if we keep sitting on the
fence, I think past experience tells us which side we're going
to fall on. So we have to make a move, and I advocate the tra-
ditional way—in my case, the Iroquoian way.

Kahnawake Chief, 1984

The previous chapter examined the evolution of traditionalist thought in
Kahnawake, culminating in a description of the key features of the
nationalist ideology at its present stage. It is worth restating here the difference between what I refer to as 'traditionalist' and 'nationalist'
thought in Kahnawake. The previous chapter demonstrated how traditionalists had provided the energy for the development of a nationalist
ideology. But the Longhouse movement as a whole is mired in conflict
over what others consider superficial aspects of the greater body of
Iroquois traditions.

The Longhouse movement has failed to consolidate its program into
a coherent set of institutions capable of exercising government authority within the community. This was not seen as presenting a problem for
the community's overall political development, because the Longhouse
movement has provided the impetus for a larger transformation. Since
the emergence of traditionalism during the 1960s, Kahnawake Mohawks
in general—the vast majority of whom are not Longhouse adherents—
have developed a nationalist ideology that integrates the key elements
of what an anthropologist identified in the 1950s as 'nativist' (Voget
1951: 222), and which were later transformed into the core principles of
the traditionalist ideology.

This general orientation to nationalism should form the focus of any
analysis of Kahnawake politics. Longhouse traditionalism has become

the benchmark of politics in Kahnawake as far as outsiders pay attention to such matters, yet other Mohawks have moved far beyond the
Longhouse people in modernizing traditional Mohawk values and principles. Where the Longhouse maintains an interpretation and strategy
based on re-implementing an old order, most Mohawks have taken the
next step toward integrating them in the new political reality.

This chapter will explore the evolution of political values among
Kahnawake's band council chiefs since the 1960s. The band council,
since 1978 referred to as the Mohawk Council of Kahnawake (MCK), and
its associated structures are the over-arching representative institutions
in Kahnawake. In terms of practical application and assertions of
Mohawk power, the band council remains the primary actor. This chapter will show how political values held by the leaders of the band council have evolved over time and may be taken to represent the changes in
political values which have occurred on a much broader scale over the
same period. As a statement or manifestation of Mohawk nationalism,
the words of the three chiefs who have served the community during its
nascent traditionalism through to the present day convey to the reader
the radical change in the tone and intensity of political values among the
leadership in Kahnawake.

RK was chief of the band council during the 1960s. His views then
and now represent a perspective formed in the pre-traditionalist era.
During his tenure, the community began to experience the first assertions of the new nationalism through the activism of the Longhouse and
the Warrior Society. RK represented most Mohawks during this period
in that his nationalism was at a stage I term 'latent', because of his still
unbroken confidence in the Canadian government's ability and willingness to protect Mohawk rights and land.

AD was chief of the band council during the 1970s. His views indicate a re-evaluation of the relationship Kahnawake had had with the
Canadian government. Previously a staunch supporter of RK, his views
by the 1970s had evolved into a rejection of the past, a realization that
Kahnawake could no longer rely upon Canada to respect and protect
those rights and lands which were so important to Mohawk people. AD's
views are also a good example of how initial attempts to integrate a traditionalist perspective resulted in a rather uncompromising shift from
one extreme to the other, a stage of nationalism I refer to as the 'revival'.

JN has been chief of the MCK since the early 1980s. He inherited an
institution created by the Indian Act, and since the beginning of his
tenure was faced with a revived Mohawk nationalism which presented a
serious challenge to the legitimacy of his position within the community
and the existing relationship Kahnawake had with Canada. JN has
responded by developing an interpretation representing a stage of
Mohawk nationalism I refer to as 'complex'. He has synthesized

traditional values and accommodated them to the demands of the modern political environment. In contrast to the intransigence of the 'revival' nationalism represented by AD, JN's perspective is sober and pragmatic.

What follows are excerpts from a set of conversations conducted with the three Mohawk chiefs revolving around their perspective on self-government or sovereignty, and political identity. A consideration of the chiefs' words illustrates the shift in political thinking over time. Changes in both the character and intensity of nationalist thinking are quite evident as the three engage the author in a discussion of essential political issues, such as motivations for seeking leadership, legitimacy, membership criteria, and political relationships. The material is presented as recorded in the belief that the chiefs' words speak for themselves.

VIEWS ON SOVEREIGNTY

RK

When did you first get involved in politics?
RK: Gee, I forget. But I was in for 19 years as a Councillor, Assistant Chief and Chief. I was young when I started.
When did you finish?
RK: I forget what year it was, but I resigned. It must have been in the 1970s.
And you don't participate in politics any more at all?
RK: No, I lost interest in Caughnawaga politics.
Why?
RK: Well, while I was Chief of the band, on my Council there were a lot of back-stabbers. And I feel the same thing is going on right now. It's just the way it is in politics here.
Could you tell me why you don't consider the Longhouse Chiefs and Clan Mothers to be legitimate?
RK: My grandfather used to tell me a lot of things about the Longhouse, how they were disorganized, how there were new Chiefs coming up all the time . . . He was a Chief in the Longhouse himself, and I think he just lost interest in it.
What about now? Is it the people who are involved or is it the system?
RK: I don't even know who's in there now. I don't pay any attention at all, after what my grandfather told me.
Is there anything the Longhouse could do, or change in any way to make you accept them?
RK: I doubt it.
So the Mohawk Council is, for you, the legitimate system of government?
RK: Yes.

Even with the problems it has?
RK: Yeah.
What are the best and worst things about the Council and an Indian Act government?
RK: They can run the reserve the right way, it's an all-right system.
Do the Canadian and Quebec governments have any authority here?
RK: Just the federal government. But they don't have the right to tell the Council anything. They are just there to protect our land.
Do you believe that we should vote in federal elections?
RK: No.
How should we participate or cooperate with the federal government then?
RK: Just getting along.
What are some of the important events in the community's history that have shaped politics?
RK: The St Lawrence Seaway, it took all our land away.
What was the Canadian government's role in the Seaway?
RK: They expropriated all our land! That was wrong. The band council tried to stop it, but it was no use because the government passed a law to expropriate the land and take whatever they wanted.
Did it change the way you thought about the government?
RK: Oh yeah. We lost trust in them.
What was the feeling in Kahnawake when the Seaway was going through?
RK: They felt bad. Look at all the farmers, they moved them off their land and right out of their homes.
Did anyone try to do anything about it?
RK: You couldn't do anything, the government just passes a law: expropriate. Even if you went to court, it wouldn't help you.
What about fighting, like they would do now?
RK: I don't think so. They wouldn't have thought of that.
Was the town different after the Seaway?
RK: Well, it changed it a little bit. We lost all of the river front, plus all the land they took.
What about the people, are they different?
RK: I don't think so.
After the Seaway, what else is important in our history? Things through the 1970s, like when the Warrior society . . .
RK: I never believed in the Warrior Society. I think they were just a bunch of radicals.
They weren't important politically?
RK: No, no.
What about after that, in confrontations with Quebec like the Cross shooting?[1]

RK: I thought that was wrong, what they did.

You were Chief in 1973 when the trouble happened, what were your views on the situation?[2]

RK: I thought we were doing the right thing for the people of Caughnawaga. I didn't want a bunch of radicals taking over.

Compared to 1973, is it the same sort of thing going on now?

RK: Well, they still have the Warrior Society. I think they do things in the wrong way.

Do you still think they are trying to take over?

RK: Yeah, I think so.

What exactly is the danger in them taking over?

RK: Gee, I don't know. I've often thought about it, and I'm sure they would put this Reserve upside down. Unstable.

What is your view on the next important development, the cigarette business?

RK: Well, you know . . . Indians are making money on it. But it was getting out of hand for a while. I thought the Provincial Police [SQ] and the RCMP would move in and crack down on everybody. But I guess they never got a chance to do it.

If it did get out of hand again, do you have any problem with the RCMP enforcing Canadian laws here in Kahnawake?

RK: The RCMP are allowed to come in here because this is federal land, eh. But not the Provincial Police.

Are the Peacekeepers an adequate police force?

RK: Well . . . for the reserve, yeah.

What were your views on the 1990 crisis situation?[3]

RK: I thought the band council would move in and try to squash it because it was bad for Caughnawaga. We couldn't get groceries . . . everything was at a standstill. I don't think they went about it in the right way.

Who was at fault during that whole thing?

RK: Well, it was because of what happened in Oka, eh.

If you had to lay blame, who would it be on?

RK: I blame it on the Warriors.

Do you agree that we had to support what was going on in Oka, or should we have stood back?

RK: We should have just considered here in Caughnawaga, and not worry about somebody else.

Do you consider the Mohawks a 'nation' or a 'people'?

RK: No, we are a nation.

What is our relationship to Canada then, as a nation?

RK: I don't think we're equals. But we are a nation and it should stay that way, we think different than the White man.

So it's all right to be a nation and still be under the Indian Act and the Canadian government?

RK: Oh yeah.
Is this something that is a permanent thing?
RK: I hope so! Because they're talking about self-government right now, eh. I'm afraid of it. I don't know if the federal government will give any more money to the bands, and if they stop giving us money they'll have no other choice but to tax us. And if they tax us, they'll break every one of us. We'll lose our homes, our land. We couldn't afford to pay it, we don't make that kind of money any more.
So you see self-government as a way for the Canadian government to cut its financial responsibilities?
RK: I think so.
Do you think the government here in Kahnawake is capable of administering self-government?
RK: I don't know if they could do it.
It's a lot more complicated than they realize?
RK: I think so.
So you're happy with the Indian Act and our current relationship?
RK: Yeah.

AD

What are the important events in our history that have shaped the way Kahnawake thinks?
AD: I always think of history in the long term from 1890 to the present. You read about how we were in the past, then you come to the rail lines, power lines, the Mercier Bridge. Then you have the border crossing case, and the continuous visits to governments about land claims . . .
What you're saying is that everything is important.
AD: Yeah, all that forms us today. That's what makes us aggressive. The war years, the draft when they used to come and pick up people. I've seen that myself, and also the RCMP raided the Longhouse when there were meetings or ceremonies going on because they weren't allowed. I've seen police raid weddings because people were drinking, and I've seen the police raid restaurants because people were drinking after coming back from New York. And then I've seen the incidents that happened with the Seaway, when our lands were expropriated.
Was that event in particular any different from the others?
AD: It was a manipulation too, in the sense that everybody opposed it, and they played families [off against each other] . . . I learned something of how the government considers you to be a collective group when the collective is in agreement with them, but when the collective disagreed with them, then they would consider you an individual. That showed how much damage they could do to the land. I was raised on that water. That was the biggest thing as far as our dislike for non-Indian people goes. Prior to that, there was a relationship where we used to have

cottage families over here, a lot of them. And then when the Seaway came, of course, it took all the waterfront, so since that time we've had a bad relationship with the non-Indian people. I use it in the same way that when White people see one Indian drinking, [they think] all Indians drink. So they took the land, now all White people are bad.

It was that much of a turning point?

AD: Sure, as far as I'm concerned people became more and more aggressive toward non-Indian people. Really. And then it was one of the first times that I know where official representation was made to the United Nations. The Seaway caused that, because I was on the Council with Matty Lazare and that was the time we made a couple of trips to New York for that.

What kind of efforts were made by the Council to oppose the Seaway?

AD: Because of those efforts, the Council became isolated as opposed to the individuals who had property.

So there was division and some people did favour the Seaway?

AD: Yes. Only the Council opposed it at that point, and of course the people who were directly affected by it. One of the things I've realized since is that the traditional people were the ones who posed a lot of questions and motivated, in an indirect way, things to happen which were to our benefit. At that time, there was some question as to their tactics, but now we understand. That goes for everything.

Do you see any change in the way the Longhouse was back then as opposed to the way it has developed since?

AD: Yeah. At that time it was the direct approach, verbal and physical. There was no office or anything. Then it changed over to a more organized way, organized in a non-Indian sense. At that time, your word was valid, as opposed to a signature, and that transition has occurred where the signature has replaced the word.

It seems to me that after the Seaway, there was a period where people were somewhat confused and nothing much happened. Is that accurate?

AD: Yeah. Canada was involved in all sorts of things like the Expo '67 and then the Olympics, it was sort of a happy time for everybody. There was a lot of work and everyone was enjoying themselves. One of the things is that in Kahnawake, when there was a lot of work, there was no problem. When there was no work, then there was movement so far as traditionalism was concerned. People had more time to think how they were affected by these things. If you look, every time there was a recession, we ran into a lot of problems internally. Every seven years something affected us.

As far as I'm concerned, one of the most important things was when we took over the United Church school and established our office there. Then we established the Peacekeepers . . .

Could you compare the way things were done before that point with what went on afterward?

AD: We used to have meetings, and it was still hidden meetings. The term 'secret meetings' came not from being secret to the Indians, but secret from government. Even at that stage, the government still didn't consider a meeting legal, unless there was an RCMP and an Indian Agent present. So we had to have meetings at somebody's garage to get discussion going. There was an off and on relationship with the government, sometimes we would send information, sometimes we wouldn't. And then Matty [Lazare]—Lazare was chief of the band council during the Seaway era when I was a councillor—and them decided to not have any Indian Agent, because he had run everything so far as administration was concerned—he had a free hand. So when we took over we found a lot of things which he had neglected to pass on to us as far as programs and funding. We found out a lot of stuff like that, so we started to become more and more involved. This was in 1964, I think. And then we started handling all the business . . . Then we got control . . .

So the Council as a governing system has developed only recently. Didn't they [Canada] only start implementing the Indian Act with the Agency in the 1930s?

AD: Yeah.

So the community's political development has moved in two thirty-year time spans; and now we're moving again.

AD: We could make it faster, but those thirty years that the government ran things have made us so dependent. We have lost a lot, and we need to change that. During that time also, the government attempted to transfer authority to the province. We had our own RCMP men, but in reaction to the government's efforts to put in the SQ here, we formed the Peacekeepers. We were trying to kick out the SQ—the RCMP were here but they weren't doing it [acting against Provincial jurisdiction] and neglecting their responsibility. And that's how it happened, these guys started volunteering and we lobbied for it. One of the biggest instances was when RK and I were called in to the RCMP Headquarters building over here. They had all the brass dressed in uniform and ribbons, with the RCMP on one side and the SQ on the other. We walked in and they told us that we had to get rid of those men because it was illegal, they were 'vigilantes'. But we had done our homework by contacting several judges on the Superior Court and got them on our side. They were looking for a solution to the problems here too, and we told the police brass that we would stop it on the condition that we work toward establishing an Indian Police Force in Kahnawake. And they said, 'all right'. So we called a big meeting with all the people, the police brass and the judges. We had the Attorney General on our side too. And then the government had to agree to establish the Indian Police here. That was a big change.

That was all related to the 1969 White Paper, eh?
AD: Everybody knows that the White Paper was a decentralization proposal by Trudeau to transfer jurisdiction over Indians to the provinces. It was rejected. But if you look back, that whole period was an attempt to do it anyway. They were just trying to legitimize their policies. The problem is that in spite of its rejection and our objections, they did transfer jurisdiction to the province. And we're living with that today. We tried to tell the people at the time that it was already taking place anyway. The one thing that worked against us through that whole period was that our own people were not ready to take on those responsibilities.
So what about after that?
AD: The thing that threw them was land claims. There was a fellow by the name of Hugh Conn working in the Department of Indian Affairs who was close to retirement, who informed us of a document dating from 1912 which stated that the government had to negotiate the rightful ownership of some territory, which they had neglected to do. We asked him for it, but he said that he would give it to us after two years, when he retired. We waited, and when he retired he gave it to us. That's what brought out the whole land claim question. This threw a monkey wrench into their transfer of jurisdiction plans. They now had to deal with land issues.

In 1972 we went to a meeting in British Columbia, and because of that document, we started to use the argument of Aboriginal Rights. Up to that point, the control of the Indian movement in Canada was in the hands of the western Indians because they had treaties. They considered themselves to be more Indian than anybody else because of the treaties. That was their attitude. So if you mentioned anything about 'Aboriginal Rights', they would say, 'no way, it's Treaty Rights'. So in 1972 we made a big speech in Vancouver at the All Chiefs Meeting. Man, they threw us to the dogs! But we maintained our position. Now they're using our argument and Aboriginal Rights to re-do treaties that are not respected. That all started here in Quebec.
What about internal changes? Like in 1973 when there was trouble here involving AIM and the Warrior Society?
AD: Not to sidestep, but in 1970 we had an arrangement in which I left to lead the CIQ [Confederation of Indians of Quebec]. So RK was the Chief then, and I was in Quebec [City].
What is your view on that situation?
AD: It's hard to talk about [RK], but I will tell you that the RCMP have ways to build you up, to make you believe that you have more authority than you actually have. He should have sat down with the traditional people.
So it shouldn't have been a situation of us versus them, and right versus wrong?

AD: We always hesitated to make it public at the time, but the people evicted were targeted for a specific reason and for actions they did as individuals, not because they were White. We even informed the outside police and the municipalities of what was going on there. So we evicted them, but couldn't name them or say why. And of course the media got hold of the fact that we were evicting people, even our own people got in on it, and assumed that we wanted to kick out all the White people here. We didn't handle it well. It exploded into a racial war because of our actions to evict certain individuals who were undesirables. But if the RCMP had just done their job, RK wouldn't have had the trouble that he had. All that reinforced the feeling that people got after the Seaway of hating White people. 1973 made it even worse.

Could you comment on the gradual development of the Longhouse since then, and the events leading up to the 1990 crisis?

AD: I think the people here are basically traditionalists. They want to be. But they haven't had good explanations of it. People said that you can't be Catholic and be a traditionalist. But now those barriers are starting to be erased, people are starting to realize that it's a question of living together. More and more people are coming because they realize the fact that in order to preserve what they have, whether it's physical or spiritual, they have to at least look at traditionalism. The unfortunate thing is that we don't have consistency, we are played one against the other. That's the residue of government manipulation. If they don't agree with what we're doing, they'll disrupt by saying, 'We're going to work with Handsome Lake, or Deganawida Longhouse, or Grand Council.' And we fall right into it. But I think that can be overcome.

If we all followed traditionalism, we would at least be talking to each other. That's why I'm back in it. Since at least 1978 my objective has been to introduce it to people in a positive way, and get people to make a decision to go back to it. Not a specific form of tradition, but traditionalism. After all, Christianity has become a tradition in Kahnawake. But I mean getting back to the Great Law and Longhouse ways.

As for 1990, I feel it was due to happen. When I returned here from my store in Quebec to help out, I realized that I had been doing all these things: talking to the Queen, the Pope, every Prime Minister since Pearson, the President of the United States, Haile Selassie . . . all about our situation, and nothing had changed. They are still taking land and imposing culture, and I said to myself that they were going to find out now, that this was the last straw. That's what it was for me. I think something can be built on that.

Concerning the question of what is happening in Kahnawake. I don't know who says [here] that cigarettes are illegal and gambling is wrong . . . the government says that. I use the example of us in the 1960s when we started the bingo. We were raided and I went to court every week for three years. We won the cases eventually, but we were told at the time that bingo was immoral and illegal and corrupting people, yet when they approved it they gave it to the church! We get caught in those types of situations. I don't even look at 'bingo' or 'cigarettes', I look at the principle. The principle is that we are independent and we can do what we want.

JN

How did you arrive at the conclusion that it's better to work within the system?

JN: It's a combination of a number of things. But you have to go back to when I first ran for office and got elected. I really did not anticipate or know what I was in for. I had no preconceived idea that I was going to change things. First of all, I wanted to find out—because I was hearing all kinds of stories about corruptness and all other kind of stuff, and I wanted to find out if this was true. And then, how [the council] related to the community and how it related to the outside. My motives for seeking office was to find out if there was a way of improving things for the community. That's what started me off, and basically, that's still the thing that motivates me. But very quickly after that, this mandate for change came about: scrap the Indian Act system, scrap the elected Council, and let's put in traditional government. So then I knew my responsibility, before I had time to figure out the other stuff about corruptness and the Indian Act. Then there was a transition that took place, a changing of the guard . . . then it was . . . me.

If you sort of fell into this position as a leader of change, who was responsible for the mandate and this push?

JN: There were a number of incidents and quite a bit of dissatisfaction with the way government was behaving. There was a time period during which the entire police force was fired and the volunteer force came in. Then we wanted to do something about the Rivermont Quarry and we couldn't get any support and assistance from the outside on that. David Cross was killed, murdered, by the SQ, and there was just a general build-up and a lot of dissatisfaction. Like in 1973 when you had the riots in the community, and the council as a whole called in the SQ and they came in and occupied the town. That led to a rebellion, a rejection if you will. And at that time there was almost a takeover, an ouster of the council. But they managed to come to a peaceful understanding and agreement. And there are still people in council after that who were a part of [that confrontation], and there still are people on council today who were a part of it. So there was a general movement of dissatisfaction, and the people said, 'Now is the time that we have to do something.' It was a buildup, it wasn't something that you could pinpoint, [it was] a gradual change. There had been a renewal of traditionalism, this

Warrior Society that started to come about at the time. The movement to take over our education system . . . we did away with the Catholic school-Protestant school division . . . a lot of things were happening to unite the people.

So this was all part of a general trend in the community towards a more traditional outlook.

JN: Towards a more traditional understanding; then they said, 'OK, this is the mandate.' And since that time, that has been the mandate which I have tried to get subsequent Councils to understand. If you think that it isn't a mandate, then go back to the public and ask them. *(laughs)* Nobody has had the nerve, I guess, or the willingness to go back and ask. I know that there has been a lot of dismay as to what traditionalism is because various things have happened in the last little while where people have put traditionalism in front of activities that have been detrimental to Kahnawake. But it is still there, and there still is some kind of achingly slow movement towards that. That's a long explanation, but it's the only way I can really describe it.

So members of your family have just got involved in different aspects of this general movement?

JN: Yeah, some people have found their calling in different areas. I decided to do it this way, and traditionalism had nothing to do with it. But suddenly . . . Boom! . . . this is the way we're moving. It was a shocker, and then it was like, 'now what do we do?' We're still trying to figure it out.

Could you explain a little more about how you see both the Longhouse system and the Council as legitimate in Kahnawake?

JN: There's a coming to grips in a lot of different sectors that there is this reality of a system that has been imposed to a certain degree on the community. To clarify: at the time there were Rotiyaner, condoled chiefs, and an acceptance that this was going to come. Even though there was a lot of resistance to the Indian Act, it still managed to work its way in. And since that time there's been an arm's-length tolerance; throughout the last 100 or so years. And since 1979, my way of looking at things was to say, 'Let's look at a way of making a transition. But let's do it in a cooperative fashion.' I've been trying to set a schedule and a time as to how it's going to come. I've had to balance the two worlds as much as I could. You can't really manage the two, but in your own mind and thinking, you try to. We also had to understand that the community had these traditional leanings, but that there was uncertainty as to what traditionalism was. Since the Indian Act, there has been created a lot of dependence on the government and the Council, whether we like it or not. So we've created institutions that are still tied to somewhere else. So if we try to create a balance, or even move to make one predominant over the other, it has to be in line with the rest of the community. And we are not going to force it through. We are going to do it on an even pace and in a way that's acceptable to the community. Part of my job is to encourage people to find out what's going on in different areas. And to get at the traditional people and tell them that there's no exclusivity, that they don't have the exclusive right to [a traditional form of government]. To say, 'Some of you sitting here in these positions may not be in them in the future.'

So in your mind, in one segment of the community the council is legitimate, and in another the Longhouse is legitimate. Therefore we have to blend the two?

JN: Well, there's gotta be a working relationship to a certain degree right now, but it's not formal. The only thing that's really formal is this Peace and Security Committee.[4] That seems to be the 'weak link' between the two (*laughs*). It's the first time we've really cooperated in a situation that wasn't a crisis; it came out of a crisis, but it's something more and not dealing only with security, it's more than that. So it's a link, a weak one, but it is a start. On both sides—and there are definite sides here, as much as we say there isn't—there is a recognition, despite the resistance, that each is important to the other. It's a matter of putting aside a little pride and personal differences and finding out what's compatible.

Your views seem to be consistent with the idea that we have a government-to-government relationship with some real linkages to Canada, rather than the radical sovereigntist view of complete independence. Could you explain that?

JN: Because that's the reality of the world right now. No matter where you go, that's the way it is. There's nothing wrong with thinking the other one, because in the back of our minds it is there, but for me I think of what's achievable.

When I asked if you thought Kahnawake was forced to accept the Indian Act system, there are two ways to interpret this question. Either we were forced by circumstances to accommodate, or we were coerced or tricked into it. Which did you mean?

JN: I meant it in terms of strong-arm tactics being used. But on the other hand, there was an acquiescence, and an acceptance that seemed to say, 'Let's see how it works.'

So you're not one of the conspiracy theorists who think we were undermined by government actions?

JN: We were to a certain degree. But if the community and those who had influence really wanted to prevent it, they could have fought, physically, instead of through political means. And the easy out for them was to blame 'The Fourteen'.

Tell me more about that.

JN: From what I understand (*laughs*) there was supposedly a vote that was taken, 14 people showed up and voted against it. Then, between here and Ottawa, somehow the votes got changed and they said the 14 had voted in favour. There's two stories to it. One is that 14 people voted for it directly in that election, and they were considered traitors. Then there's the other story that 14 did vote, against it, which was later on changed in favour of it.

There are other similar stories around too.

JN: And unfortunately, there was a 'suspicious' fire at the old Kateri Hall where the records used to be kept.

There's been a lot of 'suspicious' fires here, eh?

JN: *(laughter)* Two fires in Council halls which destroyed a lot of records.

What were the most important events in the community that have shaped your way of thinking?

JN: Well, my introduction to the education system which I have described. And also the Seaway; I don't remember the political battles, but I know it changed my parents quite a bit.

So the Seaway was important?

JN: It was a very important thing in my life, and also to a lot of other people. It revived the traditional thinking in many people. It brought a lot of people together, but it also divided a lot of people.

I always thought it did cause us to reject Canada, but now I'm also getting the sense that it divided people too.

JN: It divided people because those that were most affected by it physically and had to move their homes were coerced to accept the money. There was only one or two who refused to move right until the very end; but the others said, 'OK, we'll take the money.' Some people who live in the village said, 'Hey, it's way out there, it doesn't affect me.'⁵ So it affected us psychologically. Politically, the government came in here and took the land and rearranged things. They passed the special act of parliament. That's where the thinking of the government protecting people here changed. It was just like that. It turned people around because after that they said, 'That government isn't protecting us.' It changed the course of life in Kahnawake anyway. It was a rude awakening. I didn't feel it at the time because I was young, but that's the way it's coming down. There's a lot of bitterness still there.

That's important. Because people didn't actually feel it at the time, except for those directly affected. It wasn't a sense in the community that we were violated until much later.

JN: I think it led to a lot of problems with alcohol too. To me, when that came through, a lot of things changed for the worse, and a lot of people changed. I saw it in my own house.

Did you have to move?

JN: No, we didn't. But when you have a father who did a lot of fishing and spent a lot of time on the river . . . once that Seaway passed, it really got to him. And my grandparents too, you talk to them and find out it really affected them. It did a lot of damage, and it had an effect on the children, and it's had its effect on the grandchildren, and now great-grandchildren.

Other periods in my life time which were important were 1973. The situation with the evictions. I was married at the time, and it did create an impression on me and I asked, 'Where is this town headed?' I saw divisions again, and some battles taking place. I remember an incident at my wife's grandparents'. We had just moved into our house, and we were going down to where all the trouble was near the fire station right next to Tom Lahache's. We were going there and we had to park down the hill near the Legion. We pulled in the parking lot and there was about twenty guys standing on the roof, all armed, protecting the Legion from the Warriors. I could hear 'Lock and load,' as soon as I approached them. There was a big spotlight on me, and I asked what was going on. Then I said, 'This is terrible.' Right in our own community, look what the hell they're doing . . .

Do you think it was a different situation in 1973 than in 1990, whereas the Legionnaires then were getting their impressions of traditionalism from Wounded Knee and the takeover of a community? Or was it just divisions that already existed?

JN: There was this impression of a group of people who took matters into their own hands. And there were loyalties both ways . . . people just chose to take sides at that time. And it seemed that the popular movement was with this eviction, but you really didn't know it because you just knew there were people going house to house to make people leave. That was a popular thing to do, but the way they went about it was questionable. The Council's reaction was, 'They have no goddamn business doing it, we are the authority, etc.' I'm not exactly sure, but I think the influence was there to go to the Legion and the Knights [of Columbus] and get people to back up the Council. And then there were threats that were made, 'They were going to shut the Council Office down, they were going to shut the church down, they were going to get at the Knights, and at the Legion.' And then all of a sudden you got these guys over here thinking they have to protect themselves. And believe me, they were serious guys. But it was an internal kind of thing that time. Nobody was really against the eviction because people said, 'Yeah, well, it has to happen.' But it was like, 'Not them, we're the ones to do it.' Or 'If they're allowed to do that, then they're going to take over completely.' And actually, there was a movement on the other side to do just that.

That was sparked by an incident in which RK gave permission to this Meloche guy to build a home. It never went to a meeting, he gave him the land, he got a grant, got a welfare home! From there things just exploded. You can second-guess as to why they did that, and why the other side reacted, but it did create a lot of thinking in this community. One of my first reactions, when I saw some of the people involved on the front page of the Montreal newspaper—I was working in Montreal at the time—was, 'Here I am an ironworker earning my keep and there are those people in Kahnawake causing this problem and putting us on the front page.' I wasn't too happy with that. I wasn't too proud of it. My first reaction was that most of those people doing things had never worked in their lives. They're on welfare and they have nothing better to do. Those people there are nothing but a bunch of bums, because I knew them, and there I was working hard, and they went ahead and did something like that with no regard for anyone else.

What about after 1973, in terms of important events?

JN: After that there were other situations which only increased the drive for us to be totally responsible for everything that goes on around here. Then you move through to the 1979 incidents, and on to the time period—which you can say is still prevalent today—which you can call 'The Showdown'. The internal showdown, as well as the external showdown in which the cigarette issue came into focus, a lot of money became involved, the issue of having Warriors patrol this community. I call it a showdown because that's really what it was: a showdown as to who was going to control the law and the economy and those sorts of things.

Since the seventies, then, you see a continuation of the same pattern. Do you think it has been resolved now?

JN: The thing that made people think about whether or not we were doing things the right way was 1990. We were thrown together whether we liked it or not, and we were in a situation where either we called in the outside forces to resolve it or we take control of the situation ourselves. And that is exactly what happened; we did take control of the situation, the people of Kahnawake did. I don't care what anybody says or thinks, the Warriors may have started it off, but it was something that became too big for them. And either we were going to capitulate and say, 'Come on in and get rid of these people,' or we say we take control. Certainly from 1973 to 1990 there was a switch, where in 1973 the Legion was defending its building against a force they considered against them, whereas in 1990 they took it over. The veterans brought in the Warriors and said, 'This is your headquarters.'

Since that time there has been a de-escalation, but still a vigilance. I think that the recent survey that was done proves that there is a large part of this community that feels that we need that vigilance because they don't have a sense of security yet.[6] They still fear that the Châteauguay White Warriors, or the SQ and RCMP are going to come in and do something. They still need some form of security. It doesn't necessarily mean that we have to run around with guns though. I think everyone realizes that we had our flashpoint, we bared our teeth and growled. They growled back, and they have more 'teeth' than us. We are not going to win that war. But we still have to maintain that edge and say, 'It's very easy to get those guns out from under the bed!'

What is your sense of the future of Kahnawake?

JN: One of the main goals that I have is to establish a good strong economic base so that you do have money available to do certain things in this community. Not money that's going to go directly into individuals' pockets, but to have a better educational system and a lot of other different things.

So your goals aren't necessarily political?

JN: It's a combination of both, because the economics will also support the political. The economics also has to realize that we have to bring along that traditional baggage with us too. Some very important principles have to be reflected in the economics, not to the extent of hindering economic progress, but there are certain things that have to be embedded in there. Then on the political side, I have no difficulty towards advocating and pushing the establishment of traditional government. But it's not going to be done by a small group of people; it's gotta be open to everybody. No exclusivity; it's not going to be a club. And how do you do that? By first of all re-establishing the clans as the main political families in Kahnawake. Everybody, whether or not you have a clan or you're adopted in, has just as much right as everybody else. You break down that blood quantum barrier, and you let the clans be the ones to decide and judge who is going to participate in the system. But you have to set certain standards too, and certain things that people have to live up to.

Regarding the return to traditional government, the process is one thing, and the content another. Would you characterize your position as 'purist'—with keeping the clans, the matrilineal structure and gender-specific roles—because there are other ideas like 'modernizing' the structures?

JN: There is a lot of flexibility built into my thinking, but the clans are very important to me. Those are your political and social families. In order to move issues through the community I have not yet seen a better way of maintaining communication than relying on the extended family structure, or the clans. This is the basis of a traditional government.

VIEWS ON IDENTITY

RK

Do you think the fact that we don't pay taxes is what makes us different from everybody else?

RK: Yeah.

You do agree with the blood quantum idea and measuring 50% blood?
RK: Yes.
You consider yourself full-blooded Indian. Is this based on research?
RK: Well, through my father and mother and their parents, and all my ancestors; they were all Indians.
What about the history of Kahnawake, with all the racial mixing even way back in the 1700s? Doesn't that affect the way you think about this?
RK: No.
On the membership question, what determined whether or not a person is a Mohawk to you?
RK: If they have 50% blood.
Do you agree with Bill C-31 giving the native women their rights and status back?[7]
RK: No, the law said if they married a White man, they lose their status. Now we got all kinds of guys on the Band List over here with no Indian blood.
What about the women themselves?
RK: They should have stayed out.
We make an exception here when the woman is divorced or widowed. Then we let them come back, what do you think about that?
RK: If she married a White man, they shouldn't allow that.
What about non-Indians living in Kahnawake?
RK: That's something you can't stop. But sometimes they're a nuisance . . .
You lived for a long time in the United States, yet you still don't consider yourself an American?
RK: No.
Because you live here in Canada and get Medicare and all that, this doesn't make you a Canadian?
RK: No.

AD

What would you consider to be a Mohawk, someone who follows the traditional way?
AD: What I consider to be a Mohawk is based on 'Ohenron', 'Tekariwatehkwa', those kind of words. Which means we live in harmony, we thank, and so on. And who believes that the Great Law is the application of these principles dictating the responsibilities of the men and the women and the clans and everything, and who follows that principle. And then following those principles based on considering future generations, where the Seven Generations comes in. If you believe that you are a Mohawk; if you don't, then you're an Indian. You understand? And if you don't believe that, and its part of Iroquoian society, then you're not an Iroquois.

So in your opinion, there could be a difference between a Kahnawakeró:non and a Mohawk?

AD: Yeah.

So if I say, 'I don't believe in traditionalism,' I'm still an Indian but not a Mohawk?

AD: That's right.

And this is a political as well as cultural thing?

AD: A total existence.

So obviously you don't consider yourself American or Canadian. Is there no concept of dual citizenship in the Mohawk nation?

AD: No. But we're prepared to do like other nations have to do in this day and age, and if I have to use a foreign passport to reach my objectives, then I will. A lot of people don't look at it that way, but I do.

Are there any rights that a Mohawk, in your view, would have that other people in Kahnawake don't?

AD: Yeah, because the whole argument and concept, even as evidenced in the Constitution, is based on inherent right. Rights flow from being Mohawk and being distinct, and that's what you have to be. You have to continue and preserve that, because if you break that line, you're not preserving it and you become something else. And you don't have any argument. The inherent right and who you are has to come from a seed or a root way back. So it gives more right than to be a Kahnawakeró:non. I think that's what causes problems here, because a Kahnawakeró:non, when he's in trouble with the White man's law, will choose to use the Indian law; and when there's a problem with the Indian law he'll choose to use the White man's law. That's a Kahnawakeró:non.

That to me sometimes seems part of our basic character.

AD: That's right, and it shouldn't be. It should be based strictly on the Kanienkehaka, the Mohawk.

What about the spiritual side of it, about the differences in religion? Can a Christian be a Mohawk?

AD: I think so, provided that you follow basically the concepts of our Mohawk spirituality.

Can you tell me what things you do to qualify you as a Mohawk?

AD: Well, the ceremonies, respect for others and the land. It all goes back to the declaration which says that you follow the roots and you'll be protected by the branch. That would say that anybody could do it, you don't see any colour. They come to understand Mohawk philosophy, and they become more Mohawk than some with dark hair and all the features . . .

It's a cultural-philosophical sort of thing?

AD: Yes.

So someone like JN can be a traditional person even though he works for the Indian Act system?

AD: Yeah. Depending on what I said before, where you use other methods to reinforce your own.

What I'm trying to get at is whether there is some kind of test. What means do you use to evaluate whether someone is a Mohawk or not?

AD: I guess it would have to be more than just the idea. It would have to be someone who would practise. You know, go to the ceremonies. Or at least do something to take up the responsibility that is required there, and to understand the responsibility of the others. I guess that's why I have a lot of trouble getting people to understand it, because you have all that to understand before you can do it. Like I said, I've seen many places where non-Indian people practise it and seem to be more Mohawk than some Mohawk people, especially in Europe.

The question in my mind is this: if you don't believe in the political side of it—the Longhouse structure of government—but are committed to traditionalism in a spiritual and cultural way, are you still a Mohawk?

AD: Hmmm . . . I don't think so. Because I believe in that total line. As I said, 'the words that come before all else' applied to that system, so you have to use that system. That's what is there. If you choose something else, then it's not that system.

So there's no modifying it?

AD: No, because the attempts that have been made have screwed us up. We've tried Christianity and non-Indian political systems, and that's what has confused us. My belief is that the Great Law is there, and you have to refer to it, you can't go to the amendments like everybody else does. An amendment is made only for a specific situation. If you have a new situation, you go back to the basics and work from there.

Do you remember when you made the change in your thinking, and why?

AD: I made it surprisingly early, I think I always have thought this way. I think I wanted to use the system to try to convert it back. I think that's what dictated my whole situation. When I saw my mother and father talk about traditionalism, because we were in an elected system imposed on us, I always thought about Mohawk traditional. My objective was always to get the people to go back to that system. Even in the association we formed, that's why we called it the 'Confederation' of Indians. I wanted to make it the same way the Confederacy was organized with each group operating individually. So it was always there.

But it didn't seem to gel until a certain period. When you first started out in politics, it seemed like more of a pan-Indian ideal than anything else, and then focused later on what you're talking about.

AD: Well, we had to do that because we became involved early in our political careers with all the other Indian people, and then we realized that they weren't the same as us. We originally tried to impose [unity], but we couldn't do it. So we had to start improvising, and that's where you got the pan-Indian thinking. The most difficult part was that pan-Indian thinking decided one thing and our own people decided something else, and I was a chief in Kahnawake and President over there. I think the point was in 1978 when we were at the meeting where the people got up and said, 'We're going to go traditional.'[8] That's when I started going the other way around. Maybe people don't believe it, but [it is] a fact; the reason we first took over the Indian government here, it was to put in a traditional system.

I wanted to do that anyway, realizing that other council members had no inkling of what that system was. Then I asked the clan mothers what we were going to do, and they said we had to put people in place and all that . . . I lost . . . it went downhill. That's when I started to drink, I gave up. I got a response that shocked me. And then I came back here yet didn't become involved in anything really. 1990 was, for me, a release. When you're a chief in Kahnawake you're criticized by your own people and shafted by the government. You're in between and it's not an easy position to be in. You do things and you could feel the government manipulating you, yet you have to do them because people are depending on you for services. So after that 1990, I felt relieved.

You don't feel that the Mohawk language is essential to the Mohawk people?

AD: It is essential to the people as a whole, but not something that you have to have to be a Mohawk. It's preferable, and it's nice when you understand what's happening in the ceremonies. But you don't need it personally to be a Mohawk.

JN

When you were growing up, what was the word they used in referring to the group here in Kahnawake?

JN: It was just 'Onkwehonwe'. It's only been recently that people have started to use terms like 'Kanienkehaka'. I never heard it before that . . . maybe it was twenty years ago that I first heard the word, 'Kanienke'. Or 'Kanienkehaka'. Then I asked them what it meant, you know?

Yeah, I asked an older woman, 98 years old, and she didn't even understand the word.

JN: It's true. For me anyway, all I heard was that word 'Oriwagaineha'. The old way of doing things, the traditional way. It was used in a positive way.

When did you start thinking of yourself as a Mohawk rather than an Iroquois or a Kahnawakeró:non?

JN: That was there a long time ago, but not the term, 'Kanienkehaka'. But Mohawk was; to define ourselves specifically, we said 'Mohawk', the English term. As far back as I can remember. Or we were

'Caughnawaga Indians' or whatever. Or on many occasions among the Mohawk-speaking people here we would say, 'Kahnawakeró:non'. So if you were from somewhere else, you would say, 'What is it, what are you?' And some people would say, 'Onkwehonwe', some others would say, 'Caughnawaga Indians', and others would say 'North American Indian'. But then you would get 'Mohawk' too.

Does being from Kahnawake mean you are an Iroquois too?

JN: Yes. But I wouldn't have said that 15 or 20 years ago. We knew about the Confederacy, and everybody knew about the Six Nations, but as far as the relationship to it, nobody knew the details. It's only been in the last, maybe 15 years really that I became, first of all, curious as to why we kept hearing all this stuff and why people were encouraging us. Because I remember all the arguments that used to go on, going back even prior to that time. When I was young I used to go to public meetings and hear from what was known as the 'Defence Committee'. Some of those people are still around, people who were considered the intellectuals of the time. They were like 'anti-council'. I remember the attacks that they made . . . they talked about the Confederacy and the Six Nations and Mohawks.

How about for them, did you get the sense that it was all intellectual, or was it something they lived?

JN: I think it was partial experience, part reawakening, and partial exploitation. People used to talk about some of them living different than the way they were preaching. Like being devout Catholics at the same time as all of this, as most people were!

I can never get away from the fact, in my research, that no matter what traditional branch people are from, everyone was Catholic at one time or another in their life.

JN: Sure. But suddenly something changed them . . .

You believe that the older people were forced to accept Christianity. Was this something they told you or something you figured out?

JN: It was a little of both. In the way they explained things. It was almost apologetically explained, like maybe it was wrong for them to accept it, but there was nothing else they could really do. They were in a time period that they had to accept it. So at times I've thought about it and said, 'Why the heck did they allow that?' But then you think about it and you can't really blame them, you know? You can't fault them for what they did. I've had discussions with my parents over this, and it's almost apologetically the way they talk about it.

So they knew this yet they were very devout and committed to whatever religion they were.

JN: Also, they trusted. They put their faith and their trust in the priest, the Indian Agent, and the government was doing the right thing. It was that time period, I believe, in which this attitude that government was right, and 'You don't fight the government'. We went through stages in our history, and during this time, that's the way things were. That was the stage at which the government completely took over and implemented the Indian Act. It was a new thing for many of them. And there are still a lot of people around now who it was new for. You know all the stories about the 'Famous 14' who were sell-outs and all of that.[9] They knew all of this was not right, but they said they'd manage for awhile and later on do something about it.

So if it wasn't that these people had carried it forward from a long unbroken tradition, it fits with everyone else's experience that it was a re-creation.

JN: You talk with the older people, and hear that in the 1920s you had traditional people, 'Rotiyaner', who were sitting in church. And they played prominent roles in the church because the church recognized that these people were very important in the community.

And they didn't see anything wrong with going to church either.

JN: No, they didn't.

Do you remember what you thought of Longhouse people when you were young?

JN: Yeah, I do. It was like Longhouse people were there, but they weren't there. They didn't talk too much about them.

Where was the Longhouse when you were young?

JN: I think it was down near the river. I remember because my uncle used to have a farm down the road. Everybody used to go there when we were kids, to picnic, and they used to hire a lot of people from Kahnawake to pick vegetables. I'm pretty sure that there was a Longhouse there.

So there was no problems between them and other people?

JN: No. Even my mother-in-law, who isn't old, says that she knew all the dances. It was like they went to church, but they also went to participate at the Longhouse.

Turning to the citizenship question, living within what they call the 'state' doesn't make you a citizen of either Canada or the United States?

JN: No.

Taking part in the social programs and being subject to the laws also doesn't imply citizenship?

JN: No, as far as I'm concerned we have the unique opportunity to benefit from two worlds. Our own, in terms of being here and being tax-exempt and having other rights, as well as the spiritual side of knowing who you are and the traditions and customs. Then there's also being able to go out there and take advantage of the educational system, their economic system . . . We have the right to the two, and we should use them to the fullest extent.

But to you it's definitely a situation of leaving one world and going to another?
JN: Yes.
Could you explain why you believe that a Mohawk can also be a citizen of the United States or Canada, even though you are a strong Mohawk nationalist?
JN: We can and should have the best of two worlds. And in order to enjoy that other world out there, at times you have to be labelled, and at times you have to conform with certain things. But it's not one that you give of yourself freely, you don't say to yourself, 'Yes, I accept that; I am an American citizen.' In their system they have to do it that way, but what you're saying is, 'it's in their law that I'm part of the citizenship.' But primarily, you have your own.
I think as more and more people get out and experience things, they are realizing that you have to concede some things.
JN: But you do it without prejudice to your first loyalty.

CHAPTER SIX

THE STRUCTURE OF GOVERNMENT IN KAHNAWAKE

*The concept of mutual respect embodied in the Two Row
Wampum, in which Natives and Non-natives will not interfere
in each other's affairs, must now be brought to life . . . our 'row'
must be made strong enough to withstand any and all attempts
by foreign powers to control it . . . with the guidance, will and
authority of the people, we must simply go ahead and exercise
our right to self determination in order to maintain it!*

Mohawk Council of Kahnawake, 1993.

The previous chapters have illustrated the shift in the mindsets of
Kahnawake Mohawks away from a belief in Canadian institutions as
useful tools in safeguarding their rights and lands. Rejecting the specific framework within which the Canada-Kahnawake relationship existed has eventually led to the development of an ideology which denies
the legitimacy and rejects the authority of all European impositions in
the community. This new ideology could have led to a radical rejection
in Kahnawake of the governing band council, which is chartered under
the auspices of the Canadian Indian Act. However, the transformation of
the band council from an Indian Act agency into an institution of self-
government, and a conscious effort on the part of the council to implement the values, principles, and structures of Mohawk tradition into a
new institutional framework for Kahnawake, has resulted in its
entrenchment as the platform upon which the community will build its
future political structure.

This process is reflected best in the ideological shift in the band
council itself and the structural evolution of the council and its associated institutions within the community. In the 1940s, the band council

in Kahnawake was characterized by a complete institutional integration with the framework imposed upon Native peoples in Canada by the federal government. Despite the community's political culture, which oriented the Mohawks toward the goal of preserving their cultural distinctiveness and political autonomy, the Canadian federal system was nonetheless viewed as an adequate means of ensuring that Mohawk rights and aspirations would be realized. By the late 1950s, the band council had come to reflect a growing commitment within the community to realize true ideological independence from Canada and actually to implement an autonomous political structure to govern the community.

As detailed in Chapter Four's discussion of the revitalization of traditional Mohawk culture and its transformation of the community's political ideology, the Six Nations Iroquois Confederacy took on special prominence as a model of governance and as a source of governmental legitimacy in Kahnawake. The alternatives contained in the Iroquois Confederacy tradition contrasted radically with the old mentality, which posited a governing authority for Natives delegated from Canada. In the 1940s band council chiefs deferred responsibility for defining the terms of the Canada-Kahnawake relationship to Canadian Indian Affairs authorities. Seeking revisions to the Indian Act, they pleaded, 'We look to you to safeguard our interests and not to treat us as you have in the past' (Canada 1951: 13). Since the time of that council position, a clear break with the past has occurred. This chapter will trace the transformation.

DELEGITIMIZING THE INDIAN ACT SYSTEM

The Mohawk Council of Kahnawake has evolved away from an acceptance of the delegated governing authority principle embedded in the Indian Act, toward reflecting the principle of a locally derived legitimacy. Whereas the genesis of an overt and coordinated challenge to the legitimacy of the Indian Act band council began only in the 1960s, dissatisfaction with the character of the Canada-Kahnawake relationship, particularly in relation to the band council, has been an almost constant feature of politics in the community since the imposition of the Indian Act system in the 1890s.

As early as the late 1940s dissident elements within the community, indeed within the council itself, had publicly expressed frustration with the parameters of the relationship. In a joint statement prepared and delivered by the Kahnawake (Caughnawaga) and Akwesasne (St Regis) band council chiefs on 9 September 1950, the chiefs were clearly uncomfortable with the impositions evident in their community and the restrictions on their right to self-government:

we Indians do not wish to become Citizens of your Government or any
other Government; we are loyal to our Indian form of Government, and
we want to be free to enjoy our liberty as guaranteed to us by our Great
Constitution of the Six Nations . . . Let us live in peace, recognize our
Rights and form of Government as provided in the Treaties. Take your
Officials and Police Force off our Reserves, and let us take over the
Government and Policing, in which event you will be in a position to
say you have given us Equality. (Canada 1951: 11)

While not at that point constituting an active effort to delegitimize
the band council in Kahnawake, the 1950 attack on the imposition of
Canadian authority in the community represents a nascent movement
on the part of Mohawks to replace the Indian Act council with a representative institution modelled on the Iroquois tradition. The core issues
were community control over the administration of government and
policing. These two issues persist as the axes around which the anti-
Indian Act movement is oriented. The practical concern of local control
is combined with an ideological position which views the Canada-
Kahnawake relationship as flowing from treaties[1] between the Mohawk
nation and the Crown, rather than as a 'municipal' relationship.

The revisions enshrined in law in the 1951 version of the Act did not
reflect the aspirations of self-government expressed by the Mohawk
chiefs' presentation to the Parliamentary commission. In fact, the 1951
Act further entrenched the principles of federal control and delegated
authority through an imposed European style governing structure. This
caused a rupture between those Mohawks who had previously served as
band council chiefs and were oriented toward re-establishing a traditional order in the community, and a new group who came to dominate
the band council in the years after the 1951 revisions, seeking to promote economic development and other 'progressive' measures to further integrate Kahnawake within the federal structure and Canadian
society in general.

The dichotomy between traditionalism and an Indian Act mentality
was transformed into the major political cleavage in Kahnawake. The
evolution of the band council and the community itself since this period is the story of the infusion of a traditionalist orientation into the
imposed structures and philosophy of government among all segments
of the community. In essence, since the early 1960s the band council has
displayed a great dynamism in its adaptation of traditional Mohawk values and principles and the rejection of the Indian Act mentality by all
leaders—band council as well as Longhouse.

Members of the community initiated the shift in ideology by challenging the band council's reliance upon the Indian Act as the sole
framework for governance within Kahnawake. There were at the time

monthly public meetings at which various issues were put before the public for consideration in the development of a working consensus or to gain approval of council decisions taken previously. It was at these public debates that the band council faced increasing pressure to re-orient its approach to governing the community. The band council initially rejected any suggestion that it abandon the Indian Act framework. In response to a community member's probing question, the Chief re-affirmed his commitment to the Indian Act and dismissed the question with one of his own (MCK-BCM 02/04/65), 'What would we use if there was no Indian Act?' Over the years, he would continue to assert the old mentality in defending the idea that Kahnawake should remain under federal jurisdictional authority (MCK-BCM 04/03/71).

Facing this initial intransigence on the part of the Chief and council, community members began to take more direct action to undermine the authority of the Indian Act and to circumvent the council through the creation of an alternate institutional regime in Kahnawake. Traditionalists set out to develop a parallel system of government for their adherents, and began to assert that their institutions, predicated on traditional values and principles, were the legitimate structures of government within Kahnawake. The council reacted to this movement by clearly stating that it was the 'official' representative institution within the community.[2] In a letter to the Indian Affairs Minister, the Chief acknowledged 'the frequency of self-appointed so-called Indian representatives' challenging the band council's right to represent the community on a number of levels. He advised that 'only the elected Council should be given consideration on matters relating to the town or the people of Caughnawaga' (MCK-BCR 23/65–66).

This discord eventually resulted in a sense of extreme alienation between those Mohawks seeking an immediate rejection of the Indian Act system and the establishment of a traditional form of government, and those who were clinging to the Indian Act system as a source of stability within the community. During August and September of 1973, alienation was transformed into violent confrontation between the two factions. The violence was precipitated by a movement by the traditionalists to evict a number of non-Indians from the reserve. The ensuing confrontation pitted the Longhouse, its Warrior Society, and supporting elements from the American Indian Movement (AIM) against the band council, its police force and supporting forces from the RCMP and the SQ.

The Longhouse's demand that those non-Indians who were generally acknowledged to be undesirable elements in the community be evicted from their homes and forced to leave the reserve was a clear-cut challenge to the authority of the band council. At issue was not the merit of the non-Indian people—there was little sympathy for the non-Indians in the community—but which institution had the authority to make rules concerning membership and residency within Kahnawake. To this challenge, the council reacted by further entrenching itself in the authorities delegated by the federal government. The band council did not attempt to mediate or cooperate with the Longhouse on what was clearly a common concern of community members. Instead the Chief implemented a three-pronged strategy to confront the Longhouse's militancy: 1) the council enhanced the enforcement capability of the police; 2) it filed criminal charges against the Longhouse activists and encouraged the Department of Indian Affairs to intercede in support; and 3) it coordinated a tri-partite band council-federal-provincial mobilization to suppress the movement (MCK-BCM 08/13/73).

The split between traditionalists and the band council become more pronounced as the confrontation festered. The band council was concerned with maintaining law and order, preserving its powers under the Indian Act, and maintaining the support of the Department of Indian Affairs. The Longhouse, on the other hand, was revolutionary in that it took direct action to bring about a governing system based on the Great Law. It sought to achieve a greater autonomy and to re-establish a Canada-Kahnawake relationship based on the historic treaties of the Iroquois. The Longhouse spokesman, Louis Hall, boldly stated that traditionalists would respect no band council by-law because the federal Minister formally approved all council legislation. Hall also claimed title to the reserve lands in the name of the Six Nations Confederacy (MCK-BCM 09/07/73).

The confrontation over evictions represented a significant moral victory for the traditionalist ideology in that the band council had to concede that the problem with non-Indians resident on the reserve stemmed from the Indian Act regime and the Department of Indian Affairs' control over membership. The council agreed to test its Indian Act powers by taking its own measures to evict the non-Indian undesirables. Having demonstrated that the Indian Act was contestable, the Longhouse militants pressed the point by taking further actions, some of a violent nature, to effect immediate evictions before the council had time to engage the approval process for its evictions by-law. The council was prepared to accept defeat over the issue of whether the Indian Act provided an adequate framework for governance in Kahnawake, but it was certainly not ready to abdicate its control over the use of force within the community to achieve common goals. The council's response to the Longhouse's violent actions against the non-Indian people was to have serious long-term consequences for the community.

When the Longhouse's Warrior Society moved in dramatic fashion to remove the non-Indians from their homes on the reserve and began a series of attacks on the council building and the Chief himself, open hostilities between Longhouse supporters and band council supporters erupted in the community. The band council considered its options in light of the fact that its own police force, lacking support from outside police agencies, had resigned and the federal RCMP had deferred action as a matter of policy. The government did not enforce the Criminal Code infractions with which the council was charging the Longhouse militants. The Chief, after deliberating with his council and consulting with federal and provincial authorities, decided to accede to the SQ's condition that they would only intervene in support of the council after a formal request for action from the Chief (MCK-BCM 09/07/73). The intervention of the provincial police did little to calm the situation and in fact exacerbated the conflict, resulting in a number of violent confrontations between the factions.

The band council found itself allied with provincial authorities against segments of its own population, who were themselves allied with militants from the American Indian Movement (AIM).[3] As the confrontation dragged on, the band council came under increasing pressure to remove the provincial police forces on the reserve. In response to questions in late October concerning the continuing presence of the provincial police in Kahnawake, beyond the chaotic early days of the conflict, the Chief gave four pre-conditions which if met would prompt him to rescind the request for the aid of provincial forces: 1) all AIM personnel must be removed from the reserve; 2) Warrior Society members must surrender their weapons; 3) the Longhouse must dismantle the military-style bunkers around its headquarters; and 4) twelve Mohawks charged with criminal offences must surrender to the arrest warrants issued by provincial police (MCK-BCM 10/22/73).

The pre-conditions set by the Chief during this period demonstrate the extent to which the band council sought solutions to political problems within the community exclusively within the framework of Canadian law and the Indian Act. In the end, the pre-conditions were not met; the Longhouse retained its political momentum and continued to challenge the authority and legitimacy of the band council system. The Chief was later forced to resign, due in part to a lingering distrust and to the perception that he had led the council into collusion with provincial authorities.

The major impact of the band council-Longhouse confrontation was a victory in principle for the traditionalists, in spite of the bad taste left in Mohawk mouths by the Warrior Society's violent tactics. From this point on, the Department of Indian Affairs' jurisdictional control over the reserve was discredited, and the idea of the band council cooperating with provincial authorities became unacceptable.

The ideological triumph of the traditionalists was clearly demonstrated in the evolution of Kahnawake's police force since the confrontation. Five years after the initial confrontation, the next band council Chief found even a moderate level of integration into the Amerindian Police Force, a provincially-sponsored pan-Indian policing service linking all Indian reserves in Quebec, unworkable as a long-term solution to Kahnawake's policing needs. Kahnawake pulled its police out of the Amerindian force. The new Chief in his explanation to the public reinforced what had by that time become a dominant idea among members of the public and the band council: 'a political step was taken by pulling the Iroquois out of the Amerindian Police; the Mohawk Nation will establish and run our own police force' (MCK-BCM 08/08/78). By the end of 1978, the band council had completely rejected federal and provincial integration with respect to policing and asserted local control over law enforcement in Kahnawake (MCK-BCM 11/21/78).

The 1973 confrontation over evictions and the subsequent evolution of policing in Kahnawake is indicative of a larger pattern of politics regarding issues of jurisdiction and control. Consistently, the band council faced challenges from members of the community in regard to the level to which Canadian authorities controlled Kahnawake's institutions and structures of government. The principles undergirding the traditionalist ideology, in this case a rejection of the legitimacy of the Indian Act, became the guiding principles for the reform of the institutional structure within the community. Rather than dismantle the band council system, however, the leadership of the council sought to accommodate change and reform the institution to reflect a new thinking. The degree of accommodation and reform is even more apparent upon review of the development of revitalized linkages between Kahnawake and other Iroquois communities, under the reconstructed framework of a political union between historic nations of the Confederacy.

REVITALIZING CONFEDERACY LINKAGES

The central principle of the Iroquois political tradition is the linkage of five nations into a confederation. The history of Kahnawake reflects the erosion of that principle since the colonial era and the evolution of the various Iroquois reserves into what in the modern era were basically politically insular and independent communities. Since the 1970s, Mohawks and other Iroquois have capitalized on persistent cultural and kinship ties and moved toward reconstructing the political linkages on a number of levels.

There is no better indicator of the infusion of traditional ideology into the band council than the consistent and intense efforts made by the council to revitalize real institutional ties to other Mohawk communities, with the long-term objective of rebuilding the political power of the Iroquois Confederacy as an eventual alternative to the Canadian political framework imposed upon the community.

In the mid-1970s the band council initiated a series of pragmatic linkages with other Mohawk communities. For example, the Kahnawake (Caughnawaga), Akwesasne (St Regis) and Kanesatake (Oka) Mohawks submitted a combined land claim to most of the southern part of Quebec in 1974, building on the historic linkages and renewed sense of cooperation between the communities (MCK-BCR 44/74–75). During the 1980s, this spirit was enhanced and transformed into an explicit policy of re-creating institutional linkages according to the Six Nations model—a conscious rejection of the principle enshrined in the Indian Act and Canadian government policy which sought to isolate Indian bands at every level. A prominent band council chief stated in 1981 that the priority issues for the Kahnawake council were unifying the Mohawk nation and resolving Kahnawake's outstanding land claims (MCK-BCM 04/15/81).

Shortly after this internal commitment, chiefs of the band council—now the Mohawk Council of Kahnawake—began to participate in the meetings, deliberations, and councils of the Iroquois Confederacy's Grand Council at Onondaga Nation Territory. Participation in the public and informal affairs of the Confederacy was seen as the strongest statement of the MCK's intention to reconstitute a place for Kahnawake within the Confederacy's political structure.

The MCK's pragmatic evaluation of the value of reconstituting the Confederacy linkage is clear in the justification given for the expense involved in sending representatives to Onondaga. In response to one doubting MCK chief's questioning what was at stake for Kahnawake, another responded, 'nothing less than our political sovereignty, recognition of our nationhood, and the re-establishment of our aboriginal rights' (MCK-BCM 11/24/81).

In seeking to re-establish a place for itself and the community of Kahnawake within the structure of the Confederacy, the council was in fact acceding to the legitimacy of the traditional political body. The delegitimation of the Indian Act had extended in the minds of the band council Chiefs to their own institution. Thus by the 1980s the MCK had accepted a role as a bridging institution oriented toward facilitating the transition from an unacceptable regime to an authentic form of Mohawk government in Kahnawake.

'Going traditional', as it was known in Kahnawake, became the official policy of the MCK when the council passed a formal resolution in 1982 to the effect that 'This Chief and Council take immediate steps to make a transition from the Indian Act elective system to the aboriginal form of government which is the Six Nations Iroquois Confederacy.' The leader of the MCK government also made a personal commitment to the traditional process and promised to resign immediately if the process was halted (MCK-BCM 04/05/82).

This acceptance did not preclude the maintenance of certain elements of the band council's administrative and bureaucratic apparatus. The predominant Mohawk view on reforming governance in Kahnawake was based on a functional or pragmatic evaluation of the utility of the band council administrative structure versus the political value of increased links to the traditional Confederacy structure. The major problem with the Indian Act was, in the MCK's own words, that it politically 'ties our hands' from a nationalist perspective.

Tacitly they acknowledged that certain structures within the community that had been created under the authority of the Indian Act provided necessary and valued services (MCK-BCM 01/13/81). Beyond its utility for the mundane aspects of community governance, the Indian Act was viewed as a limiting device to prevent the Mohawks from achieving their expressly nationalist long-term objectives. Thus the MCK Chiefs were drawn to a role within the Confederacy which would give Kahnawake much more power and flexibility in its assertion of increased self-government powers.

It was decided that the MCK would press for reforms which would see the re-creation of a traditional governing structure in terms of political representation of the community and maintenance of the council's bureaucratic structure to administer the community's affairs on the local level. This is an important point: even as the MCK recognized the power inherent in resuming a place within the Confederacy, as a practical matter of governing authority, it was not prepared to abdicate responsibility for local matters. The view toward the Confederacy linkage was that all Iroquois communities shared the common goal of re-establishing a powerful indigenous alternative to the imposed Euro-American federal structures. Developing cooperation and linkages would facilitate the achievement of this common goal as well as more localized goals held by individual communities. However, there was no movement in Kahnawake to submit to any degree of local control by the Confederacy Grand Council.

The degree to which Kahnawake leaders wished to retain their autonomy even within a revitalized Confederacy was evident in their position on the relationship which existed between the Confederacy and the MCK during the Canadian Constitution negotiations in the early 1980s. The MCK held that 'Council takes the position that it is currently working WITH the Confederacy towards common goals, but not UNDER their direct authority.' Further, stating that the MCK was seeking to 'promote equal unity' with their Iroquois partners, but that it had been sure to 'reserve the right to keep its own counsel' (MCK-BCM 02/27/84).

Prerequisite to the acceptance of the traditionalist concept of proper linkages with other political communities—an exclusive integration into the Confederacy—was the disentanglement of Kahnawake from other non-Confederacy alliances and associations. The MCK movement to restrict Chiefs from participating in the affairs of national political organizations like the Assembly of First Nations (AFN)[4] is indicative of this re-commitment to the idea of Mohawk people as part of the Iroquois political world, as opposed to other newer forms of political community to which some community members had become attracted.

The Grand Chief—formerly the Chief of the council—was adamant that MCK Chiefs should not participate in non-Iroquois forms of political organization. Arguing for the maintenance of community autonomy with respect to the Assembly of First Nations, he said: 'The self-established principle of maintaining our complete autonomy quite apart from the regional or national bodies, while promoting our own credibility in dealing with matters concerning Kahnawake's primary interest is working.' He went on to stress the more practical concern, that 'These groups do not deal with sufficiently strong commitment, and are promoting a style of Indian Self-Government that is opposed to our concept of self-government' (MCK-BCM 04/09/84).[5]

Clearly, the focus on limiting those alliances and associations had the potential to detract from the effort to re-integrate with the Confederacy. In the summer of 1984, the Grand Chief and the MCK took the decision to halt all participation in the AFN and redouble their efforts toward the 'labours of the Iroquois Confederacy', with only three of the eleven council Chiefs dissenting (MCK-BCM 06/04/84). Later, a similar commitment was made with respect to efforts to re-unite the Mohawk nation, with the immediate objective of aligning policies on key issues (MCK-BCM 11/25/85). This was followed by a formal public statement disengaging the MCK from any involvement or alliance with the AFN:

> Kahnawake is not a member of the AFN group, however [sic], does participate in an observation/advisory capacity, while pursuing its goals from the Traditional Iroquois Confederacy perspective. The issue of self-government and aboriginal rights is derived from this source, rather than from the designated parameters of the Federal and Provincial governments. (MCK-BCM 12/08/86)

The mid-1980s represented a high point in terms of developing near-consensus on the issue of Kahnawake's relationship with the Iroquois Confederacy. All of the groups within the community expressed a similar commitment to re-organizing Kahnawake's institutional structure to reflect the Mohawks' rightful place within the Confederacy, and to maintaining the level of services provided by the administrative and infrastructural elements of the band council system. Even Kahnawake's largest Longhouse group, which by this time had established a Mohawk Nation Office (MNO) as a parallel institution to the MCK, was conciliatory. In response to statements that the

Longhouse should recognize the MCK's sincere efforts to reform toward traditionalism, the Longhouse responded that it 'does not intend to be solely derogatory in its views, but to simply highlight the historical purity of its source of government—The Confederacy' (MCK-BCM 08/29/87). The Grand Chief's leading opponent on his own council did not oppose the move outright and wished only for clarification and guidance from the Confederacy Chiefs themselves before committing herself to the full movement toward re-integration. She drafted a letter to the Confederacy Chiefs inviting them to meet in Kahnawake:

> in the sentiment of moving towards traditional government, requests the Grand Council's favourable decision to meet to dispel any misconceptions as to the stance and opinion of the Grand Council . . . as well as offering direction for the community to consider in adopting the traditional ways of government. (MCK-BCM 12/09/87)

During this period the MCK itself seemed to be reaching out to all segments of the community in an effort to put Kahnawake's house in order in preparation for eventual re-integration. In an introspective general review of the council and the community in 1987, MCK Chiefs addressed many of the key issues facing the community in its move to re-orient its internal affairs and external relations to a traditional Iroquois model. In doing so, the Grand Chief expressed in a vivid fashion the degree to which traditionalism had become embedded within the logic and ideology of the band council in Kahnawake:

> Our people have shown resilience, adaptability and instances of unity; the political mindedness of our people has kept our Nationhood strong with resurgences of culture and language . . . The concept of Indian Act phase-out, of nationalism, has yet to be fully presented, understood and accepted by the people. The provisions of traditional government are still above and beyond this . . . Council needs to establish a liaison with the Longhouse; it must be made clear with what matters the Council is dealing, and that the Longhouse may have to align their thinking accordingly. (MCK-BCM 04/06/87)

The MCK was at this point clearly announcing its role as the leading institution within the community and assuming the primary responsibility for advancing the re-establishment of system of government based upon Iroquois traditions.

The Council's adoption of another principle from Iroquois traditional political thought by the council was indicative of the degree to which traditionalism had permeated the MCK. Once the Indian Act had been delegitimized and the move to re-integrate Kahnawake into the Confederacy structure was underway, the council set out an explicit policy of abiding by the Two-Row Wampum concept—the traditional ideal of mutual respect and non-interference in each other's internal affairs—in relationships with the federal and provincial authorities. Late in the 1980s, the Grand Chief came out strongly against any Kahnawake involvement in national committees or treaty negotiations oriented to integrating native communities into the Canadian federal structure. It was the council's view that participation in such processes was precluded by the community's commitment to return to a traditional Iroquois structure and, according to the Grand Chief, 'our use of the Two-Row concept argument' (MCK-BCM 03/21/88).

The concept of a 'nation-to-nation' relationship, predicated on sovereignty, with Canada came into common usage as the traditional Iroquois principle of a separate relationship between native and newcomer societies was integrated into the political culture of the band council. By the summer of 1988, Kahnawake Chiefs would characterize their goals in meeting with the federal Minister for Indian Affairs in terms of 'looking for a political commitment from Canada to leave the atmosphere of the Indian Act, and to move to a Nation-to-Nation association which would entail self-determination' (MCK-BCM 07/09/88).

From the 1960s to the 1980s, the band council had integrated key elements of the Iroquois political tradition into its own operating principles and philosophy. The move to traditional government is best summarized as a policy of adopting the principles of traditional Iroquois government while utilizing knowledge of tradition in the implementation of institutions and specific mechanisms appropriate to contemporary political reality (MCK-BCM 10/15/91). By rejecting the legal and philosophical basis of the Indian Act's legitimacy within the community, the council had set the stage for a system of government based instead upon indigenous values and principles.

By seeking to re-establish a place for Kahnawake within the structure of the Iroquois Confederacy, the chiefs had laid the ground work for the re-creation of a political community based upon traditional associations. Implementing the philosophy of the Two-Row Wampum as the guiding principle of relationships with other governments ensured that none of the internal progress toward traditional government would be jeopardized by further impositions upon the community flowing from compromises to Kahnawake's sovereignty.

It seemed that at the end of the 1980s the stage was set for Kahnawake to make a giant leap forward toward its goals of re-establishing a traditional order. But the progress which had been so steady since the 1960s was undermined by developments related to the rise of Mohawk involvement in a contraband cigarette trade which imposed new stresses upon the community and whose monetary benefits distracted Mohawk people from their commitment to the traditionalist program.

Previously traditionalism had served as the political conscience of the community, and the energy behind significant reforms of the band council system was evident, but in the late 1980s the traditionalist movement was co-opted by those who used Iroquois culture and collective rights as a smokescreen for activities which contravened Canadian law and Mohawk sensibilities (Alfred 1991). Those who justified their involvement in the cigarette trade using the rhetoric and cloak of the Great Law and treaty rights cheapened the values and principles of the Iroquois tradition in the minds of those in the community who had been merely sceptical of the traditionalist program (Hornung 1991; Johansen 1993). The reform movement ground to a halt as traditionalists became obsessed with creating wealth out of the cigarette trade enterprises and funnelled a large portion of the profits into replicating or challenging the band council institutions within the community.

Constant and destructive efforts by the traditionalists to undermine the authority of the MCK as a governing institution forced the band council into a defensive posture. Mohawk involvement in the cigarette trade in fact derailed the cooperative process of internal reform which had been under way in earnest for at least a decade before 1988. With the persistent federal and provincial police intervention and with the internal factionalism resulting from the cigarette trade, traditionalist ideals were abandoned as more pressing demands for repelling external invasion and maintaining control internally daily concerned the MCK.

In the wake of numerous violent confrontations among Mohawk factions, an armed incursion by the RCMP in 1988, and a minor war with federal and provincial forces in 1990, council Chiefs reflected a community attitude in expressing frustration with the Longhouse's preoccupation with building a war chest and its confrontational strategy within the community, and with the general process of 'going traditional':

> The feeling is that it has been stalled in the 1979 mandate by adopting the stance of waiting for the community longhouse resources to come to the forefront to lead the transition process. This has proved unworkable due to the atmosphere of power-struggle . . . prevailing in recent years—and this has degenerated into factionalism . . . The Council will have to carry the ball. (MCK-BCM 10/15/91)

CURRENT INSTITUTIONS OF MOHAWK GOVERNMENT

'Carrying the ball', the MCK has served as the lead institution in developing a system of government which reflects the traditional Iroquois principles of public accountability and direct participation. The people of Kahnawake have designed and implemented a set of structures which are accountable through direct community control. Government in Kahnawake is based on this principle to such an extent that the MCK policy-making process is driven at all stages not by the initiative or pro-active energy of the leadership, but almost exclusively by input from members of the public, upon whose initiative the leaders react and translate the 'will of the people' into public policy.

In his analysis of the process of governance in Kahnawake, Ponting utilized a community development framework to explain the system in place in Kahnawake relative to those in other Indian communities in North America (Ponting 1986). He identified a number of characteristics of the band council system in Kahnawake which community development literature has also identified as key to the creation of stable and dynamic governing systems (Ponting 1986: 176-7). These characteristics may be summarized by grouping them into the four features of government in Kahnawake:

- Responsive Leadership – The MCK maintains close contact with the community through regular public meetings and open forums on special topics. The policy process is driven by input from the public, and all major policy issues are ratified by the community at a public meeting or by referendum.
- Delegation of Responsibility – The MCK has fostered a collective sense of responsibility for governance in the community by insti-tuting a system of delegated authorities for key jurisdictional areas. By creating committees made up of chiefs, specialists, and commu-nity representatives, the MCK has ensured that responsibility for decision-making on important matters such as education policy, environmental issues, and economic development is distributed widely among members of the Mohawk public.
- Institutional Completeness – Kahnawake has developed an exten-sive range of institutions leading to a self-government capability which far outstrips the legal limits of the Indian Act. These have allowed the community to make a strong claim for a revision of the framework of its relationship with the federal government.
- Aggressive Expansion of Jurisdictional Domain – The MCK has con-sistently sought to expel federal and provincial authorities from those jurisdictional areas in which the community has developed a capability for self-government.

Government in Kahnawake thus reflects, on one hand, an effort to max-imize the powers afforded Indian bands under Canadian law (Hawley 1986), and on another, the movement to replace the Indian Act relation-ship with a nation-to-nation framework which respects the inherent right of Kahnawake Mohawks to a level of self-government limited only by their level of institutional capability.

The Mohawk Council of Kahnawake governs the community under a system of political leadership whose basic structural elements are derived directly from the provisions of the Indian Act.[6] The Act allows the selection, through normal election procedures, of a 12-member band council comprised of a Chief and between one and eleven councillors based on a ratio of one member for each 100 band members. The MCK conforms to this aspect of the Indian Act, holding biennial general elections for a Grand Chief and eleven Council Chiefs who collectively serve as the political representatives of the Mohawks of Kahnawake. Operational authority for the various institutions making up the council system is vested in the MCK's Executive Committee, consisting of MCK chiefs, administrative heads of various institutions, and senior managerial staff from the MCK.

The MCK has established 83 separate programs which it administers under the umbrella of the council system. The MCK's Executive Committee maintains direct control and managerial responsibility over a number of programs grouped under various departments, including Infrastructure, Social Assistance, Membership Administration, Waste Management, Housing, Fire Brigade, and an Ambulance Service.

In key areas, the MCK has delegated complete operational responsibility to committees made up of elected community members and appointed specialized personnel. The three most important of these are in the areas of justice, with a committee overseeing the operation of the community court and law enforcement agencies; education, with a committee overseeing the administration of Kahnawake's primary and secondary schools as well as the management of post-secondary support programs; and social services, with a committee overseeing the provision of social services, counselling and support programs, including alcohol and drug abuse prevention and a substance-abuse treatment program.

The MCK derives most of its legal powers from section 81 of the Indian Act as a set of delegated authorities under Canadian law. Under the Act, band councils may pass By-Laws pertaining to various areas of responsibility, the By-Laws being for the most part subject to disallowance upon the discretion of the Minister of Indian Affairs. Under this system, the council is afforded a number of substantial powers in areas including the maintenance of law and order; merchant activity on the reserve; public games and amusements; land management; wildlife management; residence and entry on the reserve; and zoning. It may also pass By-Laws in a special area which is not subject to disallowance by the Minister: the licensing and regulation of intoxicants on the reserve.[7]

Indian bands are also afforded an authority under the Act 'where the Governor-in-Council declares that a band has reached an advanced stage of development' which allows them to tax and license commercial

activity on the reserve, but this aspect of the Act has not been implemented in Kahnawake. The Indian Act also contains provisions which
reserve certain powers for the Minister concerning land title and usage,
including powers related to the issuing of special-purpose land use per-
mits and sales, the division of reserve lands, and road construction.
These Ministerial powers are in effect in Kahnawake and have necessi-
tated the maintenance of an Indian Affairs agency on the reserve dedi-
cated to lands and estate matters.

In other areas, the MCK has made a definitive move away from the
delegated authority of the Indian Act, basing its authority instead upon
the will of the Mohawks of Kahnawake and their right to self-government, as a council policy document states: 'The Mohawk Council
derives its authority as representative of the people of Kahnawake from
the electoral process and from the community manifested in the continued support of its policies' (MCK 1990: 6). Most notably with respect
to policing, membership, reforms to the decision-making process, economic ventures, and the design of a gaming project, the council has
asserted and acted on an authority which far exceeds that afforded
bands under the Indian Act.

There are areas where the authority of the MCK overlaps with that of
the federal or provincial governments, or where jurisdiction is contest-
ed by one or another level of government. For example, section 88 of
the Indian Act stipulates that where there is no specific legislation, laws
of general application will apply to Indians. This section has resulted in
numerous conflicts over the extent of provincial jurisdiction and
authority over Indian people and over the structures and institutions on
reserves.

Another source of contention over authority is the Indian Act provision which allows for the expropriation of reserve lands by 'Consent
of Cabinet' for public purposes upon the request of provincial governments, municipalities, or corporations. This provision has led to serious conflicts in Kahnawake as the band council either attempted to
prevent the enforcement of Orders-in-Council for expropriation of
Mohawk territory, or attempted to reverse existing sales or leases to
corporations.

The extent to which provincial laws apply on reserves has been a
particularly contentious issue in which Kahnawake has strongly challenged the right of the province to enforce its laws on Indian people.
With regard to schools, for example, Kahnawake has fought on many
fronts and has achieved autonomy and control over all aspects of the
education system on the reserve. Quebec's attempt to enforce its
language laws on Mohawk children has been defeated. But in certain
areas, such as health care, Kahnawake and Quebec have a good working relationship and shared jurisdictional responsibility, highlighted by

cooperation in the provision of social services and the funding and operation of a hospital on the reserve.

The band council had revenues totalling $18.1 million in 1993.[8]
These revenues were derived from three sources: 1) a negotiated
'Alternative Funding Arrangement' with the Department of Indian
Affairs which accounted for $13.6 million, or 69% of the council's rev-
enues; 2) other sources including mortgages, interest, tickets and fines,
federal housing subsidies and federal transfers relating to employment
programs accounting for 25% of the council's revenues; and 3) miscella-
neous Department of Indian Affairs transfers for special projects or purposes, which accounted for 6% of the council's revenues.

REFORMING THE CANADA-KAHNAWAKE RELATIONSHIP

The current institutions of Mohawk government in Kahnawake, despite
the degree to which the MCK has tested the boundaries of the Indian Act
and outstripped the parameters of the band council system, are still
politically and legally within the general parameters of the existing legislative and political relationship unilaterally established by Canada in
the last century. In 1989, the MCK embarked upon an initiative to revise
the formal boundaries of that relationship. The council resolved to
divest Kahnawake of its link to the Canadian government through the
Indian Act and to take advantage of a DIAND process geared toward
devolving administrative authority and management powers to councils
(MCK-BCR #138/89-90). Kahnawake's goal was to use the DIAND-sponsored
process as a platform to entrench traditional values and promote the
reorientation of Kahnawake's internal government.

The objective—re-establishing a traditional form of government—
was reflected in the MCK's vision of a Canadian 'Inter-Governmental
Relations Act' which would abrogate the Indian Act and form a new set
of parameters for the Canada-Kahnawake relationship. Admittedly, this
contrasted with the Canadian government's goals for 'self-government',
meaning decentralization with the maintenance of existing legal and
political authorities. The MCK resolution summarizes the MCK philosophy
toward the Canada-Kahnawake relationship and illustrates clearly the
degree to which the council has integrated traditional principles.

Since the 1960s there has been a radical transformation of the MCK
as an institution. The MCK resolution on its future relationship with
Canada established an entirely different concept of the relationship
between Canada and Kahnawake than the one accepted by the council
during the 1950s and 1960s. This new paradigm is thoroughly infused
with the language and symbolism of Iroquois traditionalism. The four
main elements of the new paradigm are:

I. An assertion of the inherent sovereignty of the Mohawk nation and of a primary political allegiance to membership in the Iroquois Confederacy.

II. An assertion of ultimate and exclusive jurisdiction over Mohawk territories.

III. An assertion of the right and responsibility of Mohawks to govern their own affairs.

IV. An assertion that the Indian Act is suppressive and must be replaced.

Within the newly established paradigm, the MCK entered into negotiations with the federal government to revise the conventionally unequal relationship, to develop an accord which would recognize the need for cooperation in a number of jurisdictional areas, and to accede to the Mohawk demands for exclusive legislative jurisdiction in the following areas (MCK 1992):

1. Land and Resources
2. Education
3. Language and Culture
4. Property
5. Local Services
6. Public Health Services
7. Alcohol and Tobacco
8. Environment
9. Gaming
10. Agriculture and Wildlife
11. Transportation, Roads, and Public Works
12. Firearms and Explosives
13. Social Services and Child Welfare
14. Family Law, Citizenship, and Wills and Estates
15. Inter-tribal Trade and Commerce
16. Justice, Public Safety, and Civil Defence

Beyond demonstrating the MCK's confidence in Kahnawake's institutional completeness and its capability for self-government, the list of jurisdictional areas targeted by the council for exclusive Mohawk control point to the fact that the Mohawk conception of self-government or sovereignty is not statist. It is instead an indigenous conception based on traditional values and does not seek to replicate those institutions which are clearly beyond the capability of the Mohawks to fund, manage, or control.

The traditionalist paradigm is manifested again in a 1991 framework agreement signed by the council and the Canadian government to begin negotiations toward establishing a new relationship. In the framework agreement, the council insisted that self-government negotiations would proceed 'without prejudice to the position of the Mohawk nation regarding sovereignty and nationhood' (MCK 1991: 2). The foundation of sovereignty and nationhood, it was acknowledged by the MCK, lies not in the replication of state institutions on a local level for the Mohawk population, but in a re-institution of the traditional Mohawk form of government and the revitalization of the proper nation-to-nation relationship between the Mohawks and Canada. As the framework agreement reads, the MCK was:

> proposing to resume the implementation of the structures, institutions and modalities of the Great Law. The principles of Traditional Government provide for the qualities of both collective *and* individual rights and a matriarchal system of selection of male political representation. (MCK 1991: 1)

The new paradigm thus highlighted what the MCK believed to be the core elements of the Iroquois political tradition—a collectivist orientation and gender-based division of political roles—for the contemporary era.

Grouping the issues for which jurisdictional control was being sought and assembling core traditional values into a negotiating platform, the MCK laid out four major goals for the negotiation process: 1) the establishment of a Transitional Framework for Mohawk Governance; 2) recognition of the community's jurisdiction with respect to Justice and its authority to legislate, adjudicate and enforce laws; 3) the entrenchment of financial arrangements and a recognition of the federal responsibility to provide flexible financial support for self-government initiatives; and 4) recognition of Mohawk authority over Land Management (MCK 1991: 4–6).

Kahnawake has arrived at a point where its capabilities have outstripped the parameters established by the Indian Act. Its governing institution has become infused with a philosophy which delegitimates the structure of the internal colonialist relationship imposed upon the community by the Canadian government. The new traditionalist paradigm in Kahnawake seeks to implement a system of government based on traditional Mohawk values and which is somewhat reflective of the structures which governed Mohawk people in the pre-colonial era. But the Mohawk conception of sovereignty or self-government does not preclude them from recognizing that certain jurisdictions require a sharing of authority with other governments. Particularly in the area of financing, the Mohawk insistence on the maintenance of a formal relationship with Canada reflects a pragmatic evaluation of the political realities facing the community which tempers the ideologically driven demands for complete separation in other statist forms of ethno-nationalism.

In response to the former Chief's introspective question from the 1960s, 'What would we do without the Indian Act?' Kahnawake's leaders have refashioned the band council system, formerly an instrument of suppression, into an institutional structure which may serve as the basis for the re-establishment of Mohawk self-government. Kahnawake leads Canada in developing alternatives to the system of colonial domination of Indian nations. Through the development of an institutionally complete structure of government and the pressing of demands for increased jurisdictional control derived through negotiation and federal government recognition of community capability in key areas, the MCK has designed a realistic model for sharing jurisdictional responsibility for governing Indian people in North America in an appropriate and respectful fashion.

CHAPTER SEVEN

INTERACTIONS AND THEIR IMPACT

CONFLICT OVER TERRITORY AND MEMBERSHIP

The Great Law will come to shed light on the minds of the people . . . everyone shall become related to one another, so that it will become a single family consisting of every tribe; and they will be kind to one another, all of the people . . . Thereupon Tekahioke said, 'But what will happen should the other nations, who have continually picked on us, presently kill a few of us now that we are letting go of protecting ourselves in order to survive?'

Great Law of Peace, 15th century

Highlighted in previous chapters is the fact that Canadian government institutions have become delegitimized in Kahnawake and have been supplanted by an institutional framework based instead upon an indigenous model and value system. Understanding the history of the relationship between Mohawks and the Canadian government on the issues of land and membership is important to comprehending the drive behind Mohawk nationalism.

The internal processes revitalizing traditional principles account for only half the explanation of nationalistic assertions at Kahnawake; the impact of the pattern of interaction between Mohawks and the Canadian government has also been a determining factor in explaining the intensity—as opposed to the content—of the Mohawks' nationalistic assertions. These 'interactions' over land and membership are illustrative of the impact external factors have had in orienting the Mohawks toward a strong assertion of their goals, and away from a compromising stance with respect to the achievement of Mohawk sovereignty.

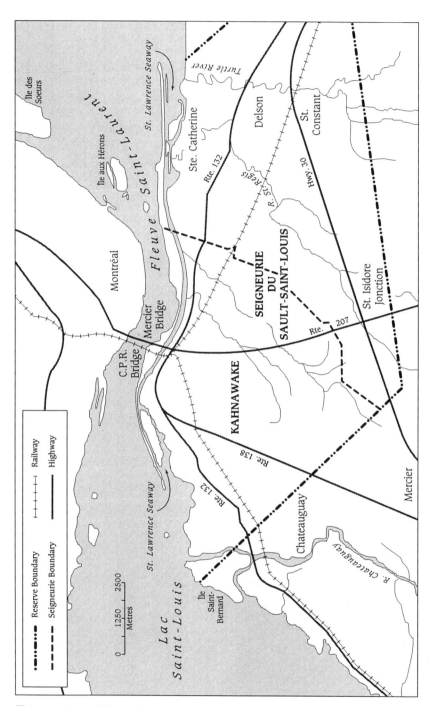

Kahnawake and its environs

INTERACTION I—THE MOHAWK LAND BASE[1]

The conduct of Canadian authorities in managing the Kahnawake land base under the Indian Act has been a major factor in undermining the Mohawks' faith in Canadian institutions. Historically, the Mohawks had placed some faith in the ability of the imperial government to safeguard their land rights through treaties and other agreements. However, as the British abandoned their empire in North America and the colonial government emerged as a new state, the Mohawks became increasingly disillusioned with the protections afforded their lands under the new regime. Confidence in the Canadian system was gradually eroded by the consistent neglect of Mohawk demands for redress concerning the alienation of Mohawks from their original land base. The erosion of Mohawk confidence in the Canadian system came to a head with the large scale expropriation of Mohawk lands in the interest of industrial development—the railways, hydro-electric power, the St Lawrence Seaway—during the early and mid-20th century.

The Seigneury of Sault St Louis

This community was established as a permanent settlement during the 17th century in an area inhabited and utilized by the Mohawk and other native nations for centuries. The reserve itself originated from two French Crown Grants, 29 May and 31 October 1680, to the Society of Jesus, for the purposes of spiritual conversion of the Iroquois and to keep them within the French sphere of influence. After the fall of New France to the British shortly thereafter, Indian title to the land was established in article 40 of the Articles of Capitulation of Montreal on 8 September 1760:

> The savages or Indian allies of his most Christian Majesty [the King of France], shall be maintained in the lands they inhabit, if they chuse to remain there; they shall not be molested on any pretense whatsoever, for having carried arms, and served with his most Christian Majesty. (Kennedy 1930: 29)

The Jesuits, however, believed that the lands were granted to them and that the Society of Jesus was the rightful owner. The Mohawks appealed to the military governor Thomas Gage for support against the Jesuits' claims and on 22 March 1762 Governor Gage ruled in favour of the Mohawks, stating:

> that the lands of 'Le Sault' are not a Seigniory of which the R.R. Jesuit Fathers can call themselves Seigniors; but that they are lands granted by His Most Christian Majesty solely to settle there Indians, who besides from their nature could not be subjected to the rights of *lods*

et ventes, High, Mean or Low Justice. His Most Christian Majesty making the grant on the only condition that the said land called 'Le Sault' shall belong to him *toute défrichée* when the said Iroquois would give it up, makes it known that his intention was not that the R.R. Jesuit Fathers would draw any advantage by the said grant. (Canada 1891: 301–2)

In the period between Gage's Judgment and the establishment of an administrative regime in Canada to manage Indian lands in 1845, it was discovered that the Jesuits had throughout their association with Kahnawake mismanaged and illegally sold off the larger portion of the Mohawks' land. This had continued into the 19th century with the appointment of British agents who continued the pattern of profiting from the sale of Mohawk lands to settlers. A report presented to the Legislative Assembly of the Province of Canada in 1845 acknowledged the situation:

> your Commissioners observe with regret, that within the last five years, two successive agents at Caughnawaga have been defaulters, and were dismissed without the recovery of their balances. Your Commissioners are of opinion that the Land affairs of the Indians in Lower Canada require examination and a stricter surveillance for the future. (Canada 1845)

The Province of Canada responded to the continuing encroachment upon Indian lands by passing legislation consolidating Canadian authority over reserved lands. The Indian Land Protection Act of 1850 was passed with the specific intention:

> to make better provision for preventing encroachment upon and injury to the lands appropriated to the use of several Tribes and Bodies of Indians in Lower Canada and for defense of their rights and privileges . . .

Unfortunately for the Mohawks and other Indians, while the Act did seek to prevent private interests from benefiting from the sale of Indian lands, it merely reserved the right for the Crown to encroach upon Indian lands. The 1850 Act did not result in the Mohawks receiving any redress for the wrongs previously committed against them, and it represented the first step in the process whereby Indian lands were gradually brought under the legislative authority of the Canadian government. Article I of the Act empowered the Governor of the Province of Canada:

> to appoint from time to time a Commissioner of Indian Lands for Lower Canada, in whom and in whose successors by the name aforesaid, all lands or property in Lower Canada, which are or shall be set apart or appropriated to or for the use of any Tribe or Body of Indians, shall be and are hereby vested, in trust for such Tribe or Body.

Thus in Canadian law since 1850, in accordance with the development of specific legislation and under an Indian Affairs regime that soon followed the Indian Land Protection Act, the lands of the Mohawks of Kahnawake have been held and managed by Canada in the name of the Crown for the Mohawks. There have been no significant events with regard to land title addressing Mohawk claims of ownership of lands illegally sold by the Jesuits or British agents, nor have there been any subsequent changes to the reserve's boundaries.[2]

The Mohawks of Kahnawake have over the years consistently sought to have the issue addressed by the colonial and Canadian authorities. British and Canadian political authorities and courts have supported the occupation of Mohawk lands and the failure of settlers to pay rents due the Mohawks. This fact has been a significant contributing factor in undermining the Mohawks' sense of trust and legitimacy in the Canadian political and legal regime. In at least eight separate actions, the Mohawks of Kahnawake have attempted to gain respect for their title of the former seigneury, or at least compensation for rents due from the occupants of lands within the Seigneury which were leased or sold without Mohawk consent. Examining the response of colonial and Canadian authorities to the Mohawk challenges in each case points to a major source of Mohawk frustrations over the course of their relationship with the settlers and their governments.

1. *Prescott v. Casot, 1798*
General Robert Prescott acted on behalf of the Mohawks in suing the Jesuits before the Court of King's Bench over the encroachment of the Jesuit seigneury, La Prairie, onto the boundary of the lands established as Indian lands within the Seigneury of Sault St Louis. The Mohawks were initially successful, but the decision was overturned on appeal during the next year.

2. *Petition to Colonial Secretary, 1807*
The Mohawks continued to pursue the boundary dispute after the unfavourable court decision, sending three men to London to put forward Kahnawake's claim before the British Colonial Secretary, Lord Castlereagh. The petition was referred to the Governor of Canada, who was instructed to inquire into the matter, and the Superintendent General of Indian Affairs and the Attorney-General. The Canadian colonial authorities all submitted reports denying the merit of the Mohawk claim on the basis of the ruling in *Prescott v. Casot,* and the fact that some Mohawks were present when the boundary line between the two seigneuries was re-drawn. The reports were accepted and endorsed by Castlereagh. This ruling is significant for our purposes in that it is a clear example of the failure of the Crown to treat the Mohawk land claim objectively. According to one legal opinion concerning the ruling:

It is worth noting that, by this time, the Seigneury of La Prairie de la Magdelaine had passed from the Jesuits, whose order had been dissolved in Quebec, to the British Crown. Recognition of the possible validity of the Mohawks' claim to the boundary strip would thus have entailed the diminution of the crown's estate in the Seigneury of La Prairie. This fact gives rise to at least an apparent conflict of interest in the Crown's treatment of the Mohawks' claim.

3. *Petition to Governor of Canada, 1820*
The Mohawks again asserted their claim to the lands within the disputed boundary to the Governor of Canada, Lord Dalhousie. Dalhousie rejected the claim outright, and in a Commission established in 1827 to register the former seigneury's tenants, he mistakenly embedded the belief that the Jesuits were the previous owners of the Seigneury of Sault St Louis.

4. *Petition to the Governor of Lower Canada, 1828–1830*
A missionary, Fr Joseph Marcoux, acted on behalf of the Mohawks in presenting a petition before the Governor of Lower Canada, Sir James Kempt, reasserting the Mohawk claim to the disputed boundary lands. Kempt was advised that both the Courts and Executive of the Province had found the Mohawks' claim to have been without merit. Marcoux pursued the matter further, expanding on his earlier petition by giving specific references to Jesuit practices which should have confirmed Mohawk ownership of the disputed lands. For example, he discussed the protocol concerning the construction of a mill on the eastern end of the Seigneury:

> the Old Mill on the Tortue River had been built by the Indians of Kahnawake to generate revenue pending their recovery of the Mill of the Sault at the mouth of the St Pierre river . . . according to the Mohawks' tradition, the Jesuits had sought and obtained the permission of their Chiefs prior to building the Mill of the Sault.

Marcoux argued that this protocol constituted formal recognition of the Indians' ownership of the lands by the Jesuits. But Kempt followed his predecessors in dismissing the Mohawk claim; referring only to the previous court and executive decisions he stated that 'Such being the circumstances, he could offer them no consolation.'

5. *Delegation to Colonial Secretary, 1830*
A delegation of Mohawks travelled to London to put forward the Kahnawake claim to the King. They were received instead by the Colonial Secretary, Sir George Murray, who rejected the claim on the basis that he was unable 'to attempt to disturb that which had already been decided by the Law'.

6. Testimony to the Commission of Inquiry into the Affairs of the Indians, 1843

Thè missionary Fr Marcoux again represented the Mohawks in 1843, presenting testimony in support of the Mohawk claim to the disputed boundary lands. The Commission's Report led to the creation of legislation in 1850 to consolidate Crown responsibility for managing reserve lands rather than to the redress of outstanding Mohawk claims.

7. Band Council Resolution Asserting Title, 1965

The band council passed a resolution on 11 September 1965 asserting a right to benefit from the lands contained within the former Seigneury.

8. Letters to Minister of Indian Affairs, 1988–89

The Mohawk Council of Kahnawake sought to have the Mohawk claim to the lands of the former Seigneury addressed by the responsible Canadian Minister. The historical grievances cited in Grand Chief Joseph Norton's letter were disregarded by the Minister, and the Mohawks were advised to submit a claim under the Canadian government's specific claims process, which consisted of a lengthy unilateral review of the claim's legal history and evaluation of its merit by DIAND, and for which there was a waiting list for entry into a resolution process of 28 Indian bands (MCK 1988).

The Mohawks rejected the specific claims approach in view of the fact that the provincial government was planning to construct a new highway through lands claimed by Kahnawake, and further expropriations were imminent. In another appeal to the Minister for a prompt resolution of the matter, the Canadians reiterated their decision to treat the Mohawk claim within confines of the specific claims process:

> I have reviewed the response and confirm my predecessor's position. The federal government's specific claim policy provides your band with an administrative process to resolve historical grievances. If an outstanding lawful obligation is demonstrated by the band through a claim submission, I will accept the claim for negotiation of a settlement. Until such time, any discussions on settlement negotiations are premature. (MCK 1989: 2)

The Minister also disregarded the Mohawk argument that the provincial construction project was a priority concern:

> You also indicated that the extension of Highway 30 will have a direct impact on the former seigniorial lands and that tripartite negotiations are required. The lands required by the Government of Quebec for such an extension will be acquired under authorities enacted by the provincial legislature. I do not see that Canada's participation in any negotiations on this project will be required. (MCK 1989: 2)

This pattern of interaction between the Mohawks of Kahnawake and Canadian authorities demonstrates how the Canadians have systematically disregarded a potentially valid land claim so as to preserve the structure of the land regime which has been implemented without the consent of the Indian landowners. On this basis alone, Mohawks have had sufficient grounds for turning away from those Canadian institutions—the courts and the executive—which have been the source of a demonstrated lack of respect for Mohawk rights. These outcomes combined with the negative experiences Mohawks have had in approaching Canadian authorities, and the lack of responsiveness on the part of the Canadians even to entertain Mohawk arguments and evidence, have resulted in the understandable rejection of Canada by Mohawks as a safe haven, in which their rights and lands will be protected.

Reserve Land Management under the Indian Act

Adding to the Mohawks' frustration concerning the erosion of their land base was the management of their reserve lands under the provisions of the Indian Act. The issue of the Seigneury lands illustrated how Mohawk title to portions of their claimed territory has been systematically ignored by Canada. Even lands which have been uncontested parts of the Kahnawake reserve have been alienated from Mohawk control by the federal government in support of corporate interests.

Through the operation of the Indian Act and the Indian Affairs regime which has been established in Canada, the Minister for Indian Affairs retains authority over land management on Indian reserves and has the power to sell or lease land for public purposes. Kahnawake's location directly across the river from Montreal—for three centuries Canada's largest city—has resulted in the community being targeted as a site for locating various works supporting the expansion of Canada's rail network and the electrification of the Montreal area.

The Canadian government has in land management shown a callous disregard for the Mohawks' right to control development within their lands. The Indian Act powers assigned to the Minister have been used to expropriate large amounts of territory from the reserve without Mohawk consent, and without either monetary or other forms of compensation to the community. The presence of railways, highways, and electric towers cross-cutting the reserve is a source of anger for Mohawk people in Kahnawake, and the gradually accumulating frustration due to the piecemeal erosion of the Mohawk land base has tainted the Canada-Kahnawake relationship for over a century.

Listed below to illustrate the manner of Canadian management of Mohawk lands are the various surrenders and their purposes, from the time of the imposition of the Indian Act in Kahnawake late in the 19th century up to the St Lawrence Seaway construction—which will be dealt with separately. It is worth comparing the surrenders initiated and consented to by Mohawks and those which were completed at the discretion and under the authority of the Minister for Indian Affairs:

Mohawk Surrenders (individual or band council)

Date	Purpose
9 Nov. 1887	Surrender of village lot by a Mohawk
17 Nov. 1912	Surrender of stone rights for rail wharf
15 March 1915	Surrender of stone rights
1921–1932	Leases for Kanawaki Golf Club
25 April 1930	Right of way for Bell Telephone
27 May 1932	Surrender for stone rights
16 Dec. 1932	Surrender for stone rights
25 Nov. 1949	Right of way for Bell Telephone

Federal Government Land Surrenders in Kahnawake

Date	Purpose
15 Oct. 1884	Lease to non-Indian
17 Feb. 1888	Sale to Atlantic and Northwest Railway
7 Dec. 1895	Sale to Southwestern Railway Company
12 June 1896	Sale to Southwestern Railway Company
23 April 1897	Right of way to New York Central Railway
17 Sept. 1897	Right of way to Canadian Pacific Railway
28 Feb. 1898	Authorization for CPR to lay water pipe
4 July 1898	Land to Atlantic and Northwest Railway
17 Sept. 1898	Right of way for road construction to CPR
13 Jan. 1899	Land to Atlantic and Northwest Railway
11 April 1909	Surrender of stone rights
7 June 1910	Authorization to extend CPR station
24 Jan. 1911	Right of way to CPR
8 June 1911	Right of way to Canadian Light and Power
12 May 1911	Island east of village sold
6 June 1912	Land sale to CPR
30 Sept. 1912	Land sale to CPR
14 Mar. 1913	Land sale to CPR
18 Mar. 1913	Land sale to CPR
5 June 1914	Land sale to CPR
3 May 1917	Island west of village awarded to Quebec
29 May 1930	Right of way to Canadian Light and Power Company
7 Dec. 1932	Expropriation for construction of bridge
4 May 1933	Right of way to Hydro-Quebec
9 Mar. 1936	Right of way for bridge approach road
21 Dec. 1940	Widening of highways

31 Mar. 1950	Right of way to Hydro-Quebec
21 May 1950	Right of way to Hydro-Quebec
21 Dec. 1954	Right of way to Bell Telephone
2 June 1955	Taking of Indian interest in Seigneury

With the exception of individuals surrendering property for the construction of schools and leasing lands to a private golf club, all of the Mohawk surrenders revolve around the generation of revenues for the band council out of the operation of stone quarries in remote areas of the reserve. The federal surrenders, on the other hand, involve mainly land sales and permanent rights of way to railway and electric companies in the core residential and agricultural areas of the reserve. The zealousness of the federal government in parcelling out the Mohawk land base is thus evident from the very beginning of Canadian administration of the reserve.

The St Lawrence Seaway

The most significant of government surrenders of Mohawk land in terms of both the sheer area involved and the long-term destructive impact on the Canada-Kahnawake relationship were the St Lawrence Seaway expropriations. The Seaway project should be viewed in the larger context of Canada's development of a national transportation infrastructure and within the framework of the Canada-United States relationship. However, the local impacts of the selection of Kahnawake lands as a key portion of the Seaway were tremendous. The design of the Seaway called for the channel to run directly through the oldest residential and historical section of the community; it entailed the expropriation of an entire portion of the reserve, separating the village from, and denial of Mohawk access to, the river where Mohawks had traditionally lived and worked for centuries.

An Order-in-Council authorized the federal government to surrender parts of the reserve to the St Lawrence Seaway Authority, and on 16 September 1955 and 9 February 1956, the expropriations were effected and plans to construct the Seaway were implemented. The band council resisted the expropriations from the start, and challenged the legitimacy and morality of the project to no avail. Individual Mohawks were directly affected by the expropriations if they lived within the sectors slated for construction of the channel or ancillary works, and many homes were destroyed or relocated over the course of the project.

Resistance by individuals was precluded by the enforcement of the expropriation orders by the RCMP. The band council became the sole focus of efforts to counter the expropriation orders and prevent the implementation of the Seaway. At this point in their history, the Mohawks of Kahnawake continued to seek redress within the legal parameters established by the colonial relationship—that is, by relying upon arguments affirming the validity of ancient treaties and the trust responsibility of the federal government to Indian bands under the Indian Act.

Immediately after the Order-in-Council, the band council began launching legal challenges and petitioning every level of government within the colonial power structure in protest of the expropriations. Band council records show a total of 35 resolutions passed during 1956 and 1957 pertaining to the Seaway. Each one is indicative of a different aspect of the Mohawks' frustration and anger and of the exhaustive appeal Mohawks devised to counter the federal actions.

The council sought to have Mohawk rights as owners of the Seigneury lands respected by arguing that the expropriations violated still valid covenants between the Mohawk people and the descendant government of the imperial authorities. The council conveyed:

> a protest in the strongest terms to the Government of Canada and the Department of Indian Affairs at the violation of its ancient right to the possession of its land at Caughnawaga . . . derived from sacred treaties and proclamations from the French and English Kings. (MCK-BCR #317/56–57)

Receiving no response from the federal government on its appeal to honour, the band council turned to the legality of the project given the specific powers afforded Indian governments under the Indian Act. Band councils are delegated the authority to control residence and access to the reserve and to pass by-laws dealing with trespass by non-Indians on reserve lands. To this effect, the council passed a resolution to 'order the Minister to take immediate proceedings to oust the following corporations, as we find them to be trespassers', listing a number of companies involved in the construction of the Seaway and who were benefiting from earlier surrenders, including the St Lawrence Seaway Authority, Mirron-Manibec, Warncock-Hersey, Hydro-Quebec, and the Canadian Pacific Railway (MCK-BCR #333/56–57).

With no action on the trespass issue from the Minister, the council sought to prevent further surrenders by the federal government by making explicit the community's withdrawal of its consent to erosions of its land base. Attacking the legal authority of the Minister under the Indian Act to manage and control the sale of Mohawk lands, the council:

> pledged themselves to adopt every means possible and within their power to preserve the Reservation of Caughnawaga in its entirety . . . no surrender of lands or any form of acquiesence to land surrenders will be forthcoming. (MCK-BCR #349/56–57)

Further to this end, the council challenged the validity of the Order-in-Council authorizing the expropriations, given that the Indian Act established a relationship of wardship predicated on a trust responsibility toward Indian bands by the federal government. The trust Mohawks had placed in federal authorities was the foundation of their tolerance of the colonial structure which had been imposed upon them, and they asked the Minister to condemn the Seaway project 'as a flagrant breach of trust on the part of the Government of Canada' (MCK-BCR #350/56-57).

These and many other resolutions appealing for the Minister to intervene on behalf of the Mohawks did not yield any positive result. The Mohawks then recast the tone of their appeals from honour, and abandoned the effort to convince the Minister to assume his trust responsibility, initiating instead a legal strategy to challenge the Seaway project and the federal government's management of reserve lands in court. The council retained the services of three McGill University professors as legal counsel in this endeavour. Frank Scott, Emile Colas, and Gerald Ledain were hired to 'oppose the shameful invasion and disgraceful slicing away of the Caughnawaga Reservation' (MCK-BCR #353/56-57). In advancing the legal strategy, the council stated further:

> Let it never be said that this present duly elected Council have ever consented to cede or surrender any portion of our Sovereign Territory which is now being invaded, and that, we will always have the Honour to protect our people and our posterity according to our treaties. (MCKBCR #353/57)

This January 1957 use of the word 'invaded' marks a departure for the council from a deferent voice to a more radical statement of the Mohawk position. The invasion theme is reflective of a traditionalist view of the relationship between Canada and Kahnawake based on a nation-to-nation basis. It is a theme which became increasingly relevant in Kahnawake in the years following the Seaway expropriations, and which saw its genesis in a series of statements expounding on the concept of an armed invasion and criminal trespass emanating from the council in 1957 (MCK-BCR #354, #355, #411/56–57).

In its efforts to halt the project the council soon exhausted all legal manoeuvres and was abandoned by the Minister. As Mohawks began to move from their homes, the sense of betrayal was palpable. What more could the council do to oppose the destruction of Kahnawake? The answers that would emerge a generation later were inconceivable to Mohawk leaders in the 1950s. They could do nothing except harbour a growing sense of resentment and a general perception that Canada had failed Kahnawake. As a final statement on the Seaway expropriations, perhaps intended as self-justification should subsequent generations see the Seaway as a sell-out, the council set out an eloquent and angry condemnation. It made clear that the lands at Kahnawake:

> have never been ceded, sold or surrendered and belong to the Band of Caughnawaga Indians as a whole, regardless of any rights, alleged or pretended of Conquest, Expropriation or otherwise. We cannot conceive of how any non-Indians can have the audacity to pretend claim to any lands occupied by Indians, when we Indians are the primordial inhabitants placed here by the Great Spirit and universally recognized as the only true Citizens of North America. Humanity blushes at the events of this period of Colonial History and Dictatorship, and Usurpation. (MCK-BCR #412/56-57)

The Legacy of Betrayal

As part of the survey on governance issues Kahnawake Mohawks were asked whether they thought that 'DIAND and the Canadian government will protect Mohawk lands and rights.' Seventy-seven per cent of the respondents disagreed; eleven per cent more stated that they were unsure. Interviews conducted in conjunction with the survey confirmed that the faith Kahnawake Mohawks once had in Canadian institutions had completely evaporated, in large part due to the experience of the Seaway. Mohawks were uniform in expressing the sense that their trust had been destroyed either by the experience of the expropriation itself or, for younger Mohawks, by the vivid image of the betrayal described by parents or grandparents.

There are many specific memories and perceptions concerning the Seaway experience, with the common thread that they are all negative. Some people have located the end of an idealized era of tranquillity and harmony in the internal squabbles over the proper response to the Seaway—stating simply that 'it ruined things'. An MCK Chief views the Seaway era as the beginning of the process which has led to the division of the community. He perceives some families to have 'sold out' in accepting individual compensation for expropriation, leading to a lasting sense of animosity between groups in the community which persists to this day. While this view is not representative of the general perception in Kahnawake, it is in line with other Mohawks' view that the experience with the Seaway poisoned Kahnawake's relationship with Canada.

Mohawks who were adults during the Seaway era shed light on the non-confrontational stance adopted by the community. The main regret of a 90-year-old woman was that the community's historic link to the riverside was lost. Even so, she did not conceive of her husband and father and other members of the community leadership at the time taking action beyond legal or political challenges to confront the government project. Her view represents a sense of resignation to the fact that Indians were wards of the federal government and subject to the whims of the interests represented by the government under the Indian Act. In response to a direct question: why the Mohawks did not fight the expropriations, all she could answer was that fighting was no use at the time because the RCMP would enforce Canadian laws and, with respect to Mohawk land, 'they would take it anyway'. In the end, despite the difference in approach between older generations and young Mohawks, she stated a common belief; as a result of her experience in the Seaway era, she had concluded wryly that 'you don't trust the government'.

There is a noticeable distinction between Mohawks who were directly affected by the Seaway expropriations and those who were not. The fact that a Mohawk's home was re-located or farm seized understandably seems to have engendered a more intense reaction to the Seaway in the first generation. Interestingly, the most intense reaction has come to characterize the general community perception in second-generation Mohawks, who did not experience the Seaway expropriations first-hand. For example, a man whose family was dispersed in the wake of the destruction of his home by the Seaway continues to harbour great personal animosity toward the Seaway expropriations and has transmitted that feeling to his son who expresses similar perceptions. Thus a man in his 30s who did not experience the Seaway directly can state that the Seaway was 'the last straw' in the humiliations suffered by Mohawks under the Indian Act, causing the community to develop a stance so that the land surrenders 'would never happen again'.

Even where the first generation was not personally affected by the Seaway—the family had not been forced to move or give up land—there is some recognition that the Seaway was a negative factor in other people's lives, and this perception is transferred to the second generation. Thus, the 25-year-old daughter of a Mohawk not affected directly could state that things in Kahnawake were 'nice before the Seaway' and that the expropriations were unacceptable because 'the government took our land'.

Having acknowledged that the immediate impact of the Seaway upon people and the physical aspect of their life in the community was negative, some more philosophical Mohawks point to the long-term implications of the Seaway as having been ironically positive. If the Seaway is viewed as the catalyst for the community's rejection of the Canadian government's legitimacy, then, as a Longhouse Chief and the MCK Grand Chief agree, the Seaway is responsible for activating the traditionalist movement in Kahnawake. The legacy of the Seaway betrayal in Kahnawake thus contributes to the high intensity of the Mohawk assertion of independence.

INTERACTION II—MEMBERSHIP

Control over Indian community membership has been a goal of the Canadian government since the imposition of the Indian Act in the late 19th century. Subsequent versions of legislation regulating Indian government and federal Indian Affairs policy have maintained provisions outlining criteria for Indian 'status'. Like other Indian communities, Kahnawake has been subjected to shifting federal regulations concerning Indian status and periodic re-definitions of the criteria of Indianness under the Indian Act. Coinciding with the effect that erosion of traditional cultural values had on community membership during the 19th and early 20th centuries, reliance upon imposed European definitions of status eroded the community's social fabric, fostering political factionalism and the gradual inculcation of European notions of citizenship among generations of Mohawks who were forced to accommodate the Indian Act system.

Previous chapters have shown how, beginning in the 1960s, Kahnawake Mohawks began to assert jurisdiction over many areas in their community, including membership. As part of the traditionalist movement and the eventual development of a nationalist ideology in Kahnawake, imposed Canadian definitions of Indian status and criteria for eligibility to reside within Mohawk territory were explicitly rejected by the Mohawks. Control over membership and the definition of Mohawk status was recognized as the core power necessary to re-create a community based upon traditional Mohawk values.

The most recent imposition of membership criteria upon the community occurred in 1985, with the 'Bill C-31' amendment to the Indian Act. The community has reacted to such impositions in the area of membership by asserting control. In this case, in response to the federal government's expansive re-definition of Indian status, the community implemented a highly selective and closed set of criteria for membership.

Kahnawake as a community had traditionally been extremely receptive to the integration of outsiders. Mission records from the early period of the community's history confirm that Mohawks at Kahnawake had continued the traditional Iroquois practice of adopting and assimilating captives, resulting in a diverse racial mixture within the Mohawk community.[3] Even into the modern era, Kahnawake Mohawks accepted many non-Native people through marriage and among those residents who came to enjoy community membership and later formal recognition of this membership through inclusion as status Indians when the Indian Act system was implemented in Kahnawake during the 20th century.[4]

By the time Kahnawake Mohawks took specific measures to re-gain control over membership in the early 1970s, the community had been

living with an imposed set of membership criteria for at least a generation. Residents had developed a disposition to reject their historically
inclusive approach to membership and had adopted instead a closed
approach to defining status. Community members perceived that their
previously inclusive philosophy had resulted in the erosion of the
Mohawk culture in Kahnawake. They had also assimilated the racialist
philosophy of membership entrenched in the Indian Act. Kahnawake's
new position blended elements of the Indian Act's reliance upon
European notions of 'race' (alien to traditional thinking) and the indigenous contemporary goal of maintaining cultural distinctiveness.
Essentially, it reflected the Mohawks' appropriation of the specific
means used in White society to accomplish indigenous ends.

At a public meeting in January 1972, a Mohawk woman initiated discussion of the proper community response to a recent Ontario court ruling challenging the Indian Act's denial of Indian status to women who
married non-Indian men. She urged the council to support formally the
federal Justice Department's appeal of the ruling and to request the
Minister of Indian Affairs to launch a separate appeal. The reason, she
stated, was that any further expansion of the categories of Indian status
would result in the 'destruction of the Indian race through saturation of
non-Indians' (MCK-BCR #75/72–73). Her views represented a growing perception among Mohawks that their culture and rights were threatened
by an influx of non-Native people into the community through intermarriage with Mohawks, and the belief that the most effective means to
combat this threat was in the imposition of a strict, racially based set of
membership criteria.

Census data for the period indicate that as of 1965 only 4.5% of band
members had in fact gained Indian status through marriage (Katzer
1972: 105). As well, overall non-Native residency on the reserve was
declining from a high of 796 persons, representing 28% of the total
reserve population in 1961, to fewer than 500 persons, representing less
than 10% of the total reserve population by 1972 (Katzer 1972: 111, 177).
Despite this, there was a heightened sensitivity to the issue of non-
Native residency on the reserve and the marriage of Mohawks to non-
Native people, arising from the fact that the rate of intermarriage had
risen substantially since the 1950s (Frideres 1993: 338). This sensitivity
was reflected in the creation of a local committee to examine the issues
surrounding membership and to propose a course of action for the band
council with respect to membership policies.

The committee was made up of Mohawk women and was charged
with reviewing internal policies and developing recommendations to be
presented to the recently established parliamentary committee reviewing the Indian Act. The committee returned to the council with a set of
recommendations in January 1978 which focused solely on the rules

concerning intermarriage (MCK-BCR 01/19/78). The recommendations came to form the basis of the council's policy on intermarriage, but the committee was noticeably silent on the more basic issue of criteria for membership, which the committee recommended be discussed further in a public forum.

Discussion of the issue continued in conjunction with consultation by the council with community members. Canadian and international courts had delegitimized Canada's Indian Act membership policy on the basis of an inherent gender discrimination against women, and the federal government had begun consultation with Native groups to reform the Indian Act rules on membership. Kahnawake Mohawks were conscious of the federal government's plans to make the Indian Act criteria more expansive and to allow Native women to marry non-Natives without any loss of status—a right Native men had always been afforded. In November 1981 the MCK established a formal policy challenging the federal government's authority and the further imposition of any rules concerning membership. The MCK consolidated the research it had conducted within the community and designed a policy which was explicit in its goal of undermining federal authority by creating membership rules which contradicted those established by DIAND. Specifically, the MCK committed to a policy with three key elements (MCK-BCM 11/27/81):

1. Eviction of non-Indians resident on the reserve,
2. A moratorium on mixed marriages, and
3. Establishment of a biological measurement.[5]

The community was in general agreement with the council's approach and the tenets of the new policy on membership, although there was some dissent from Longhouse people, who felt that reliance upon biological criteria was in opposition to the traditional Mohawk values on membership (MCK-BCR 12/22/81). The MCK developed two rules based on these principles, and the principle of evicting all non-Natives from the reserve was abandoned:

- *Moratorium on Mixed Marriages:* The MCK implemented a rule which stated that any Mohawk who married a non-Native after 22 May 1981 would lose the right to residency, land holding, voting, and office-holding in Kahnawake.
- *Kahnawake Mohawk Law:* On 11 December 1984 the MCK implemented a biological criterion for future registrations which required a 'blood quantum' of 50% or more Native blood.

Kahnawake's current membership regulations thus represent a community consensus established in 1984. Subsequent changes in the federal Indian Act rules on membership and developments within the community have made the membership issue a major sticking point in the relationship between the Mohawks and Canadian authorities. It is evident that Kahnawake's abandonment of traditional Mohawk values regarding membership and its adaptive 'racial' biological approach is rooted in an effort to counter recent attempts by the federal government to impose membership criteria upon Mohawk people, who view the proper authority for decisions concerning membership as located within Kahnawake.

Revised Indian Act Rules on Membership: Bill C-31

The Canadian government revised the Indian Act in June 1985 to eliminate certain gender discrimination within the Act—the particular offending sections stipulated that Indian women who married non-Indians would lose their legal status as Indians. The series of amendments which effected the change also included the partial devolution of control over membership to Indian bands, resulting in what has become known as a 'two-tiered' membership system with a distinction made between Indian status on the federal level and band membership on the local level. The new system created a situation where the federal government defined and imposed membership criteria for those communities which did not design and implement a local code in accordance with the Indian Act. In effect, where the new Indian Act theoretically allowed for band-controlled definitions of membership criteria, only those local membership codes which were acceptable to the Minister and which conformed with Canadian laws were ratified and formalized by DIAND.

Kahnawake's membership rules were never codified, and the Mohawks did not seek the approval of the Minister in establishing them. Thus the community faced a situation where the federal rules were legally binding, yet the local practice operated under a completely different set of criteria. Generally, the Bill C-31 amendments resulted in a huge increase in the number of status Indians, each one assigned Indian status on the basis of his or her familial linkage to an Indian band. Band councils for the most part opposed the Bill C-31 revisions, arguing that the heavy influx of new Indians would place an unbearable strain upon the resources and land bases of established Indian communities. The attempt to implement Bill C-31 since 1985 has confirmed the fears expressed by the band councils, and band councils have used the limited powers extended them under Bill C-31 to counter the imposition of new membership criteria upon their communities (Canada 1990). Many communities, like Kahnawake, have devised local rules which explicitly counteract the goals of Bill C-31 for substantial philosophical as well as more base political and economic reasons.

Kahnawake's resistance to Bill C-31 is rooted not only in practical concerns regarding the availability of housing and land and the increase in program costs, but also in political considerations arising out of the ongoing drive for enhanced local control. Both are important in understanding how a hard-line approach to the membership issue has become a key feature of the nationalist project in Kahnawake.

The practical effect of Bill C-31 upon the demand for resources in the community was a major factor in shaping Kahnawake's resistance to the legislation's implementation. Communities across Canada had expressed concerns that the costs associated with programs in areas such as education, health, justice, housing, and social assistance would outstrip the resources allocated by the federal government to Indian band councils (Canada 1990: V, 52–61). In Kahnawake, due to the high number of Bill C-31 registrants—1,253 individuals—who had been awarded status by the federal government, and the community's limited land base, the potential for overtaxing programs was great.

A financial impact study commissioned by the council in the late 1980s confirmed much of the community's fear in this regard (MCK 1989b). Contrasting the impact of normal growth with growth due to the influx of Bill C-31 registrants in key administration sectors, the study projected moderate increases in costs under normal growth and a huge increase considering the potential integration of Bill C-31 registrants into the programs administered by the council. The fact that approximately 25% of those registrants would seek to establish a residence on the reserve was also considered. The results of the study are summarized in Table 7.1.

The community perceived that the Bill C-31 registrants who were assigned Indian status by the federal government were going to cause shortfalls in the areas of program and service delivery. In an era characterized by massive reductions in the amount of federal support for Indian governments in key areas such as education and overall reductions in the level of support in other areas (Angus 1990), the financial impact study validated this perception as a basis for forming MCK policy in response to the new federal policy.

Table 7.1 MCK Bill C-31 Financial Impact Study, 1988-1997		
	Normal Increase	Bill C-31 Increase
Elementary Education	89%	174%
Higher Education	31%	87%
Health / Social(Child)	119%	275%
Health / Social (Adult)	74%	201%
Justice (Court & Police)	86%	193%
Social Assistance	64%	193%
Housing	73%	82.5%

Kahnawake, like many other communities, resisted the implementation of Bill C-31 on deeper considerations than economics. The federal government's own research confirmed that many Indian bands opposed Bill C-31 and the re-integration of Bill C-31 registrants for a host of reasons including social and cultural, political, and legal concerns (Canada 1990: III, 13–24). The major factors in inducing resistance among band members to Bill C-31 have been the lack of consultation in the legislation's design phase and the complete lack of consideration for impacts upon the social and political life of the communities in the implementation phase.

The federal government reported that a typical negative comment on the attempted integration of Bill C-31 registrants focused on the erosion of 'the native lifestyle', and the rifts caused by the imposition of new membership criteria:

> Bill C-31 has effectively disrupted community life because it has created rifts among family members and amongst community members . . . There has been an inordinate amount of energy, time and money spent with little regard for the social, emotional and psychological impact; consequently, there is bigotry and fighting because of the misunderstanding . . . Bill C-31 has segregated and labelled people: those who were living here before against those returning. (Canada 1990: III, 20)

The negative impact of Bill C-31's imposition is also seen in legal and political conflict between communities like Kahnawake seeking to enforce their own codes—unrecognized by the Minister—and Bill C-31 registrants assigned status in the band who do not meet the local criteria. Kahnawake's rules have been challenged in federal courts by individuals seeking band membership, and the MCK has been defiant in asserting its exclusive jurisdiction over membership matters. Litigation has become a common recourse for addressing membership matters:

> One band is involved in two law suits and a possible third. The first sets the band against Bill C-31; the band wants the freedom to control its own membership. This litigation has sparked division within the band, which has led to a second suit—by Bill C-31 registrants against the band and the government concerning the slowness of the reinstatement process. (Canada 1990: III, 23)

In the wake of the unilateral federal imposition of the Bill C-31 membership criteria, and in consideration of the economic and social bases for resistance, Kahnawake has implemented local membership rules reflecting a hardened stance with respect to the right of the community to control membership.

Mohawk Law on Membership[6]

Kahnawake's current rules on membership are derived from three
sources: 1) the 1984 Kahnawake Mohawk Law regarding citizenship; 2)
the 1981 Moratorium on mixed marriages; and 3) the Indian Act. Given
the disparities among the three sources of the Law in terms of goals and
philosophy, current regulations governing membership in the community are somewhat inconsistent and are generally conceded to be ineffec-
tive in promoting a coherent vision of Mohawk identity and the further
entrenchment of traditional values. Nonetheless, the community continues to accept the MCK policy as its guidelines for membership rather
than implement a system based upon the Bill C-31 rules. The MCK policy
itself has five main elements:

- 'Mohawks of Kahnawake' are those persons whose names appeared
  on the band membership list prior to 1981, irrespective of blood
  quantum,[7] and all those persons who possess at least 50% Mohawk
  blood quantum and whose parents were listed on the band membership list.
- Persons who possess at least 50% Mohawk blood quantum, but are
  not included on the band membership list previously, may apply for
  instatement as a Mohawk of Kahnawake upon their marriage to a
  Mohawk of Kahnawake.
- As of 22 May 1981, any Mohawk who marries a non-Native relin-
  quishes all legal, economic and political rights as a Mohawk of
  Kahnawake.
- The Kahnawake band membership list supersedes the DIAND 'Indian
  Registry' in determining status as a Mohawk of Kahnawake.
- Non-Native children adopted by Mohawks remain non-Native.
  Mohawk children adopted by non-Natives retain their Mohawk sta-
  tus and are eligible for instatement upon successful completion of
  a blood quantum verification.

Thus, the formal rules which constitute the MCK's membership policy
clearly represent an effort to enforce the principles developed in
Kahnawake during the 1970s and early 1980s, in response to anticipated
shifts in the federal position with respect to the definition of Indian status. However, there is a growing perception in the community that the
MCK's rules are flawed. Although they reflect a commitment to locally
defined criteria, they are inconsistent with the larger effort to retrench
traditional Mohawk values. To test the vigour of the ideas contained in
the MCK's existing rules, members of the council's Membership
Committee were interviewed during December 1990 and asked to present their views in the context of the new political reality created by the
traditionalist critique and the impact of Bill C-31:

- On the issue of a 50% blood-quantum standard and the maintenance of the Marriage Moratorium—There is a general consensus that both the 50% blood quantum minimum and the moratorium should remain in effect.
- On the issue of whether blood quantum was a proper means of determining a person's eligibility for membership—The consensus is that blood quantum was an effective, though not ideal, means of determining eligibility.
- On the issue of the legal and political status of those persons who do not possess 50% blood quantum, but who have some Mohawk blood—There is no consensus, although there is general agreement that 'blood' is only one factor among several that determines whether or not a person is a Mohawk.
- On the issue of whether Mohawk status could be alienated from a person who was born a Mohawk—All agreed that persons born Mohawk remain so forever.
- On the issue of what specific elements constitute the Mohawk identity—All agreed that being Mohawk meant participating and attempting to perpetuate the cultural and historical legacy of the Mohawk nation. Although the members could not objectively define a Mohawk, specific references were made to their distinctiveness, pride, and aggressive defence of legal rights as a distinct people in North America.
- On the issue of the relative importance of race, culture, residence and political or legal rights in determining status as a Mohawk—All agreed that language and culture were important as the vehicles that transfer the Mohawk identity over generations, but all agreed that Mohawk language proficiency and cultural knowledge are not absolutely necessary to be considered Mohawk. All agreed that residence in a Mohawk territory is not necessary, but that some form of contact should be maintained so that the social and cultural ties to the Mohawk people are not lost. Most members felt that 'Indian' physical characteristics were ideal because they helped an individual identify himself as an Indian, and represented the difference between Indians and non-Indians. But all agreed that in today's reality, physical resemblance to some Indian ideal is not a necessary part of being a Mohawk. All agreed that the legal or political status awarded or denied a person by a government—MCK or DIAND—does not independently affect whether or not that person is or is not a Mohawk.
- On the issue of the basic values which distinguish Mohawks from other communities—Some Mohawk values cited were pride, a sense of Mohawk self-determination, and a dedication to the community. Most members mentioned the fact that culture and

language were valuable in themselves and that a central Mohawk value was the protection and perpetuation of the difference between Mohawks and the rest of society.

- On the issue of rights and responsibilities in a Mohawk community —All agreed that collective rights of the community were of a higher value than any individual rights, although a number of members did respond that individual rights were also important, and not to be considered lightly. Some of the responsibilities of Mohawks cited were: to maintain a sense of tradition and family ties to the community, to respect elders and their wisdom, to participate in community affairs, and to preserve the land.

- On the issue of the difference between Mohawks and other Natives with respect to consideration for membership status—All agreed that there is an obvious difference between Mohawks and other Natives, but that this difference does not affect the desired effect of Kahnawake's membership regulations, and that other Natives should be considered equal with Mohawks as far as the marriage regulations were concerned.

Despite differences of opinion among members of the Membership Committee on almost all of the issues discussed in the course of the interviews, there exists a general consensus on the major elements of the community's membership regulations and a unanimity of conviction of the goals and objectives of the policy. All agreed that the goal of a membership policy should be to safeguard the rights of Mohawks over non-Mohawks within Kahnawake, and to perpetuate Kahnawake as a distinctly Mohawk community in the face of continuing pressure to assimilate politically and culturally into non-Native society.

In the view of the Membership Committee, it is true that all persons born Mohawk remain so forever; needless to say, the difficulty is in determining whether or not a person is born a Mohawk. Mohawk identity clearly has two components: culture and race. The racial component of a person's identity is simple to determine once a standard is decided upon, and Kahnawake has decided upon a standard of a minimum of 50% blood quantum. The Mohawks of Kahnawake have accepted the standard that anyone who possesses at least 50% Mohawk blood quantum is a Mohawk regardless of adherence to the culture or integration into the social fabric of the community. For persons possessing less than 50% blood quantum, status as a Mohawk is determined taking into account cultural and social factors.

The cultural component of the Mohawk identity is more complex. It is dependent upon nebulous factors such as values and participation rather than an easily measured factor like blood quantum. Certain factors are identified as indicators of whether or not a person is living life as a Mohawk: pride in the Mohawk heritage; knowledge of the Mohawk culture and language; and participation and contribution within the Mohawk community. Mohawk values are collective as opposed to individual in orientation, where the collective good overrides the good of any one individual. Individuals are important, but in the formulation of membership policy the rights and values of the Mohawk community as a whole are protected when they conflict with non-Mohawk and non-Indian rights and values.

The views expressed here by the Membership Committee are generally representative of the spectrum of opinion within the community. To comprehend the importance of the views expressed by Mohawk people on the issue of identity, one thing must be understood: in Kahnawake there is a consuming fear of assimilation. It is for the most part this pervasive fear of further erosion of the Mohawk culture and the loss of a racial difference which drives Kahnawake's policy. The community's development of stringent, racialist membership regulations can be seen as an attempt to create a bulwark against the pressures which could undermine the basis of Mohawk distinctiveness. This motivation is clearly represented in the public justifications for the 1981 Marriage Moratorium:

> Because of the many concerns that have been expressed by the people of Kahnawake and the necessity of maintaining Indianism in the Kahnawake Mohawk Territory it is imperative that this Moratorium be implemented . . . It will be difficult for this moratorium to be accepted by some of the people, but everyone must try to understand that certain steps must be taken in order that future generations will survive as Indian People. (MCK 1981)

On Kahnawake's efforts to counteract proposed changes in the Indian Act, and on the establishment of a blood quantum system, the council was adamant in asserting that 'What Kahnawake is presently involved in is not racism, not discrimination nor is it sexism. It is plain and simple survival of a distinct and unique culture that requires some very strong laws and regulations to protect the future' (MCK 1984: 3).

The Mohawks have withstood consistent efforts on the part of the federal government, and the more passive influence of non-Native popular culture, in order to endure as a recognizable political and cultural community. In the face of renewed efforts on the part of the federal government, through Bill C-31, to impose an externally devised definition of 'Mohawk' upon the community, Kahnawake has responded by challenging the federal government's definition. It has itself erected a boundary devised according to community consensus and designed not only to protect the cultural and racial borders of the Mohawk community, but to advance its nationalist political goals as well.

The Radicalization of the Membership Issue

From the perspective of a Canadian public and government which has recently eliminated gender discrimination in its own laws and now seeks to make Indian band membership rules conform to Canadian interpretations of individual rights, the most contentious issues in Kahnawake's membership policy are the blood quantum requirements and the community's ban on intermarriage with non-Natives. Kahnawake is often portrayed by Canadian politicians and intellectuals as a radically racist community seeking to impose a form of racial purity (*Globe and Mail*, 3/17/94: A-1; 3/19/94: B-1; *Montreal Gazette* 3/16/94: A-9; 3/19/94: B-1). But Kahnawake's approach is far from radical given the process of identity formation for Indian peoples which has developed in the modern era. The political environment shapes the community's struggle to maintain some form of delineation between Mohawks and non-Mohawk people.

The process of identity formation within Indian communities has, at least since contact with European cultures, had two key elements: culture and race (Clifton 1989). Hertzberg's landmark study of modern Indian identity relates how Indian communities have had difficulty coming to terms with the increasing salience of racial criteria: 'The idea of race was both important and quite ill-defined, sometimes being equated with "nationality", sometimes with "culture", and sometimes with biology' (Hertzberg 1971: 23). As communities have become more confident in the use of racial criteria, the relative importance of the two elements varies according to the specific cultural, political and economic context within which the community operates. Indian people originally focused exclusively on cultural factors when determining membership, but a radical shift in the context of the identity formation process has caused a change in the relative importance of racial criteria in determining membership.

Clifton, in his study of the vagaries of Indian identity in those communities which face the most intense assimilative pressures, describes lucidly how this has occurred:

> Originally, no North American society subscribed to the idea of biological determination of identity or behaviour. Indeed, the most common identity question asked of strangers was not, 'What nation do you belong to?' or 'Of what race are you?' Instead, when confronting unknown people, they typically asked, 'What language do you speak?' They were disinterested in skin colour, the standard Euro-American sign of racial identity. On the contrary, they stressed as criteria of group membership learned aspects of human nature; language, culturally appropriate behaviour, social affiliation, and loyalty . . . However, modern Indians—who are all of composite Native and Euro-American biological ancestry, and who have long since absorbed much Euro-

American cultural knowledge—think differently. Today, most use the standard American or Canadian principles of assigning group identity, which are determined by blood. (Clifton 1989: 11)

Clifton does not fully appreciate the complexity of the identity formation process in the traditional era. The Iroquois, for example, integrated people without regard for race, but maintained a political distinction between adoptees and native born people. Adoptees were given a 'name hung around the neck'—which potentially could be removed—and were not eligible for certain political roles within the community. Nonetheless, his characterization of the shift in thinking in communities like Kahnawake is accurate.

The reasons for the increased reliance upon racial criteria are rooted in Euro-American governments' consistent efforts to destroy Native cultures and the resulting erosion of the traditional values once predominant in Native communities. To rely strictly on cultural criteria would imply the existence of a unified cultural community, where membership would be determined by the consciousness and manifestation of cultural knowledge within an individual. But in Kahnawake, as in many Native communities, the erosion of that unified cultural complex has destroyed the consensus which once existed on what may be considered authentic or valid elements of cultural knowledge (Alfred 1991). In the absence of a framework for making culture-based determinations of membership, Indian communities in the modern era have been forced to accept race-based criteria.

As in Anderson's description (1990: 95) of the interplay between the fluid nature of the culture-based boundaries of nationhood and the concrete precision of institutional criteria for inclusion in the state's citizenry, Kahnawake Mohawks become conscious of the need to balance the two. But in the context of an internal colonialism which continues to impose a formal economic and political dependency upon the state, Indian communities have come to rely primarily upon the precise institutional rules which govern state-like enterprises.

In the past, both American and Canadian institutional rules on membership centred on racial criteria—Canada focusing exclusively on race and the United States combining racial and cultural components (Clifton 1989: 10). But in recent years the trend at the national level in both countries has been toward an increasingly inclusive definition of Indian status, which has led to the retention, in Canada at least, of a primarily racial set of criteria, but with a broadening of the requirement for status to the point that a person with any Indian blood at all is considered 'aboriginal'—either status or non-status Indian, or mixed blood Métis—and due the rights and privileges previously reserved for members of recognized Indian bands.

The trend in Indian communities themselves, as was demonstrated in Kahnawake's experience with respect to the reintegration of Bill C-31 registrants, is toward exclusivity. This reaction is due in equal parts to the perception of a continuing effort by non-Native governments to shape Native societies according to a White vision, to the desire to safeguard what has been preserved thus far in terms of culture and racial distinctiveness, and to a hostility toward persons who would take advantage of the monetary benefits accorded to status Indians in terms of increased access to special federal programs.

This three-pronged reaction to inclusiveness and the factionalism which has resulted from the federal government's attempt to impose members upon Indian communities is illustrated vividly in Hertzberg's discussion of the meaning of the 'reservation' (Hertzberg 1971: 313–16). The Mohawks of Kahnawake, shaped by the traditional revival and the desire to safeguard the gains that have been made with respect to self-government, place a high value on the reserve community as a symbol of their survival. Canadians, on the other hand, have viewed the reservations in earlier eras as prisons where Indians were to be held, and in the contemporary era as a focus for the progressive reformation of backward societies shaped by the impact of previous injustices. Indians who either escaped the 'prison' by rejecting their home community, or who were never integrated into their parents' communities, see the reservations as a refuge in one form or another. Reservations are viewed as useful for grounding their sense of Indian identity, providing respite from the pressures of life in the dominant society, or leading to economic benefits in the form of tax breaks or better access to government programs for Indian people.

What is an appropriate framework for deciding who is and who is not a member of the reservation communities? Contrasting views of the essential nature of Indian communities co-exist among different constituencies. The band councils representing the majority of reserve residents and band members operate on a retrenchment impulse, seeking to provide closure by protecting the existing community from further erosion on any level. The Canadian government, recently made by the courts to honour liberal principles with respect to Indian people, operates on a reform impulse, seeking instead to alter the policies it once sponsored within Indian communities—policies now unacceptable to Canadians. Finally, the Indian people who were alienated for various reasons from their communities operate on a benefit impulse, which seeks to maximize the utility of the reservation for promoting their own interests, without making a significant commitment to the community itself.

Each one of these impulses figures into the calculation of the appropriateness of a set of rules governing membership in Indian communities. Communities like Kahnawake have continued to rely upon locally defined racialist criteria because they provide the strongest and most clear-cut protections against the formulations proposed by those who would reform or simply benefit from the reserve communities—impulses represented in the federal Bill C-31. The retrenchment of racialist policies is also promoted by the fact that social, economic, and political conditions continue to make the Kahnawake-style membership policy relevant and useful to that community given its nationalist political culture: 1) some Mohawks continue to intermarry with non-Natives; 2) biology continues to be an important factor for fixing social identity throughout society—ethnicity and gender-based social and political identities are increasing; 3) the popularity of assuming an Indian identity has grown and is at present high; and 4) there are special rights and monetary benefits derived from Indian status, if not residence on a reservation (Clifton 1989: 10). To this may be added the fact that the Canadian government has yet to vacate its authority under the Indian Act with respect to membership and still pronounces the definition of an Indian and administers Indian status for the vast majority of bands. In short, all of the conditions which led Kahnawake to devise and impose its present membership policy continue to be salient factors in pushing the community toward retrenchment.

Membership and Closure

In the context of Kahnawake's nationalist project, the community's membership rules are not radical so much as they are a manifestation of the basic need of any community to create a culturally and politically appropriate boundary between its members and others. Resistance to the concept of independently defined membership criteria can only come from a perspective which does not value the Mohawks' inherent right of self-determination. To deny the Mohawks of Kahnawake the right to determine for themselves what the boundaries are between theirs and other communities is itself inherently colonial. It leads to the imposition of what Walzer (1983: 28) has called a 'simple equality' where a single boundary is imposed upon a multiplicity of communities. The Mohawks are advocating a Walzerian 'complex equality' where the differences between communities are reflected in the existence of many culturally-specific boundaries—and membership policies.

Walzer's communitarian philosophy reflects the same instinct embedded within Mohawk nationalism: a fundamental concern for the preservation of independent communities as the framework for protecting individual rights and governing diverse groups within a pluralistic society. Given the lack of consensus within the Mohawk community on the specific value and priority of key elements of traditional culture, and the pressures and fears associated with the scarcity of resources for program funding and land availability, for the Mohawks as with Walzer membership has become a question of distributive justice. For both, the existence of independent political communities 'capable of arranging their own patterns of division and exchange, justly or unjustly' is of prime importance (Walzer 1983: 31).

It is important that the discussion be premised on the right of communities to establish criteria according to their own priorities and values. Kahnawake's rejection of Bill C-31 and the conception of rights embedded in the Canadian constitution are understandable given the Mohawk view that the Canadian Charter of Rights and Freedoms is another culturally specific Euro-American ideal imposed upon Native communities. The fact that Indians did not in the pre-contact era determine membership by racialist criteria is irrelevant; Native cultures evolve like any other in response to changes in the social and political environment. For generations, race has formed one of the central bases for defining boundaries in Indian communities. The Mohawks have established for themselves a basis for what Walzer refers to as 'closure' that is appropriate to their goals and within the parameters created by the various political and economic pressures facing the community. Walzer (1983: 39) argues convincingly that:

> The distinctiveness of cultures and groups depends upon closure and, without it, cannot be conceived as a stable feature of human life. If this distinctiveness is a value as most people (though some of them are global pluralists, and others only local loyalists) seem to believe, then closure must be permitted somewhere.

Thus presented, the argument is a philosophical justification for the pragmatic steps taken by Kahnawake Mohawks to protect their boundaries. The Indian Act was and is an imposed definition of Indian identity put in place to destabilize Indian communities in the hopes of eliminating them as stable features of human life—and of the Canadian political landscape. The Mohawks have at least since the 1970s recognized the aim of the Canadian government in this regard. They have challenged the Canadian government to respect the right of Native peoples to self-determination.

In so openly challenging Canada on the membership issue, the Mohawks of Kahnawake have reacted to what they perceive as a threat to their existence as a distinct group and dared Canada to honour its multicultural and pluralistic nature (Taylor 1993). The Mohawks' success in this effort is crucial, for 'Admission and exclusion are at the core of communal independence. They suggest the deepest meaning of self-determination' (Walzer 1983: 62).

CHAPTER EIGHT

THE RISE OF NATIVE NATIONALISM

Many Onkwehonwe *are too afraid to fight for their rights.*
They have been browbeaten to a state of hopelessness. They
shall have to be inspired to stand . . . and fight for their future
and for the future of seven generations ahead . . . Then, there
are those who can fight and are ready to put their nation in
its rightful place among the nations of mankind. They are the
leaders of the present and the future.

Karoniaktajeh, 1979

The Kahnawake case has demonstrated that through the revitalization
of traditional indigenous cultural symbols, and the re-implementation of
key elements of traditional indigenous political institutions, the
Mohawks were able to construct a viable alternative ideology in opposition to further integration into the Canadian state. The re-emergence
of traditional values and principles in Kahnawake nationalism is an
important indicator of the fact that, in terms of both identity and institutions, ethno-nationalism in the Native context is more than rooted in
the past—it is the present manifestation of a continuous assertion of
national self-determination. Thus the 'Mohawk nation' is not an invent-
ed or imagined community as those who see nationalism from an instrumentalist perspective would argue.

Mohawk nationalism draws its symbols and identity from an existing cultural complex, and bases its institutions upon structures which
were operational in Iroquois country until the modern era. While an
instrumentalist view is clearly not supported here, there exists no
evidence to support the validation of an opposing primordialist view.
The traditionalism which has come to form the basis of Kahnawake
nationalism is not purist in the sense of being an ideology of strict

re-implementation of previous social and political forms. Mainstream nationalism in Kahnawake is characterized by the selective revitalization of key elements within an existing culture, a self-conscious and syncretic reformation leading to the creation of an identity and institutional framework strongly rooted in tradition but adapted to modern political reality.

The overall pattern of interaction between the community and the state importantly influences the intensity of the nationalist assertion. In Kahnawake, the development of viable alternatives to Canada from within an existing cultural complex was the first stage leading to the radical assertion of nationhood which characterizes the community. That Kahnawake had long suffered abuses and injustices under internal colonialism, culminating with a massive land expropriation and direct threats to the communal right to determine membership criteria, led to Mohawk perception that further integration with Canada would jeopardize their autonomy and distinctiveness. There was, in effect, a negative evaluation of the Canadian institutional framework.

This interpretation differs from conventional views on the factors which lead to the revitalization of nationalist movements after periods of latency. While rational-choice theorists concentrate solely on various economic disparities as the root causes of heightened assertions of nationalism, the Kahnawake case has shown that negatively perceived patterns of interaction on other axes also lead to the re-evaluation of existing frameworks. In this interpretation, the pattern of interaction is not limited to the economic realm, and it affects mainly the tone and intensity of the nationalist assertion—which itself derives primarily from the imperatives of the internally-driven process of reformation and re-evaluation. The pattern of interaction, negatively perceived, supported the development of alternatives to the state and the assertion of nationalist goals.

A nationalist ideology may be viewed along a temporal axis as the consolidation of a particular set of goals and a determinate level of intensity. Shifts in the form and intensity of the nationalist ideology occur as the community evolves and interacts with the state, and a consensus develops as to the appropriateness of the existing relationship and institutional framework. If a negative evaluation emerges, a shift in identity is initiated and institutions must respond in order to remain relevant within the context of the reformed identity, and to reflect the imperatives of the principles inherent in the emergent political culture. Those institutions that remain salient through the transformation are retained and re-oriented to accommodate the new reality; those that fail to display the requisite institutional responsiveness are jettisoned.

Thus in the Kahnawake case, the negative pattern of interaction facilitated the development of a radical form of nationalism because the

Mohawks could turn away from the state and revitalize a pre-existing set of traditional institutions as the basis for their nationalist project. The band council has remained viable as well because it has demonstrated an institutional responsiveness by accommodating the turn toward traditional Iroquoian values and has integrated key elements of the Iroquois political philosophy into its own structure.

Figure 8.1 Explanatory Model: Ethno-Nationalism (Native)				
	Starting Point	Phase I	Phase II	Phase III
Identity:	'Traditional'	Latent	Revival	Complex
Institutions:	Traditional	Colonial	Traditional	Syncretic
Interactions:	Cooperative	Cooptive	Confrontational	Crisis

KEY ELEMENTS

Interactions

The pattern of interaction between the Native community and other communities, later the 'state', forms an integral element of the explanatory model. Early interactions between Native peoples and the newcomer societies, despite the disastrous long-term effects on Native society, occurred in an atmosphere of respect. Well into the relationship, Native peoples like the Mohawk were accorded a political status by Euro-Americans concomitant with their importance as trading partners and military allies. Notwithstanding the vast divergence in long-term objectives, both Native and newcomer societies approached their relationship cautiously, consciously guarding the principles of respect, non-interference, and harmonious co-existence enshrined in many treaties—which may for the purposes of this explanation be termed a 'cooperative' pattern of interaction.

As the newcomer societies consolidated into independent states and embarked on their own 'nation-building' projects, from the perspective of Euro-American society the relative importance of alliances and trade with Native peoples declined and the pattern of interaction shifted. No longer inter-dependent with Natives, Euro-Americans began to ignore the principles of the earlier relationship and established a form of internal colonialism by imposing an institutional regime predicated on a wardship status for Native peoples and designed to usurp indigenous control. Oriented toward the erosion and eventual destruction of the social, cultural, and political integrity of Native societies, this second pattern of interaction may be termed 'cooptive'.

traditional institutional framework, did Native identity begin to integrate concepts appropriate to the task of challenging the hegemony of Euro-American institutions.

From the traditional identity to what may be termed the 'latent nationalism' phase, Native communities maintained their traditional institutions during the early period of accommodating a shifting political reality in which their power and autonomy were eroded by the consolidation of Euro-American societies. The nationalism remained latent in its assertion because of the generally insulated existence of Native communities and the lack of a coordinated threat to the integrity of Native societies.

Within the context of this latent nationalism, absent any concerted effort to assert a political distinction, Euro-American institutions were imposed and accepted in Native communities. Gradually, the Euro-American goal of undermining Native society and the cooptive nature of the relationship became clear. The negative evaluation of the existing framework led to a reform of the collective identity and the consolidation of a second phase, which may be termed 'revival nationalism'. This reformed nationalist identity created a foundation for restructuring of the institutional frame on a traditionalist basis. Similarly, as the traditionalist frame and the pattern of interaction which resulted were evaluated over time, the nationalist identity reformed again in response, and entered what may be termed the 'complex nationalism' phase.

This model thus presents an explanation of the rise of nationalism in the Native context centring on three main factors, each of which is necessary but not sufficient in itself. It views nationalism as a consistent feature of the Native political culture, and explains differential levels of assertion by positing three phases of Native nationalism. It is the interplay of institutions and key events within the context of a set of values and particular self-conception which results in a change in the form (phase) of nationalism. There is a synergistic relationship between all three of the factors, with changes initiated as a result of an internal evaluation process.

COMPARATIVE FRAMEWORK

The view of nationalism revealed here accommodates an explanation of different levels of assertion not only along a temporal axis for a single community, but also for differences among various Native groups. The model hinges on the interplay of factors which are particular to a specific temporal location and cultural and political context. By comparing the historical development of the relationship between the community and the state, and the degree to which a basis exists for developing traditional indigenous alternatives to the state-sponsored identity and institutional framework, an understanding of the form and intensity of the community's nationalist assertion may be discerned.

A community like Kahnawake—and to a certain extent all Mohawk and Iroquois communities—has developed a strongly asserted and radical form of nationalism because of the maintenance of the Iroquois cultural complex and the continuing existence of the Iroquois Confederacy structure as an idealized institutional framework. These are strong and viable alternatives to the Canadian state. Combined with a consistently negative pattern of interaction with Canada, the Mohawks of Kahnawake have developed a form of nationalist ideology which at its core rejects Canada and turns inward toward the traditional ideal. The political goals which result are oriented not towards integration, but toward satisfying the autonomy-driven imperatives of the Iroquois political culture.

Within the context of the model, most other Native communities in Canada are not faced with the same array of conditions which would lead to a Kahnawake-like nationalism, either in form or intensity. The unique conditions of Kahnawake's experience have pushed the community toward an extreme autonomist position, but other communities have not had the consistent negative pattern of interaction, or are lacking a sufficiently developed or remembered indigenous political framework upon which to base a traditionalist movement.

The traditional indigenous nature of the identity-institution alternative is important, because even if Native communities reject the specific framework of the existing relationship with Canada, institutions developed as alternatives will not be oriented toward a high degree of autonomous assertion unless they are based on indigenous values and principles, which differ radically from those which form the basis of Euro-American systems. That is, a form of Native nationalism which rejects the existing framework and develops alternatives based on Euro-American values, principles, and models, will not contain the autonomy-driven imperatives of an indigenous-based nationalism.

The radically autonomous Iroquoian position contrasts at a basic level with the form of nationalism present in most other Native communities, which seeks reform within the existing parameters of Canadian federalism through mechanisms such as the creation of a third order of government or the delegation of municipal, regional, or provincial status for Native governments. There is of course some commonality between the two forms of nationalism—both seek to preserve the existence of a cultural distinction between Native peoples and Canadians, and both seek a greater level of political authority to accomplish this end. The basic difference between the Mohawks of Kahnawake and other Native communities is the existence within Kahnawake of a unified cultural and political complex forming a viable alternative to Canada. There is as well a consistent pattern of inter-action which has pushed Kahnawake to reject Canada and embrace the traditional ideal.

Other Native communities may have undergone the same process of progression from a cooperative to a cooptive pattern of interaction with an identical imposition of colonial institutions, leading to a negative eval-uation of the framework current within the community. However, as they begin to form a nationalist ideology in response to the negative evalua-tion, their evolution is necessarily oriented toward integration with Canada because of the lack of a distinctively indigenous political-institu-tional alternative framework. Where most Native communities seek redress in the reform of Canadian constitutional law, the Mohawks of Kahnawake seek to re-structure the relationship in a more essential way through the creation of a truly confederal Canada and the re-implemen-tation of a Native-Canada relationship based on the principles of the *Kahswentha*—the Two-Row Wampum, embodying the ideal of mutual respect for the cultural and political autonomy of each society.

The Mohawk view of a confederal Canada represents the ideal of a flexible and constantly negotiated settlement between many communi-ties grouped under the state rubric. The ideal is consistent with their goals of maximizing community sovereignty and autonomy within lim-its imposed by feasibility and a pragmatic assessment of the require-ments to preserve the structural, political, and cultural integrity of each community. The Mohawk ideal is imprecise by nature: it does not seek a fixed arrangement of jurisdictional authority or a concrete distribu-tion of power. Rather, its inherent flexibility leads to a constant re-eval-uation of community capabilities and a periodic re-consideration of the appropriateness of the existing confederal power-sharing arrangement.

With reference to the explanatory model, where Kahnawake is char-acterized by the 'complex' form of nationalism which is predicated on a modified traditional institutional framework, most other Native com-munities are characterized by the 'latent' form of nationalism in which it is still possible to satisfy the imperatives of the identity within the internal colonialist framework. These Native communities develop institutional objectives in line with the existing Canadian framework and the state responds favourably, reinforcing a positive evaluation on the part of the Native community. Thus the development of an identity and form of nationalism which present a radical challenge to the exist-ing framework is precluded.

Native communities which fall into this pattern are accommodated easily by the state, because the imperative within this limited form of nationalism is simply to redress the material disparities which emerge between Native and non-Native populations in Canada. From this perspective there is no fundamental injustice beyond the differential in material conditions because, having accepted a course which leads eventually toward inclusion, albeit as a distinct 'national' or 'cultural' community, in Canada, conflicts are viewed as part of the normal tensions which arise as boundaries (cultural and political) are adjusted within states.

Communities like Kahnawake are problematic for the state and pose a significant challenge to the maintenance of an internal colonial regime. The radical form of nationalism is predicated not only on the maintenance of a cultural distinctiveness, but also on the magnification of the political sovereignty of the Native community. The traditionalist basis of the radical nationalist ideology highlights the injustice inherent in the history of Euro-American impositions and the coercive maintenance of an internal colonial political relationship. In direct contrast to the limited form of nationalism, the radical form of nationalism at its very core contains an imperative to resist further erosions of the community's national sovereignty. It is this imperative which drives the radical nationalism in Kahnawake. Even as the nationalist ideology moves from a simplistic purist traditionalism characteristic of the 'revival' phase to the syncretic phase identified as 'complex', the drive to incorporate key principles within the traditionalist political philosophy remains strong.

The diversity of traditional cultures and the range of historical experiences in the modern era have led to major differences in the form and intensity of nationalist assertion among Native peoples. The 'spectrum of assertion' outlined below conveys the nature of the differences among Native political goals—as well as the implications for the state's ability to accommodate the various forms of nationalism.

The comparison of Native goals is based on the degree to which the community seeks autonomy from the state. One pole is a 'limited' degree characterized by an assertion of powers limited to the preservation of a cultural distinctiveness and the legislative authority to maintain that distinctiveness. The opposite pole is an 'extensive' degree characterized by an assertion of state-like powers toward the magnification of national sovereignty in addition to the preservation of a cultural distinctiveness.

The spectrum may be used to illustrate the progression of a particular community like Kahnawake along a temporal axis. Kahnawake has moved over the course of the modern era from a very localized set of goals promoting stability in its latent nationalist period, through to a set of reformative goals advocating change relative to the state in its revival nationalist period, to the current phase of a complex nationalism characterized by a coherent and consolidated set of crisis-provoking goals which seek to actualize a radical form (from a statist perspective) of Mohawk national sovereignty.

The spectrum may also be used as a gauge of the form and intensity of the nationalist assertion of various Native communities at any one time. In 1995, Kahnawake's nationalist ideology is complex and oriented toward an extensive assertion of sovereigntist goals. The nationalism of other Native communities, in terms of the extent to which the are seeking autonomy from the state and the degree to which they have developed a viable institutional alternative, may be gauged at other points along the spectrum. The explanatory model and spectrum of assertion presented here thus provide not only a way of understanding the historical development of a set of political goals within a Native community, and a means to appreciate the qualitative differences between the goals and strategies present in various Native communities.

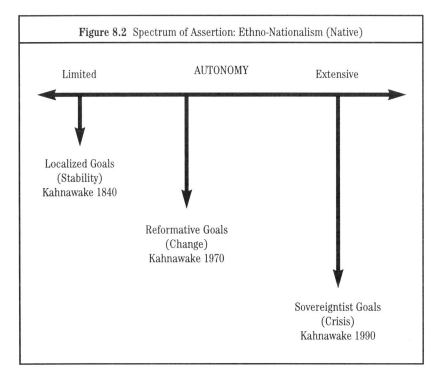

Figure 8.2 Spectrum of Assertion: Ethno-Nationalism (Native)

Limited   AUTONOMY   Extensive

Localized Goals
(Stability)
Kahnawake 1840

Reformative Goals
(Change)
Kahnawake 1970

Sovereigntist Goals
(Crisis)
Kahnawake 1990

This study has attempted to provide an understanding of the continuing refusal of Native peoples in North America to assimilate state institutions within their own societies. The refusal has come in varying intensities and in different forms, but Native communities in North America all represent to some degree the struggle of peoples throughout the world who have been subjected to colonial impositions and who through their political actions are attempting to fashion justice out of an inherently unjust history. The success of this struggle is recognized today as the key to Native peoples' survival into the 21st century.

Although this study has focused on the Mohawks of Kahnawake in particular, some general conclusions may be drawn from the Kahnawake experience on themes which transcend the local experience and which may inform a greater understanding of the nature of nationalism and the dynamics of state-nation relations.

The Essentialist Fallacy

The dominant question in studies of nationalism and political identity has been primordialism versus instrumentalism. One perspective sees unbroken tradition and continuity with the past, while the other sees conscious manipulation of traditions and cultural inventions in the emergence of nationalist ideologies. Both are in fact wrong because in spite of their disagreement they represent an essentialist fallacy either way. There is no simple answer to the question, 'Do ideologies/peoples/nations/cultures change or not?' They of course change—and they do not. The Kahnawake case has shown that in Native cultures at least there exists a stable core which forms the basis of the political culture and nationalist ideology. There are also peripheral elements within the culture which are malleable and which do shift and transform, rise and fall in importance and relevance according to shifts in the political context and according to the exigencies of the general political and economic climate.

The Contradictions of Colonialism

This study has concluded that the structural framework of the relationship between Canada and Native peoples is unjust in its imposition of Euro-American institutions in Native communities, and is based on a fundamental injustice manifested in the consistent denial of Native nations' right to self-determination. As such, Canada is characterized by a system of internal colonialism. The Canadian state has addressed the internal contradictions of internal colonialism—most notably the disjuncture between Canadian and Native cultural and political values, and the lack of demonstrated consent to the Canadian constitution on the part of Native peoples—through efforts to normalize a form of integrative state nationalism. And by attempting to destabilize, negate, or eliminate other forms of nationalism rooted in ethnicity.

The contradictions are rooted in the opposing conceptual bases for the ethno-nationalist and state nationalist assertions. State nationalism's imperative is incorporation, while ethno-nationalism has a core of separatism. Where Canada has fallen short is in the failure to recognize the medium between the two extremes. The Canadian state has not incorporated the persistent Native ethno-nationalism into its own structure and identity. By attempting to impose Euro-American values and institutions, eliminate rooted indigenous cultural complexes, and supplant long-standing institutions, Canadians have created a country which holds little appeal for those Native people who have retained or revived the essential nature of their own traditional culture.

There is a basic difference between the statist and Native forms of nationalism. The constituent elements of both, and of all nationalistic movements, are similar. It is in the rank-ordering or prioritizing of the elements that the core of the difference emerges. Each cultural complex creates a framework in which the elements are structured and interact differently, creating a distinctive form of nationalism. The crux of the problem for states like Canada is related to the hegemony of what is referred to by Asch as a 'plebiscite' nationalism whose defining feature is a 'common subjective attachment to the same state' (Asch 1988: 38). It operates on the principle that only in the collective forming the majority of the population does the right to self-determination reside. In a society like Canada with hundreds of Native nations denying the legitimacy, to one degree or another, of the values contained in the dominant political culture as a framework for their government, the premise of outright majority rule is clearly problematic.

With respect to those people within the society who do not transfer legitimacy to the state, the right to self-determination in the state's view is forfeited. This is unjust from the perspective of the national minority, even ignoring the fact that in Canada's case Native nations for the most part never gave express consent to inclusion within the state or society. Notwithstanding this fact, stability in spite of the contradictions is possible if a national minority embarks on only a local assertion of autonomy. This is facilitated by either the success of the state in accommodating the interests of the national minority, or in the failure of the national minority to develop a sufficient alternative institutional framework or an alternative political identity rooted in a distinct culture.

Instability within the state results from a national minority's broader assertion of difference on a cultural and political level. The instability is fostered by either the state's failure to accommodate the national minority's interests, or the national minority's success in developing viable alternatives to the state-oriented identity and institutional framework.

THE PERVASIVENESS AND PERSISTENCE OF ETHNO-NATIONALISM

The general conception of nationalism is in need of re-evaluation. Where many observers see the global rise of ethnic-based nationalist assertions as aberrations or anomalies, this study leads to the conclusion that nationalism is a persistent and growing feature of political life in all plural or multi-ethnic societies. It has gone beyond other contemporary analyses of nationalism which have concentrated on ascribed features of group identity or territoriality in the creation of political identities. Kahnawake has demonstrated the saliency of race as a feature of national political identity, even in a context of racial-biological ambiguity which would seem to indicate a reliance upon other factors such as language or residency. The model has demonstrated the necessity of considering the historical roots of ethno-nationalist assertions in mediating or at least understanding the conflict between ethnic groups and states. In this sense, it is useful as a means of analysing ethnic nationalism in other contexts and as a framework for understanding confrontations comparatively.

The Kahnawake experience has shown that the solution to the instability arising from the engagement of persistent and pervasive forms of ethno-nationalism with state nationalism is not to deny or suppress the rights of the national minority. The solution to instability lies in the state's exhibiting the flexibility necessary to incorporate minority national values and institutions into a framework of interaction which accommodates basic ethno-nationalist goals. In societies like Canada, which were founded on the suppression of Native nations and which maintain an internal colonialist regime, a fundamental restructuring of the relationship will be required to manifest a respect for Native nations' right to self-determination.

The basic goals of even the most radical form of Native nationalism are oriented primarily toward preserving cultural distinctiveness and achieving the level of governmental autonomy required to preserve the principle of national sovereignty. The degree of national autonomy required is dependent upon the perception of the state's ability to accommodate their interests. The relationship has entered a crisis stage in Canada only because of the state's inability to accommodate these goals within its institutional frame. Should the state restructure the relationship, reform its own institutions, or accommodate the principle of Native national sovereignty, the conditions leading to instability and further increased demands for autonomy would evaporate.

The ideal structure for plural or multi-ethnic societies flowing from this study is an evolutionary form of state nationalism which re-interprets its incorporative imperative. Canada as the ideal plural state would not attempt to eradicate Native cultures or to impose European institutions upon Native peoples whose political cultures have evolved in completely different circumstances and conditions. Canada in this view would abandon the Eurocentric project and initiate an incorporative project geared toward ensuring that state institutions come to reflect the cultural diversity of the national minority populations who have never consented to or participated in the construction of the state.

Unfortunately, the ideal state exists only in theory. The reality of the dynamic between states and nations is a continuing Eurocentric incorporative project which alienates Native peoples and fosters a further intensification of ethno-nationalist assertions to guarantee the preservation of basic elements of the minority culture.

In the assertion of nationalist goals, the tenaciousness of communities like Kahnawake can only be understood through an appreciation of the reality that for Native peoples, unlike English, African, Asian, or French-Canadians, each community is the exclusive locus of a unique culture. The unique importance of the Native drive for self-determination is evident in the context of French-Canadian and Mohawk nationalism. Quebec nationalism is predicated on the goal of preserving the French language in North America, a legitimate goal but one that pales in consideration of the fact that any further erosion of Mohawk culture and language would bring the Mohawk nation to the brink of extinction. Therein lies the significance of Native nationalism. In their drive to resist Canadian efforts to eliminate their nation, the Mohawks of Kahnawake have re-awakened an independent spirit, a spirit which animates all Native people who hear the voices of our ancestors calling out to save our people.

NOTES

Chapter One

[1] Onontio and Colar were the Native language words used by the Iroquois for the Governors of New France and New York, respectively. The Iroquois translated the name of the first Frenchman to occupy the post, Montemarse, and used it for all subsequent Governors. They converted the first Dutchman's name, Corlear, to an Iroquois pronunciation and used it similarly (Newell 1965: 23).

[2] For a more substantial treatment of non-state ethnic nationalism and ethnic conflict involving non-state actors see Esman (1994), Montville, ed. (1990), and Horowitz (1985).

[3] Esman (1994) has captured the differences I am referring to in his discussion of variations among politicized ethnic movements in terms of political goals, where 'hegemony, autonomy, and inclusion' as discrete objectives distinguish movements.

[4] This ambiguous identity is reflected in the simultaneously independent and unified political relations between communities of the Iroquois Confederacy and the Mohawk nation. The only way of determining whether the communities will be unified or separate is to undertake an issue-specific analysis of the political situation at hand. Generally, issues which may be characterized as cultural, or those which affect the legal status of individuals as Iroquois or as Mohawks, inspire unity. In contrast, there are many ideological differences within and between communities, and almost complete independence with respect to economic development.

Chapter Two

[1] I do not share the viewpoint represented by the French Jesuit quoted above, and many other latter-day cultural 'essentialists' who believe that such a clear distinction between 'us' and 'them' is self-evident. I doubt there was ever a sound basis for contemplating cultures in terms of exclusivity and unadulterated authenticity. Culture, including political culture, is always evolving, with elements of the previous present accommodating those of the new present.

[2] These proto-Iroquoians had links to the pre-historic Ohio River Valley Adena and Hopewell moundbuilder societies. This group, which included other native nations in the northeastern part of the continent, are cultural descendents of the meso-american societies which migrated into North America and established themselves in present day Texas and Arkansas (Jennings 1993: 68–73), and have a continuous archaeological presence in the area from the Point Peninsula phase dating from 700–1000 A.D. The Owasco tradition, from

1000–1300 A.D., saw the break-up of a monolithic Iroquoian group and the development of more differentiated agricultural and longhouse-living societies (Snow 1984: 245).

[3] The word Hochelaga was noted by the French as the name used by the inhabitants of the old volcanic mountain island when Cartier arrived in the early 16th century. It is probably an adaptation or corruption of the original inhabitants' own word for themselves or for the newcomers. To his ear, Cartier's hosts greeted him with the word *Ononchehaka*. In Mohawk, this word would mean roughly 'people of the mountain'. By contrast, the true Mohawk words *Otsira:ka*, meaning 'place where the fire is'—or *Oshehaka*, meaning 'people of the hand' in reference to the European manner of greeting—would be more appropriate renderings.

[4] For the Iroquois, the metaphor of a longhouse served many purposes. A longhouse was the structure they lived in, the name by which they referred to themselves—'longhouse builders', a metaphor for their concept of government and social organization, and also a geographic description of the combined west to east locations of the Mohawk, Oneida, Onondaga, Cayuga and Seneca nations which made up the Confederacy.

[5] It was during this period that several French Jesuits became martyrs in North America in the conflicts between the Iroquois and their northern enemies. Among the best known are Fr Isaac Jogues and Fr St Jean de Brébeuf. St Jean de Brébeuf was killed during an attack on Huronia in 1649. Fr Jogues was captured by the Mohawk among the Huron and killed at the village of Kahnawake in 1646 (Béchard 1976: 37–8).

[6] The presence of missionaries within a native nations' territory was seen as a sort of insurance policy against hostile or retaliatory attacks by the French military authorities (Trigger 1976: 815).

[7] The French government dispatched the Carignan-Salières regiment to Quebec. This 1200-man unit was a professional force made up of tested regulars and veterans of battlefields in Hungary and the Antilles (Stanley 1960: 12). Even so, the first march into Kanienke was a failure. Led by the inexperienced Remy de Courcelles, it was undertaken in the dead of winter; the column lost its way and was ambushed by the Mohawk just outside of Albany. A second march in the fall of 1666 led by the French Lieutenant-General in America, the Marquis de Tracey, was more successful.

The French and their Indian allies marched into the Mohawk Valley and destroyed all of the Mohawk villages and food stores. But they were not confronted by Mohawk warriors as they had expected, finding instead only some old men occupying the Mohawk towns (Fenton 1978: 469; Béchard 1976: 84). The warriors had made a tactical retreat into the surrounding hills, causing a French officer to remark out of frustration, 'in the distance could be seen the barbarians, loudly hooting on the mountain' (Grassman 1969: 84).

[8] Finding the Mohawk villages deserted and encountering no resistance save for the taunts of Mohawk warriors in the distance, on 17 October 1666 de Tracey

read an Act of Possession. It stipulated that with the planting of a cross, a display of the King's arms and three shouts of 'Vive le Roi', Kanienke was thereby made French territory in the minds of the Frenchmen (Grassman 1969: 84).

[9] In 1710, the British brought four Mohawk chiefs to Boston, where they displayed the armaments of the British Army and Navy. They went so far as to place the chiefs in a dinghy in the middle of Boston harbour, surround them with battleships, and fire a cannonade to demonstrate the effect and force of British arms. From Boston, the chiefs went on to London and an audience with Queen Anne, where they were introduced to the attractions of British culture and society (Viola 1981: 14–15).

[10] For a detailed historical treatment of the formation of Kahnawake as a distinct community during the period from 1667 to 1760, see Green (1991).

[11] The felicitous irony of a strong Catholic sentiment taking hold in the same village that produced the slayers of Jogues and Brébeuf was not lost on the Jesuit missionaries. One commented: 'In the number of believers, among the nation of the Agnie, those of the village of [Kahnawake] have taken the first rank, as if this were due to the blood of the martyrs' (Thwaites 1959: v. 63, 169)

[12] In terms of numbers, from 1668 to 1679, among all of the Iroquois nations over 4000 adults were baptized. Of these, the Jesuits considered about half to be insincere 'death-bed' conversions, leaving the number at approximately 1800 'sincere' conversions to Christianity. The average conversion rate was 20% among all the Iroquois, and substantially higher among the Mohawk (Richter 1985: 7).

[13] In 1744, for example, the Mohawks of Kahnawake negotiated a neutrality agreement among the Iroquois Confederacy, the English, and the French to protect the French fort at Niagara and the English fort at Oswego from wanton destruction during an imperial conflict (Stanley 1963: 216).

[14] The Seven Fires was a short-lived, loose political association of formerly French-allied Native nations under the leadership of the Mohawks at Kahnawake.

Chapter Three

[1] The following incident illustrates Kahnawake's lowered stature in the eyes of their former allies in the Canadian capital. Marie Therese *Kanonwiiostha* was the last Kahnawake Mohawk to have been born in one of the ancestral Mohawk River Valley villages. The parish pastor appreciated the symbolic value of the recognition of this elder's centenary anniversary in Kahnawake, and requested on behalf of the Mohawks a formal recognition by Canada. The government's response was a curt dismissal of the request. An Indian Affairs clerk wrote to the pastor: 'the [Minister] is not here to acquaint him with your letter relative to the poor centennial squaw' (Devine 1922: 410). It must have dawned on the Mohawks that they were confronting a new era; whereas for hundreds of years before, governors and generals had taken account of their power and influence in the calculations of international politics, the balance of power was now such

that lowly bureaucrats were insulting them using derogatory language and dismissing simple solicitations on behalf of the elders.

[2] The War Department maintained only a partial and incomplete record of the Indian veterans of the Civil War. Initially, Indians were legally barred from service in the Union army. But resulting from the efforts of Gen. Grant's aide-de-camp Ely Parker, who was himself a Seneca, there were eventually as many as 300 Iroquois who served during the course of the war. Accurate data are impossible to ascertain because the Indians used fictitious names, and the lack of post-war claims is due to the common but untrue belief that Indians were ineligible for military benefits. Positive identification indicates that Iroquois communities supplied at least 161 soldiers and sailors, and one marine. Scattered references corroborate Kahnawake and Akwesasne—another Mohawk community located near Cornwall, Ontario—representation in that total (Armstrong 1978: 80–2; Stacey 1959: 256–8; Donaldson 1892: 16).

[3] Under the command of a Lt-Col Denison, Kahnawake provided two commissioned officers and 54 enlisted men who served as expert guides on the treacherous Nile River rapids (Stacey 1959: 256–8).

[4] For a detailed discussion of the historical and ideological roots of the Indian Act see Titley (1992).

[5] 1944 United States v. Claus, 63F.Supp.433; 1945 Albany v. United States, 152F.2d.267.

[6] The Royal Proclamation of 1763 contained legal guarantees of the nation-to-nation relationship between the British Crown and Indian nations. It also contained language which was later interpreted to place a responsibility on the federal government to protect the interests of 'Indian and lands reserved for Indians'. This later led to the formation of the contemporary relationship through enshrinement of the concept in section 91(24) of the British North America Act and later section 35 of the current Canadian Constitution. Specific to Kahnawake, General Gage, the military governor of Lower Canada in 1762, put forward a decision concerning the ownership of the Seigneurie de Sault St Louis in favour of the Mohawks and against the Jesuit order which had, in Gage's opinion, illegally disposed of sections of the territory while managing the lands in trust (see Chapter Seven).

Chapter Four

[1] Postal locates the origins of the 'Famous Fourteen' myth, referred to in the next chapter, in this incident. Having challenged Thunderwater and the people's faith in him, the Mohawk lawyer incurred the wrath of the community. In his election bid for a seat on the band council, he received only 14 votes.

[2] The condolence ceremony effects the formal installation of a Chief in the Iroquois tradition.

[3] Kahnawake has always been characterized by a pattern which allows for the short-term and occupation-related residence away from the community with

the maintenance of a permanent home in Kahnawake. One indication of this pattern's constancy is in the Canadian Census data where, out of the total population of Kahnawake Mohawks, the proportion of a Mohawk's life spent in his home community ranged from 93% in 1884 to 94% in 1968 (Katzer 1972: 151)

[4] This section draws from the author's research previously published in French as 'La Victoire de l'Idéologie Iroquois: Kahnawake au XXe siècle', *Recherches Amérindiennes au Québec* 22, 4 (Hiver 1992–93).

[5] The Peacemaker, according to tradition, appeared among the Iroquois early in the 14th century, and the Iroquois established a system of government based on the *Kaienerekowa* soon after (Fenton and Tooker 1978). For a discussion of the Confederacy in relation to its representation of democracy, and its influence on later attempts at the design of federal systems, see Grinde and Johansen (1991) and Johansen (1982).

[6] In terms of numbers, this group has always been the largest traditionalist faction. Overall, the number of people affiliated with a Longhouse has grown tremendously since the 1960s. Longhouse people were previously a small minority in Kahnawake. In a 1965 survey of 830 residents, only 3% or 28 people identified as Longhouse in contrast to 83% or 689 who identified as Catholic (Katzer 1972: 261). By 1973 there were approximately 100 Longhouse people, or 5% of the population, as determined by the band council (MCK-BCR 09/19/73 p. 212). Current numbers are difficult to ascertain with any degree of certainty due to the lack of identifiable and consistent criteria and to the heavy overlap in identification with Longhouse spirituality and band council politics. Nonetheless, a conservative estimate of active Longhouse members in Kahnawake ranges from 20 to 30% of the total population, or approximately 1000 people.

[7] This section draws from the author's research into Mohawk views on self-government conducted for the Royal Commission on Aboriginal Peoples during 1992, and on the author's unpublished paper completed for the Commission and entitled 'The Meaning of Self-Government in Kahnawake'.

[8] It should be noted that there are at least four different versions of the *Kaienerekowa* in circulation today. Originally an oral document, it was translated into written form during the 19th century by various interpreters. A version transcribed by Seth Newhouse in 1903 remains the one most closely adhered to by most of the Iroquois Longhouses. The central core of the story remains consistent, but there is much disparity in emphasis and detail which has led to disagreement among the Iroquois as to the specific content of the Kaienerekowa as a 'law', particularly in the effort to make it a set of guiding rules for government in the contemporary era. There remains one individual, Cayuga elder Jacob Thomas, capable of reciting the oral version from memory. For a discussion of the Kaienerekowa's various interpretations, see Vecsey (1991).

[9] At least one respondent took a unique perspective on the strengths and weaknesses of the band council structure in Kahnawake. Citing the difference of opinion concerning the legitimacy of the Indian Act and the overall ineffective-

ness of the MCK as a political institution, the young woman endorsed the status quo, stating: 'It engenders opposition and critical thinking and action in the community. In this way promoting diversity—part of what defines Kahnawake and makes it a dynamic and exciting place in the political landscape.'

[10] The survey was conducted during the author's research for the Royal Commission on Aboriginal Peoples and polled 80 Mohawks representing different political factions, using a questionnaire for standardized questions and as a basis for open-ended interviews.

[11] There is some support for the idea of imposing taxes on non-Mohawk individuals and business interests within Kahnawake (29% of the survey respondents). This illustrates an ideological aspect of the tax issue in Kahnawake. One of the prevailing myths in the community is that 'Indians don't pay tax'. This of course flows from the partial implementation of Indian Act rules in the community. The tax exemption granted in the Indian Act is perceived as a sort of treaty right due all Indians by virtue of their status as members. Another aspect is that Mohawks recognize the correlation between the legitimacy of taxes and the existence of a representative and effective government. Most Mohawks reject the idea of taxes at least in part because existing government institutions are viewed as not truly representative, stable, or effective.

[12] Kahnawake has failed to support a number of proposed enterprises: a lacrosse stick manufacturing plant in partnership with an American company; a warehousing and air freight centre in partnership with another aboriginal nation; a shopping complex, and most recently a plan involving a hotel and casino complex in partnership with an American company.

[13] For a discussion of the Iroquois Confederacy's influence on federalism, see Grinde and Johansen (1991) and Johansen (1982).

[14] It is clear that Mohawks do not consider Quebec an important element in the make-up of Kahnawake's future external relations. The prevailing view in the community is that Quebec is simply a sub-unit of the Canadian federal state. Quebec's provincial status precludes its being considered as an independent political entity. This is reflected in the wide margin of difference between the number of survey respondents who favoured full or partial linkages with other entities (from 85% to 93%) and those who favoured full or partial linkages with Quebec (55%).

Chapter Five

[1] A Mohawk (David Cross) was shot and killed in his own driveway by Quebec Provincial Police (SQ) officers during a scuffle which ensued after Cross and his brother, suspected of impaired driving, were chased on to the Reserve by the police. The SQ officer who killed Cross was acquitted of manslaughter charges, even though Cross was armed only with a stick.

[2] In 1973, members of the American Indian Movement and the newly formed Kahnawake Warrior Society attempted to evict a number of non-Indian people from Kahnawake and threatened to overthrow the elected Council and

implement a 'traditional' government. RK responded by confronting the Warrior Society, and ultimately appealed to the SQ and the Royal Canadian Mounted Police (RCMP) for assistance in containing the movement. Violent clashes and rioting followed the SQ's deployment in Kahnawake.

[3] In July of 1990, Mohawk communities in Quebec became embroiled in a long and violent confrontation with the Province, now commonly referred to as the Mohawk Crisis of 1990. The Crisis was sparked by a land dispute between the Mohawks of Kanehsatake and the municipality of Oka, but quickly turned into a complex stalemate with internal and external ramifications for all three Mohawk communities (see Alfred 1991).

[4] The Peace and Security Committee was formed in the wake of the 1990 crisis to ensure cooperation between the MCK and the Warrior Society on matters of internal policing and protection of Mohawk territory from threats posed by the SQ and the RCMP forces still present in Kahnawake.

[5] Before the Seaway, most Kahnawake Mohawks resided in rural areas near the limits of the reserve, or in the 'Village' which consisted of the old part of Kahnawake surrounding the Catholic church and fortified town, or on 'The Point' bordering the river. It was mainly lands located in the Point area that were expropriated by the Seaway.

[6] The MCK conducted a survey in 1992 concerning the issue of maintaining armed checkpoints at entrances to the community. The vast majority of Mohawks supported the idea of maintaining some sort of presence at the borders.

[7] Bill C-31 refers to the 1985 amendments to the Indian Act which were intended to redress sexual discrimination and bias against Indian women inherent in the law. The main focus of the change was to give status back to Indian women who had lost their legal status as Indians and band membership by marrying a non-Native (see Chapter Seven).

[8] At a public meeting in 1978 following months of discussion on the subject of traditionalism and the desirability of implementing a traditional form of government, Akwesasne Longhouse Chief Tom Porter gave a pivotal address which overwhelmed the people of Kahnawake and led to a mandate for the MCK to return to traditionalism.

[9] The 'Famous Fourteen' is a common story in Kahnawake, telling of a group of people who, in different ways in different versions of the story, ratified the Indian Act and allowed for the dissolution of Kahnawake's 'traditional' government and the implementation of an elected government. Another version of its origins is offered in the previous chapter's discussion of the Thunderwater Movement.

Chapter Six

[1] The Mohawk chiefs listed a number of treaties which form the basis of their relationship with Canada and the United States: 1) Treaties of 1759 and 1791 with King George III guaranteeing no molestation by colonial authorities; 2)

Treaty of Peace and Friendship, 1784, which accepted Indians as nations; 3) Treaty of New York, 1774; 4) Jay Treaty, 1794, which established the fact that there are no international borders for Indians in North America; 5) Treaty of 1794 confirming the sovereignty of the Six Nations; 6) Northwestern-Anglo Treaty, 1873; 7) Grant of King Louis XIV, 1680; 8) General Gage's Judgment, 1762; 9) Imperial Proclamation, 1766; 10) Royal Proclamation, 7th October, 1763; 11) Treaty of Ghent, Article 9 which restores Indian possessions but which was not complied with; and 12) Treaty of 1754 (Canada 1951: 11).

2 While the official position of the band council was clear, some members of the council began to question their function and to consider the growing perception of the Indian Act's illegitimacy, as well as their association with the imposed institution. For example, during a meeting on the establishment of a traditionalist primary school, a band councillor was asked what the Longhouse opinion of her was. She was told by a clan mother that she had 'alienated' herself by becoming an elected chief and that the Great Law is the only legitimate governing authority in Kahnawake (MCK-BCM 10/10/72).

3 AIM supported and advised the Warrior Society in various ways. At the height of the conflict, AIM advised the Warrior Society to remove the band council from power. AIM members were later removed as trespassers by the police.

4 The Assembly of First Nations (AFN) is Canada's national organization formed to represent Indian band councils and their collective interests to the federal government.

5 There was some dissent on council concerning this matter. Some chiefs saw the withdrawal from national-level political organizations as an isolationist and detrimental policy. The view was that 'isolationism is not beneficial to Kahnawake', and 'retaining simple observers status at working sessions . . . takes away from Kahnawake's best interests' (MCK-BCM 04/09/84).

6 Information on the administrative structure, authorities and financial aspects of the band council system in Kahnawake is derived from public documents, notably the MCK's monthly newsletter and a recent institutional overview; see MCK (1990); MCK (1993b).

7 The council is also afforded a number of, from a contemporary perspective, comical powers under the Act which betray the paternalistic Victorian origins of the band council system: the council may regulate the activities of domestic animals; it has authority to act against the spread of noxious weeds; and it may make regulations on bee-keeping practices and the keeping of chickens.

8 The MCK has also recently integrated a formerly autonomous program called the Kahnawake Economic Development Authority (KEDA). This federally-funded economic development initiative had revenues of $9.2 million in 1993 and disbursed moneys through a number of programs geared toward promoting the growth of business enterprise in the community. These include a Business Assistance Program, an Employment Subsidy Program and a Loan Guarantee Fund. It should be noted that these figures on MCK revenues and expenditures do not include the budgets of key institutions in areas such as education,

social services and health which operate as autonomous community-controlled structures with their own budgets and funding sources.

Chapter Seven

[1] Information contained in this section is derived in part from confidential documents and legal opinions relating to Kahnawake's claim to the Seigneury lands. The author acknowledges the contributions of the MCK's former legal counsel Dr John Hurley in this regard. For detailed information relating to the various surrenders of reserve lands discussed in this chapter, see Ornstein (1973).

[2] Minor adjustments have been made with respect to the division of the reserve into sections and the subsequent re-unification of the reserve, as well as the expropriation and subsequent return of a small island on the eastern end of the reserve. See Ornstein (1973).

[3] The mission records for the pre-modern era contain 425 pages of original birth, baptismal and marriage notations and are catalogued into family histories dating from 1735 to 9 February 1903. The records indicate that many non-Native child captives, as well as adult Native captives from other nations, including a large number of Abenaki during the years 1761–1763, Onondaga, and Hurons de Lorette, were adopted into the community during this period. Usually, there is a notation of the birth date and parentage of the person, although there are some cases where only the place of origin is known. All captives were given Christian and Mohawk names and were assimilated into the community as Mohawks—many assuming leadership roles in both the political and military sphere. Some non-Native captives married more than once, and at least two (John Stacey and Jarvis McComber) took non-Native wives themselves after they had become assimilated into the Mohawk community. See *Dictionnaire Généalogique des Familles Iroquoises de Caughnawaga* (1901).

[4] Kahnawake Mohawks generally began utilizing French and English surnames in the early 19th century. Most surnames in Kahnawake are derived from the adaptation by a Mohawk of a common European name, the invention of a name, or the derivation of a name from the clergymen who ministered in Kahnawake. Mission records indicate the extent to which family names in Kahnawake represent the influx of non-Natives, distinguishing between those names assumed by Mohawks and those names originating with a non-Native immigrant to Kahnawake who had married into the community. As early as 1909, 30% of the family names in Kahnawake (48 of 182) were of documented non-Native origin. See *Table Alphabétique des Noms français et anglais des Iroquois de Sault-Saint-Louis Caughnawaga* (1916).

[5] The biological measurement came to known as Mohawk Blood Quantum. A person's blood quantum is determined by analysing his genealogy and calculating a percentage based on the number of non-Native ancestors present within a certain number of generations. Thus a Mohawk who has a White grandmother would be assigned a Mohawk Blood Quantum of 75%, 25% of his ancestors being non-Native.

[6] Information contained in this section is derived from the author's research into membership issues and evaluation of the MCK's membership policy conducted at the MCK during the period December 1990 and January 1991. The results of this research have been presented internally to the MCK in other forms.

[7] According to the MCK, 'Mohawk blood quantum is an estimation of the amount of Mohawk blood possessed by an individual. It shall be based on an investigation into the person's genealogical history of no more than three preceding generations, beyond which all ancestors of Mohawk lineage will be assumed to possess one hundred per cent Mohawk blood quantum. Mohawk blood quantum shall be based on an established and documented paternity agreed to by both parents' (MCK 1992b: 3).

BIBLIOGRAPHY

Government Documents and Primary Research Materials

Dictionnaire Généalogique des Familles Iroquoises de Caughnawaga. 1901. St Francis Xavier Mission, Kahnawake.

The Eastern Door (Kahnawake)

The Globe and Mail (Toronto)

Government of Canada. 1990. *Impacts of the 1985 Amendments to the Indian Act (Bill C-31), 5 Vols.* Ottawa: DIAND.

_____. 1951. *Minutes of Proceedings and Evidence, No. 1.* House of Commons Session 1951. Special Committee Appointed to Consider Bill No. 79, *An Act Respecting Indians.* Ottawa: King's Printer.

_____. 1901. Chief Surveyor, 'Letter to Minister Concerning Offer to Purchase Doncaster Reserve'. Interior Department, Ottawa, 15 May 1901.

_____. 1891. *Indian Treaties and Surrenders from 1680 to 1890.* Ottawa: Brown Cumberland, Queen's Printer. Volume II Appendix, Documents G, H, pp. 293–304.

_____. 1845. *A Report on the Affairs of the Indians in Canada.* Journals, Vol. 6, Appendix 'T,' Section III.

Mohawk Council of Kahnawake. 1993a. Documents on File. *Some Principles for Communal Laws in Kahnawake (Draft),* Canada-Kahnawake Relations Office.

_____. 1993b. Documents on File. *Onkwarihwa'shón:'a* 2(5).

_____. 1992. Documents on File. *Legislative Powers of the Mohawks of Kahnawake,* Canada-Kahnawake Relations Office.

_____. 1992b. Documents on File. *Mohawks of Kahnawake Membership Code: Draft One.*

_____. 1991. Documents on File. *Agreement on an Agenda and Process for the Negotiation of a New Relationship Between The Mohawks of Kahnawake and Canada,* Canada-Kahnawake Relations Office.

_____. 1989. Documents on File. Minister, Ottawa to Grand Chief Norton, Kahnawake, 3 May 1989.

_____. 1989b. Documents on File. *C-31 Financial Impact Study.*

_____. 1988. Documents on File. Minister, Ottawa to Grand Chief Norton, Kahnawake, 21 September 1988.

_____. 1984. Documents on File. *Kahnawake Mohawk Law, 11 December 1984.*

_____. 1981. Documents on File. *Marriage Moratorium, 22 May 1981.*

_____. (MCK-BCM). Documents on File. In *Minutes of Band Council Meetings, 1955-Present.*

_____. (MCK-BCR). Documents on File. In *Band Council Resolutions, 1955-Present.*

Mohawk Nation Office (MNO). Collected Documents, 1988–1990. Kahnawake.

The Montreal Gazette

Public Archives of Canada (PAC-RG10). Microform Collection. In *Records Relating to Indian Affairs.* Vol. RG10. Red Series. Ottawa.

Le Soleil du St Laurent (Chateauguay, Quebec)

Royal Commission on Aboriginal Peoples (RCAP). 1993. Public Hearings. *Exploring the Options: Overview of the Third Round.* Ottawa: Canada Communications Group.

Table Alphabetique des Noms francais et anglais des Iroquois de Sault-Saint-Louis Caughnawaga. (1916) 1949. St Francis Xavier Mission, Kahnawake.

Secondary Source Research Materials

Alfred, Gerald R. 1991. 'From Bad To Worse: Internal Politics in the 1990 Crisis at Kahnawake'. *Northeast Indian Quarterly* 8, 1 (Spring 1991): 23–32.

Almond, Gabriel A., ed. 1990. *A Discipline Divided: Schools and Sects in Political Science.* Newbury Park, CA: Sage Publications.

Anderson, Benedict R. O'G. 1990. *Language and Power: Exploring Political Cultures in Indonesia.* Ithaca, NY: Cornell University Press.

_____. 1983. *Imagined Communities: Reflections on the Origin and Spread of Nationalism.* London: Verso.

Angus, Murray. 1991. *'And the Last Shall be First': Native Policy in an Era of Cutbacks.* Toronto: NC Press Ltd.

Armstrong, Virginia Irving, ed. 1971. *I Have Spoken: American History Through the Voices of the Indians.* Athens, OH: Swallow Press.

Armstrong, William H. 1978. *Warrior in Two Camps: Ely S. Parker, Union General and Seneca Chief.* Syracuse: Syracuse University Press.

Asch, Michael. 1992. 'Political Self-Sufficiency' in *Nation to Nation: Aboriginal Sovereignty and the Future of Canada*, Diane Englestad, ed. Concord, Ont.: Anansi Press.

Bailey, Alfred G. 1933. 'The Significance of the Identity and Disappearance of the Laurentian Iroquois'. *Royal Society of Canada — Proceedings and Transactions* 3, 27: 97–108. Ottawa.

Barsh, Russel Lawrence and James Youngblood Henderson. 1980. *The Road: Indian Tribes and Political Liberty.* Berkeley: University of California Press.

Béchard, Henri. 1976. *The Original Caughnawaga Indians.* Montreal: International Publishers.

Blanchard, David Scott. 1982a. *Patterns of Tradition and Change: The Re-Creation of Iroquois Culture at Kahnawake.* PhD dissertation, University of Chicago.

Blanchard, David. 1982b. 'To the Other Side of the Sky: Catholicism at Kahnawake, 1667–1700'. *Anthropologica* 24: 77–102.

Blumenfeld, Ruth. 1965. 'Mohawks: Round Trip to the High Steel'. *Trans-Action* 3: 19–21.

Bobet, Ellen. 1989. *Indian Self-Government and Community Control in Canada: A Case Study of Kahnawake.* MA thesis, Carleton University.

Boldt, Menno. 1993. *Surviving as Indians: The Challenge of Self-Government.* Toronto: University of Toronto Press.

Bowden, Henry Warner. 1981. *American Indians and Christian Missions: Studies in Cultural Conflict.* Westport: Greenwood Press.

Brass, Paul R. 1991. *Ethnicity and Nationalism: Theory and Comparison.* New Delhi: Sage.

Campeau, Lucien. 1988. 'Roman Catholic Missions in New France' in *History of Indian-White Relations.* Vol. 4, of *Handbook of North American Indians,* Wilcomb E. Washburn, ed. Washington, D.C.: Smithsonian Institution.

Carse, Mary. 1949. 'The Mohawk Iroquois'. *The Archeological Society of Connecticut Bulletin* 23: 3–53.

Cassidy, Frank. 1989. *Indian Government: Its Meaning in Practice.* Lantzville, B.C.: Oolichan Books.

Chapdelaine, Claude. 1991. 'Poterie, Ethnicité et Laurentie Iroquoienne'. *Recherches Amérindiennes au Québec* 21, 1–2: 44–52.

Chevrier, Lionel. 1959. *The St Lawrence Seaway.* Toronto: Macmillan.

Clifton, James A. ed. 1989. *Being and Becoming Indian: Biographical Studies of North American Frontiers.* Chicago: Dorsey Press.

Colden, Cadwallader. [1727–47] 1958. *History of the Five Nations Depending on the Province of New-York in America.* Ithaca, NY: Cornell University Press.

Connor, Walker. 1973. 'The Politics of Ethno-Nationalism'. *Journal of International Affairs* 27: 1–20.

———. 1978. 'A nation is a nation, is a state, is an ethnic group, is a', *Ethnic and Racial Studies* 1: 377–99.

Cornell, Stephen. 1988. *The Return of the Native: American Indian Political Resurgence.* New York: Oxford University Press.

Cross, F.L., and E.A. Livingstone, eds. 1983. *The Oxford Dictionary of the Christian Church*, 2nd ed. Oxford: Oxford University Press.

Delâge, Denys. 1991a. 'Les Iroquois Chrétien des "Réductions", 1667–1770: I—Migration et rapports avec les francais'. *Recherches amérindiennes au Québec* 21, 1–2: 59–70.

_____. 1991b. 'Les Iroquois Chrétien des "Réductions", 1667–1770: II—Rapports avec la Ligue Iroquoisie, les Britanniques et les autres nations autochtones'. *Recherches amérindiennes au Québec* 21, 3: 39–50.

Devine, E.J. 1922. *Historic Caughnawaga*. Montreal: The Messenger Press.

Donaldson, Thomas. 1892. *Indians: The Six Nations of New York* in *11th United States Census*, Extra Census Bulletin. Washington, D.C.: United States Government Printing Office.

Englebrecht, William. 1985. 'New York Iroquois Political Development' in *Cultures in Contact: The Impact of European Contacts on Native American Cultural Institutions, A.D. 1000–1800*, William Fitzhugh, ed. Washington, D.C.: Smithsonian Institution.

Englestad, Diane. 1992. *Nation to Nation: Aboriginal Sovereignty and the Future of Canada*. Concord, Ont.: Anansi Press.

Esman, Milton J. 1990. 'Political and Psychological Factors in Ethnic Conflict' in *Conflict and Peacemaking in Multiethnic Societies*, Joseph V. Montville, ed. Lexington, Mass.: Lexington Books: 53–64.

_____. 1994. *Ethnic Politics*. Ithaca, NY: Cornell University Press.

Fenton, William N. 1955. 'Factionalism in American Indian Society'. *Actes du IV Congrées International des Sciences Anthropologiques* 2: 330–40. Vienne.

Fenton, William N. and Elizabeth Tooker. 1978. 'Mohawk' in *Northeast*, Vol. 15 of *Handbook of North American Indians*, Bruce Trigger, ed. Washington, D.C.: Smithsonian Institution: 466–80.

Fleras, Augie and James Elliot. 1992. *The Nations Within: Aboriginal-State Relations in Canada, the United States and New Zealand*. Toronto: Oxford University Press.

Freilich, Morris. 1963. 'Scientific Possibilities in Iroquoian Studies: An Example of Mohawks Past and Present'. *Anthropologica* 58, 2: 171–86.

Frideres, James S. 1993. *Native Peoples in Canada: Contemporary Conflicts*, 4th ed. Scarborough, Ont.: Prentice-Hall Canada.

Frisch, Jack A. 1975. 'The Iroquois Indians and the 1855 Franklin Search Expedition of the Arctic'. *Indian Historian* 8, 1: 27–30.

Gehring, Charles T. and William L. Starna, trans. and eds. 1988. *A Journey Into Mohawk and Oneida Country, 1634–1635: The Journal of Harmen Meyndertszden Bogaert*. Syracuse: Syracuse University Press.

Gellner, Ernest. 1983. *Nations and Nationalism*. Ithaca, NY: Cornell University Press.

Ghobashy, Omar Z. 1961. *The Caughnawaga Indians and the St. Lawrence Seaway*. New York: Devin-Adair.

Grassman, Thomas. 1969. *The Mohawk Indians and their Valley: Being a Chronological Documentary Record to the End of 1693*. Albany, NY: Magi Books.

Green, Gretchen Lynn. 1991. *A New People in an Age of War: The Kahnawake Iroquois, 1667–1760*. Doctoral dissertation, The College of William and Mary.

Grinde, Donald A. and Bruce E. Johansen. 1991. *Exemplar of Liberty: Native America and the Evolution of Democracy*. Los Angeles: American Indian Studies Center, UCLA.

Hamilton, Edward. 1963. 'Unrest at Caughnawaga or the Lady Fur Traders of Sault St Louis'. *Fort Ticonderoga Museum Bulletin* 11, 3: 155–60.

Hauptman, Lawrence M. 1986. *The Iroquois Struggle for Survival: World War II to Red Power*. Syracuse: Syracuse University Press.

Hawley, Donna Lea. 1986. *The Indian Act Annotated*, 2nd ed. Toronto: Carswell.

Heisler, Martin O. 1990. 'Ethnicity and Ethnic Relations in the Modern West' in *Conflict and Peacemaking in Multiethnic Societies*, Joseph V. Montville, ed. Lexington, Mass.: Lexington Books.

Hertzberg, Hazel W. 1971. *The Search for an American Indian Identity: Modern Pan-Indian Movements*. Syracuse: Syracuse University Press.

Horowitz, Donald L. 1985. *Ethnic Groups in Conflict*. Berkeley: University of California Press.

Hornung, Rick. 1991. *One Nation Under the Gun: Inside the Mohawk Civil War*. Toronto: Stoddard.

Jenness, Diamond. 1955. *The Indians of Canada*, 3rd ed. Ottawa: National Museum of Canada.

Jennings, Francis. 1984. *The Ambiguous Iroquois Empire: The Covenant Chain Confederation of Indian Tribes with English Colonies from its Beginning to the Lancaster Treaty of 1744*. New York: W.W. Norton and Company.

———. 1985. *The History and Culture of Iroquois Diplomacy: An Interdisciplinary Guide to the Treaties of the Six Nations and Their League*. Syracuse: Syracuse University Press.

———. 1993. *The Founders of America: How the Indians Discovered the Land, Pioneered in It, and Created Great Classical Civilizations; How They Were Plunged into a Dark Age by Invasion and Conquest; and How They Are Now Reviving*. New York: W.W. Norton and Company.

Johansen, Bruce E. 1982. *Forgotten Founders: How the American Indian Helped Shape Democracy*. Boston: Harvard Commons Press.

_____. 1993. *Life and Death in Mohawk Country*. Golden, CO.: North American Press.

Katzer, Bruce. 1972. *The Caughnawaga Mohawks: Occupations, Residence and the Maintenance of Community Membership*. PhD dissertation, Columbia University.

Kennedy, W.P.M. 1930. *Statutes, Treaties and Documents of the Canadian Constitution 1713–1929*. Toronto: Oxford University Press.

Kip, William Ingraham. 1846. *The Early Jesuit Missions in North America*. New York: Wiley and Putnam.

Kulchyski, Peter. ed. 1994. *Unjust Relations: Aboriginal Rights in Canadian Courts*. Toronto: Oxford University Press.

Kwartler, Richard. 1980. 'This Land is Our Land: The Mohawk Indians v. The State of New York' in R.B. Goldman, ed., *Roundtable Justice: Case Studies in Conflict Resolution*. Boulder: Westview Press.

Lafitau, Joseph François. [1724] 1974. *Customs of the American Indians Compared with Customs of Primitive Times*. 2 vols. William N. Fenton, ed. Elizabeth Moore, trans. Toronto: The Champlain Society.

Leder, Lawrence H., ed. 1956. *The Livingston Indian Records, 1666–1723*. Gettysburg, PA: Pennsylvania Historical Association.

Long, J. Anthony. 1990. 'Political Revitalization in Canadian Native Indian Societies'. *Canadian Journal of Political Science*, 23, 4: 751–73.

'Indian Treaties'. 1856. *Collections of the Maine Historical Society* Ser. 1; 4, 4: 123–44. Portland, ME.

Mabee, Carleton. 1961. *The Seaway Story*. New York: Macmillan.

Marshall, Catherine and Gretchen B. Rossman. 1989. *Designing Qualitative Research*. London: Sage Publications.

Mathur, Mary E. Fleming. 1973. 'The Case for Using Historical Data: Third Generation Tribal Nationalism'. *Indian Historian* 6, 4: 14–19.

_____. 1975. 'The Body Polity: Iroquois Village Democracy'. *Indian Historian* 8, 1: 31–47.

Meadwell, Hudson. 1989. 'Ethnic Nationalism and Collective Choice Theory'. *Comparative Political Studies* 22, 2: 139–54.

Mohawk Council of Kahnawake. 1990. *Institutions of Mohawk Government in Kahnawake: An Overview*, 2nd ed. Kahnawake: MCK.

Montville, Joseph V., ed. 1990. *Conflict and Peacemaking in Multiethnic Societies*. Lexington, Mass.: Lexington Books.

Newell, William B. 1965. *Crime and Justice Among the Iroquois Nations*. Montreal: Caughnawaga Historical Society.

Noon, John A. 1949. *Law and Government of the Grand River Iroquois.* Viking Fund Publications in Anthropology, No. 12. New York: Viking Fund.

North American Indian Travelling College (NAITC). 1984. *Traditional Teachings.* Cornwall Island, Ont.: NAITC.

Norton, Thomas Eliot. 1974. *The Fur Trade in Colonial New York, 1686–1776.* Madison: University of Wisconsin Press.

Ornstein, Toby. 1973. *The First Peoples of Quebec: A Reference Work on the History, Environment and Legal Position of the Indians and Inuit of Quebec,* 3 vols. Montreal: Native North American Studies Institute, 3: 108–18.

Philpot, Robin. 1991. *Oka: dernier alibi du Canada anglais.* Montreal: VLB Éditeur.

Ponting, J. Rick. 1986. 'Institution-Building in an Indian Community: A Case Study of Kahnawake (Caughnawaga)' in J. Rick Ponting, ed., *Arduous Journey.* Toronto: McClelland and Stewart Ltd.

Postal, Susan Koessler. 1965. 'Hoax Nativism at Caughnawaga: A Control Case for the Theory of Revitalization'. *Ethnology* 4: 266–81.

Ra'anan, Uri. 1990. 'The Nation-State Fallacy' in *Conflict and Peacemaking in Multiethnic Societies,* Joseph V. Montville, ed. Lexington, Mass.: Lexington Books: 5–20.

Rabinow, Paul and William M. Sullivan, eds. 1987. *Interpretive Social Science: A Second Look.* Berkeley: University of California Press.

Richter, Daniel K. 1983. 'War and Culture: The Iroquois Experience'. *William and Mary Quarterly* 3rd Ser., 40: 528–59.

———. 1985. 'Iroquois versus Iroquois: Jesuit Missions and Christianity in Village Politics, 1642–1686'. *Ethnohistory* 32, 1: 1–16.

———. 1992. *The Ordeal of the Iroquois: The People of the Iroquois League in the Era of European Colonization.* Chapel Hill: University of North Carolina Press.

Robinson, Percy. 1942. 'The Origin of the Name Hochelaga'. *Canadian Historical Review* 23: 295–6.

Salée, Daniel. 1993. 'Identities in Conflict: Quebec and the Aboriginal Question'. Paper Presented at the Atlantic Provinces Political Science Association Annual Meeting, Antigonish, N.S., October, 1993.

Scruton, Roger. 1982. *A Dictionary of Political Thought.* London: Pan Books.

Smith, Ermaninie. 1883. 'Life Among the Mohawks of the Catholic Missions of Quebec Province'. *Publications of the American Association for the Advancement of Science* 32. Philadelphia.

Smith, James. [1780] 1978. *Scoouwa: James Smith's Captivity Narrative.* Columbus, OH: Ohio Historical Society.

Snow, Dean R. 1984. 'Iroquois Prehistory' in *Extending the Rafters: Interdisciplinary Approaches to Iroquoian Studies*, Michael K. Foster, ed. Albany: State University of New York Press.

Stacey, C.P., ed. 1959. *Records of the Nile Voyageurs, 1884–1885: The Canadian Voyageur Contingent in the Gordon Relief Expedition.* Toronto: The Champlain Society.

Stanley, George F.G. 1949. 'The Policy of "Francisation" as Applied to the Indians during the Ancien Regime'. *Révue d'Histoire de l'Amérique Française* 3: 333–48.

_____. 1950. 'The First Indian "Reserves" in Canada'. *Révue d'Histoire de l'Amérique Française* 4: 178–210.

_____. 1960. *Canada's Soldiers.* Rev. ed. Toronto: Macmillan.

_____. 1964. 'The Six Nations and the American Revolution'. *Ontario History* 56: 217–32.

Steinmo, Sven et al., eds. 1992. *Structuring Politics: Historical Institutionalism in Comparative Analysis.* New York: Cambridge University Press.

Surtees, Robert J. 1985. 'The Iroquois in Canada' in *The History and Culture of Iroquois Diplomacy: An Interdisciplinary Guide to the Treaties of the Six Nations and Their League*, Francis Jennings, ed. Syracuse: Syracuse University Press.

Taggart, C.H. 1948. *Caughnawaga Indian Reserve: Report, General and Final.* Ottawa: Department of Mines and Resources.

Taylor, Charles. 1993. *Reconciling the Solitudes: Essays on Canadian Federalism and Nationalism.* Montreal-Kingston: McGill-Queen's University Press.

Tehanetorens. 1972. *Wampum Belts.* Onchiota, NY: Six Nations Indian Museum.

Thwaites, Ruben Gold, ed. 1959. *The Jesuit Relations and Allied Documents: Travels and Explorations of the Jesuit Missionaries in New France, 1610–1791* (1896–1901). 73 vols. Reprinted facsimile in 36 vols. New York: Pageant Book Co.

Titley, E. Brian. 1992. *A Narrow Vision: Duncan Campbell Scott and the Administration of Indian Affairs in Canada.* Vancouver: University of British Columbia Press.

Torok, Charles H. 1965. 'The Tyendinaga Mohawks: The Village as a basic Factor in Mohawk Social Structure'. *Ontario History* 57, 2: 69–77.

_____. 1966. *The Acculturation of the Mohawks of the Bay of Quinte.* PhD dissertation, University of Toronto.

Trigger, Bruce G. 1968. 'Archeological and Other Evidence: A Fresh Look at the "Laurentian Iroquois"'. *American Antiquity* 33, 4: 429–40.

_____. 1976. *The Children of Aataentsic: A History of the Huron People to 1660*. 2 vols. Montreal and London: McGill-Queen's University Press.

Vecsey, Christopher. 1991. *Imagine Ourselves Richly: Mythic Narratives of North American Indians*. New York: Harper Collins.

Verdery, Katherine. 1993. 'Whither Nation and Nationalism?' *Daedalus* (Summer 1993): 37–44.

Villeneuve, Larry. 1984. *The Historical Background of Indian Reserves and Settlements in the Province of Quebec*. Ottawa: DIAND.

Viola, Herman J. 1981. *Diplomats in Buckskins: A History of Indian Delegations in Washington City*. Washington, D.C.: Smithsonian Institution Press.

Voget, Fred W. 1951. 'Acculturation at Caughnawaga: A Note on the Native-Modified Group'. *American Anthropologist* 53, 2: 220–31.

_____. 1953. 'Kinship Changes at Caughnawaga'. *American Anthropologist* 55: 385–94.

_____. 1956. 'The American Indian in Transition: Reformation and Accommodation'. *American Anthropologist* 58: 249–64.

Walworth, Ellen H. 1926. *The Life and Times of Kateri Tekakwitha: The Lily of the Mohawks, 1656–1680*. Albany, NY: J.B. Lyon Co.

Walzer, Michael. 1983. *Spheres of Justice: A Defense of Pluralism and Equality*. New York: Basic Books.

Waters, Mary C. 1990. *Ethnic Options: Choosing Identities in America*. Berkeley: University of California Press.

York, Geoffrey and S. Pindera. 1991. *People of the Pines: The Warriors and the Legacy of Oka*. Toronto: Little, Brown.

INDEX

Mohawk Trail Longhouse, 84
Mohawk Valley, 33, 38-43
Mohicans, defeat by *Togouiroui*, 43
Montreal-Albany trade route, 44-5
Montreal island, pre-contact history, 28
moratorium on mixed marriages, 165,
    169-70, 172
mourning war, 33
Murray, George, 154
Myiow, Stuart, Sr, 84
mythic narrative, 20

nationalism, 66, 179; comparative
    framework, 183-9; ideology and
    politics, 87-102; in Kahnawake,
    19-23; key elements, 180-3; Mohawk,
    16, 83, 178; nation-centred model,
    8; and Native politics, 12-16; and
    political power, 9; Ra'anan's theory,
    10-11; radical form of, 179-80;
    Western, 8-9
Nation-to-Nation association, 140, 147
native, and newcomer societies, 182
Native peoples: and dominant society,
    7; *Onkwehonwe*, 19
Native rights, 100
nativism, 70-2, 76, 105
Neutral nation, 35
New Amsterdam, 30
New France, and Mohawk nation, 30
New Indian, 77
nominal leaders, 79
non-Indian: behaviour and young
    people, 61; eviction of from
    reserve, 132-4
non-Native institutions, 7
non-statist nationalist ideologies, 9
non-Western nation building, 10-11
Noon, John A., 83
Norton, Joe, 84, 155

occupations, post-colonial era, 54
'occupation territory', 26, 28-9
off-reserve Mohawks, 60
Ohio River Valley mound-builder
    societies, 26
Oka, 41; crisis (1990), 93, 100, 109,
    114

Oneida nation, 19, 31, 77-8
Onkwehonwe, 19, 37
Onkwehonwe Tehatiisontha
    (Christians), 43
Onkweshona, Sky World spirits, 37
Onondaga Longhouse, 71
Onondaga nation, 19, 31, 35; and
    Diabo case, 59; and Iroquois
    Confederacy, 77-8, 136; traditional
    council government, 68
oppression, 13
oral traditions, 28
oratory skill and mass communica-
    tion, 76
Order-in-Council, and St Lawrence
    Seaway Authority, 158-60
'original beings', 19
Oshernenon, 28, 42

pan-Indian: policing service, 135;
    political organization, 12; political
    unions, 47, 72
paradigm, 146-7
participatory political process, 78
Patton, Charlie, 84
Peace Chiefs, 36
Peacekeepers, 3, 111-12
Peace and Security Committee, 117
'people of the flint', 19
'people of the Longhouse', 19
'the people', meaning of, 80-1
'people who live by the rapids', 19
persistence, 73-7
Petition to Colonial Secretary (1807),
    153
Petition to Governor of Canada
    (1820), 154
Petition to Governor of Lower
    Canada (1828-1830), 154
Phillips, Joe, 66
Pierron, Father, 42
Pine Tree Chiefs, 36
plebiscite nationalism, 189
police. *See* Amerindian Police Force;
    Indian Police Force; Quebec
    Provincial Police; RCMP
policing, community control of, 131
political action, and Longhouse, 65